Aggression and Violence

SOCIAL INTERACTIONIST PERSPECTIVES

Aggression and Violence

SOCIAL INTERACTIONIST PERSPECTIVES

RICHARD B. FELSON AND
JAMES T. TEDESCHI, EDITORS

AMERICAN PSYCHOLOGICAL ASSOCIATION, WASHINGTON, DC

First printing April 1993
Second printing October 1995

Published by the
American Psychological Association
750 First Street, NE
Washington, DC 20002

Copies may be ordered from
APA Order Department
P.O. Box 2710
Hyattsville, MD 20784

This book was typeset in Century Condensed by Harper Graphics, Inc., Hollywood, MD.

Printer: Braun-Brumfield, Inc., Ann Arbor, MI
Cover illustration: Stephanie Shieldhouse, Jacksonville, FL
Cover design: Minker Design, Bethesda, MD
Technical editing and production coordination: Cynthia L. Fulton

Library of Congress Cataloging-in-Publication Data

Aggression and violence : social interactionist perspectives / edited by Richard B.
    Felson and James T. Tedeschi.
      p.   cm.
    Includes bibliographical references.
    ISBN 1-55798-190-6 (acid free paper)
    1. Social conflict.   2. Aggressiveness (Psychology)
3. Violence.   I. Felson, Richard B.   II. Tedeschi, James T.
HM136.A29 1993
303.6—dc20   92-36152
                                                                                              CIP

Printed in the United States of America

We dedicate this book to Sharon, Jacob, and Benji Felson and to Val, Brad, Jamie, Nancy, Ann Anthony, and Alexander Tedeschi

Contents

Part Three: Legitimation of Aggression

Part Four: Violence Against Women

Contributors

James R. Averill, Department of Psychology, University of Massachusetts at Amherst

Mary Pat Baumgartner, Department of Sociology, Rutgers—The State University of New Jersey

Richard B. Felson, University at Albany, State University of New York

Jack P. Gibbs, Department of Sociology, Vanderbilt University

Michael R. Gottfredson, Department of Sociology, University of Arizona

Travis Hirschi, Department of Sociology, University of Arizona

Mark Keating, Department of Psychology, State University of New York at Buffalo

Joseph M. Mikolic, Department of Psychology, State University of New York at Buffalo

Amelie Mummendey, Department of Psychology, University of Méenster, Germany

Mitchell S. Nesler, Department of Psychology, University at Albany, State University of New York

Sabine Otten, Department of Psychology, University of Méenster, Germany

Martin Patchen, Department of Sociology, Purdue University

Robert Peirce, Department of Psychology, State University of New York at Buffalo

Dean Pruitt, Department of Psychology, State University of New York at Buffalo

Mark C. Stafford, Department of Sociology, University of Washington

James T. Tedeschi, Department of Psychology, University at Albany, State University of New York

Hans Toch, School of Criminal Justice, University at Albany, State University of New York

Preface

The two editors of this volume are professors in different departments at the University at Albany, State University of New York (SUNY). Rich Felson is a social psychologist in the Sociology Department, and Jim Tedeschi is a social psychologist in the Psychology Department. Each of us was independently developing a course on human aggression and violence for advanced undergraduates. Our intellectual paths had crossed many times because we had very similar interests, particularly in the topics of self-presentation and aggression. In 1982, we were both invited to a conference on aggression in Bielefeld, Germany. We decided to travel together and to take a side-trip to Paris for a few days of sightseeing. We enjoyed each other's company and were stimulated by each other's ideas.

Over the past 10 years, we have served together as members of dissertation committees and as examiners for qualifying examinations. In 1986, we combined students and co-taught a human aggression course. It was a positive learning experience for both the students and us, and we have continued to co-teach the course once a year since that time. One problem that we faced was that there was no good textbook or sourcebook that we could use to represent our evolving view of the field of aggression. Each year the reserve librarian lived in fear of our forthcoming list. The readings ranged over a wide variety of topics: biology (hormones, brain centers, etc.), frustration–aggression theory, learning theory (modeling, instrumental learning, etc.), mass media effects, social conflict, power and influence, attributions of responsibility and blame, concern for social justice, retribution, revenge, family violence, criminal behavior, personality factors, and so on.

It became clear to us that what we saw as similar or relevant processes were frequently compartmentalized and maintained as separate theoretical and research areas in social science. Thus, scholars who studied social conflict and the use of threats and force never used the term *aggression,* and those who studied aggression did not view the work on social conflict as relevant to their interests. Similarly, social psychologists who studied coercive power did not conceive of threats and punishments that were used to achieve interpersonal objectives as "instrumental aggression." These and other examples of demarcations that have evolved in various subdisciplines seemed arbitrary to us and contributed to a rather nonsocial view of human aggression—as an almost involuntary behavior pushed out by internal processes in the individual such as frustration, arousal, or instincts. We began to develop a wider perspective that places the individual in a social context in which competing interests generate conflict. From our point of view, the use of coercion is one means for resolving conflicts, establishing justice, and maintaining status. We now refer to this as a *social interactionist perspective*.

In the summer of 1989, we first broached the idea of convening a conference of scholars from different disciplines and research areas. The idea was to establish and cross-fertilize communication lines among top scholars in areas that were seldom thought to fall within the same intellectual domain. The conference titled "Social Interactionist Approaches to Aggression and Violence" convened in Albany, New York, on April 5 and 6, 1991. It was sponsored by the SUNY Department of Sociology under the annual series known as the "The Albany Conference." Not everyone we originally invited could attend, but those who did made up a distinguished group. The two days and nights we spent together were stimulating and enjoyable.

When we planned the conference, we also considered generating an edited book from the papers presented by the participants. However, we were aware that papers presented at conferences are written (and sometimes not written at all) for rather short presentation times and are simplified and even dramatized for a face-to-face audience. These considerations led us to ask participants to prepare chapters for a book that would be based on the basic ideas presented at the conference but that would be longer, more detailed, and more technical than the conference papers.

One of the conference participants was unable to contribute a chapter because of time constraints. Amelie Mummendey was unable to attend the conference but was able to contribute a chapter. After the conference, we found out that Michael Gottfredson and Travis Hirschi, both eminent criminologists, had written a paper that was directly related to our perspective. After expressing regret that they had not been invited to our conference, we invited them to contribute to this book.

We did not impose our social interactionist perspective on any of the contributors to this book. In our view, they are social interactionists, although they may not define themselves as such. It is our job as editors to indicate why we think they are and how each chapter of this book elucidates some aspect of our viewpoint. We will do that in the introduction.

We wish to thank Louise Tornatore and Joan Cipperly for their assistance, the editors at the American Psychological Association, and the anonymous reviewers. We appreciate the financial support of the SUNY Department of Sociology, the SUNY Department of Psychology, the Research Foundation of the State University of New York Conversation in the Disciplines, and the Division of Research, University at Albany.

Richard B. Felson
James T. Tedeschi

Social Interactionist Perspectives on Aggression and Violence: An Introduction

Richard B. Felson and James T. Tedeschi

A ggression and violence are studied in a variety of disciplines. Unfortunately, there tends to be little interdisciplinary communication, even when theoretical viewpoints coincide. As a result, some scholars are not aware of what is going on outside their own disciplines. This leads to a failure to recognize the common elements in the studies of conflict, social power and influence, aggression, violence, and crime. An important goal of this book is to foster a common identity for scholars working in different fields who have a similar theoretical orientation.

One factor that maintains segregation in the social sciences is the use of different methodologies. Psychologists typically focus on laboratory research, whereas sociologists and criminologists are more apt to use field-related methodologies. These methodological preferences are reflected in the phenomena studied. Psychologists typically examine competitive behavior in conflict situations and aggressive responses (e.g., shock delivery) to provocations. Sociologists and criminologists, on the other hand, are more apt to examine naturally occurring events, such as homicide, assault, rape, and family violence. Although most of the contributors to this book use similar theoretical approaches, they use a diverse set of methods: laboratory-oriented experimental research, social surveys, crime data, observational data, and qualitative research. We view the diversity of methods as a strength because we recognize limitations in each method.

The contributions to this volume deal with theoretical issues related to what we identify as a *social interactionist approach* to aggression and violence. A social interactionist approach rests on four basic principles. First, it interprets aggression as instrumental behavior—as a means to achieving certain values or goals. For example, aggression may be used to influence others, to establish and protect valued social identities, or to achieve justice or retribution.[1] Thus, the approach is consistent with rational-choice approaches to criminal behavior (e.g., Cornish & Clarke, 1986). It also considers the role of costs and other factors that inhibit the use of aggression. It is therefore compatible with criminological theories that stress internal and external controls (e.g., Hirschi, 1969) and routine activities that produce opportunities for violence (e.g., Cohen & Felson, 1979).

Second, a social interactionist approach is critical of the view that aggression is "pushed out" or "compelled" by inner forces, such as aggressive energy, instincts, hormones, brain centers, thanatos, and frustration. Instead, aggressive behavior is viewed as a normal consequence of conflict in human relations. When interests diverge, aggression is one strategy that individuals use to achieve compliance. When someone is thought to have engaged in a norm violation, aggression is equivalent to punishment.

Third, a social interactionist approach treats situational and interpersonal factors as critical in instigating aggression. This leads to consideration of the behavior of antagonists and third parties as well as of the actor. Outcomes are not predetermined but are a function of the dynamic interchange that occurs as aggressive incidents escalate.

Fourth, the approach emphasizes the phenomenology of actors, whose values and expectations are important in the evaluations of decision alternatives. Actors often view their own aggression as legitimate and even moralistic. Thus, beliefs about justice and equity, the assignment of blame, and the accounts that people give to excuse or justify their behavior are central. The approach is therefore compatible with and borrows from attribution theory and equity theory (e.g., Donnerstein & Hatfield, 1982; Rule & Nesdale, 1976).

Although scholars within this tradition share some general principles, they focus on different social processes. Some emphasize the use of aggression to exercise influence (cf. Tedeschi, 1983). Threats, punishments, or bodily force may be used to coerce others into providing benefits for the actor. For example, robbery offenders typically use contingent threats—"Your money or your life"—to elicit compliance from victims.

Other scholars focus on the use of aggression as a form of informal social control (e.g., Averill, 1982; Baumgartner, 1984; Black, 1983; Felson, 1984; Goode, 1971; Luckenbill,

---

[1] *The theory's emphasis on motives distinguishes it from a symbolic interactionist approach.*

1977). Much of what is referred to as *aggression* consists of punitive actions that attempt to redress some grievance or injustice. These punitive actions may also be intended to influence the target. Their goal may be to prevent continuation of the undesired behavior or to deter others from performing similar behavior. These goals correspond to the concepts of specific and general deterrence associated with the criminal justice system. Note that social control plays a dual role in aggressive behavior. People engage in aggression as a form of control, and they are more likely to engage in aggression, particularly severe forms, when they are less subject to internal and external controls (see Hirschi, 1969).

A number of researchers have shown the relation between perceived wrongdoing and subsequent aggressive reactions that may escalate to a spiral of conflict (Averill, 1982; Kadushin & Martin, 1981; Mummendey, Linneweber, & Löschper, 1984; Tedeschi, Smith, & Brown, 1974; Wolfe, 1985). For example, Felson (1984) emphasized social control processes in a study of the sequence of events in aggressive interactions. He found that violent incidents usually begin when someone believes that a rule has been violated. The agent of social control may then accuse or admonish the offender, and unless accounts are given to explain the alleged violation, he or she may engage in some form of punishment (cf. Schonbach, 1990). When this act of punishment is perceived as an attack, retaliation is likely. These perceptions and reactions may lead to similar reactions by the other person, resulting in an escalatory cycle (Patterson, 1982).

A key predictor of aggression is the perception by people that they have been attacked. People retaliate because they want to deter the antagonist and others from future attacks and because they view retaliation as an act of justice. Some scholars have emphasized social identities in their explanations of why people retaliate when they are attacked. According to this explanation, people retaliate to maintain favorable identities. Evidence of the roles of honor and face-saving in aggression is provided in Toch's (1969) study of interaction between police and civilians, in Felson's (1978, 1982) research on the effect of third parties on the escalation of aggressive incidents, and in experimental studies of the effect of an audience on aggressive behavior (e.g., Borden, 1975).

Aggressive behavior may be dispute related or predatory, although there are mixed cases. Dispute-related incidents develop out of grievances and involve social control reactions to perceived wrongdoing. Social identities play a role in their escalation. Predatory actions, on the other hand, are directed against parties that, even from the actor's point of view, have done nothing provocative. They usually involve acts of exploitation wherein individuals use the target for some purpose, such as demonstrating their power or forcing compliance. Although homicides and assaults are more likely to involve disputes, robbery, rape, and bullying are typically predatory acts. Most of the chapters in this volume focus on aggression that is dispute related.

Although a social interactionist approach to the study of aggression emphasizes situational factors, it recognizes that individual characteristics are important. For example, Tedeschi (1983) predicted a greater likelihood of aggressive responses from people who lack the confidence or ability to use other forms of influence. In addition, given our previous proposal that perceived injustice is the origin of many aggressive interactions, it could be suggested that people who frequently break rules and fail to provide accounts when they break these rules are more likely to become involved in aggressive conflicts because they elicit punishment from others (Felson, 1992).

Organization of the Book

This book is divided into four parts. The first part focuses on the role of social and other forms of control and the use of coercion to express grievances. The second part attempts to link the literature on aggression with the literature on social conflict. The authors in the third part examine how individuals attempt to legitimize their aggressive behavior. The assumption is that aggressive behavior is more likely when it can be legitimized. The final part focuses on violence toward women, with chapters on domestic violence and sexual coercion.

In chapter 1, Tedeschi and Nesler elucidate the processes involved in the perception of norm violations and the reactions of individuals to them. The identification of wrong-doing is referred to as the *naming process* and is affected by the values of the individual, social comparisons with relevant others, and the norms believed to apply to the conduct in question. The next step is the *blaming process* whereby the injured party makes a judgment about the degree of responsibility and blame that should be attributed to the actor. Blame attributions elicit anger, which, in turn, is associated, along with beliefs about possible forms of retributive justice, with the formation of a grievance. There are a number of alternative actions that a grievant may choose, including doing nothing, exculpating the target from blame, forgiving the target, making claims for restitution or apologies, and punishing the offending target. In their contribution, Tedeschi and Nesler examine each of these processes and the conditions that affect the choice of alternative actions.

In chapter 2, Gottfredson and Hirschi offer a critique of traditional theories of aggression. They argue that most measures of aggression in laboratory experiments are inversely related to aggressive behavior outside the laboratory and reflect compliance to legitimized demands of experimenters rather than aggression. Gottfredson and Hirschi also question the adequacy of the notion of an aggressive personality. They present evidence that most repeat criminal offenders are versatile: They do not specialize in violence or any other type of crime. In other words, knowing that individuals have committed violent crimes does not help one predict what crime they will commit next. In addition, criminals engage in many other undesirable behaviors, including smoking, drinking, gambling, and reckless driving. Combined with the evidence that most criminal acts are opportunistic rather than planned, Gottfredson and Hirschi argue that criminals have a problem with impulsiveness or self-control. For them, lack of self-control is the key individual factor in criminal violence.

Gottfredson and Hirschi interpret the evidence on the versatility of criminals as disconfirming both the frustration–aggression hypothesis and the literature on media effects. If the violent person engages in a variety of deviant and criminal acts, then one must look to individual differences that explain this pattern. Theories of aggression that focus on levels of frustration, aversive stimuli, or exposure to models and media violence cannot explain the general behavioral tendencies of people who engage in violence.

In chapter 3, Stafford and Gibbs focus on the incidence of grievances, disputes, and violence in larger social units. They are critical of the subculture of violence as an explanation for these patterns. The formal theory they present examines how the level of control in a particular social unit affects both the frequency of grievances and the number of violent disputes. The general principle is that disputes and violence are likely to be more prevalent in social units with low levels of control. *Control* is a broad term that includes self-control and social (human) control, as well as control over inanimate objects and biological processes. Efficacious control reduces the likelihood of disputes and increases the likelihood that these disputes will be handled in nonviolent ways when they arise. Because some disputes result in violence and because violence can result in homicide, efficacious control is likely to reduce the homicide rate.

The concept of control, as presented by Stafford and Gibbs, may be useful in understanding the variation in the frequency of violence across social units, such as social classes, nation states, ethnic groups, and age and gender groups. In the case of more severe forms of aggression, variations across social units are substantial. Age and gender differences are particularly strong: Interpersonal violence is committed predominantly by young males. Traditional social psychological theories of aggression have failed to explain these patterns.

The second part of the book links the literature on conflict and aggression. In chapter 4, Pruitt, Mikolic, Peirce, and Keating bring together the literature on aggression with the literatures on negotiation, mediation, procedural choice, and dispute management systems. They focus on the use of "struggle tactics" or instrumental aggression designed to achieve victory or avoid defeat in social conflict. Struggle tactics include threats, harassment, positional commitments, and the imposition of time pressures. Pruitt et al. describe conditions that affect the use of struggle tactics versus alternative approaches to conflict, such as problem solving, yielding, and seeking arbitration or mediation. The likelihood that a person will use struggle tactics is in part a function of the success one anticipates with more pacifistic approaches. Pruitt et al. find that people generally prefer these more pacifistic procedures for settling disputes. They usually attempt to discuss issues with the other party in a dispute and prefer direct negotiation to third-party arbitration of the conflict. Struggle tactics are ordinarily listed last or next to last as a procedural choice.

The use of aggression often elicits retaliation and reciprocal harm from the target person. The principle of *lex talionis* (an eye for an eye) may be a universal rule (Gouldner, 1960). In chapter 5, Patchen examines this rule as it applies to the use of both threats and punishments in international and interpersonal interactions. He generally finds that reciprocal coercion is more complicated than a simple tit-for-tat process. Among the factors involved are the magnitude of provocation, the relative changes in behavior by the provocator over time, and the disparity between one's own behavior and the behavior of the other person. A rational choice model is presented as a way of organizing the existing literature and generating testable hypotheses.

In chapter 6, Mummendey and Otten focus on interaction rather than the actor as the unit of analysis. An aggressive interaction usually involves an aversive event that is the result of some action that was freely chosen by an actor and that violates some norm, at least from the target's point of view. The key determinant of whether the conflict escalates is a divergence in perspectives. This divergence depends in part on actors' confidence about their judgments and their willingness to consider alternative interpretations. If each party quickly decides on an interpretation, it is unlikely that they will entertain alternatives. Dogmatism or rigidity is a key individual factor affecting aggression from this point of view because it leads to the rejection of the accounts that antagonists give for their behavior and to a failure to negotiate a mutually acceptable definition of the situation. Mummendey and Otten apply these ideas to both interpersonal and intergroup aggression. They argue that in the intergroup situation, there is a greater likelihood that actors will not consider alternative points of view and, thus, a greater likelihood of escalation. They also review a series of experimental studies that are relevant to their perspective.

Some acts of aggression elicit strong moral condemnation, others elicit respect, but many elicit ambivalence or different reactions from different audiences. In an effort to deflect or mitigate negative moral judgments and avoid punishments or retaliation, individuals often legitimize their coercive behavior. Individuals are more likely to use aggression when they feel that they can justify it to themselves and/or others. The chapters in the third section examine the legitimation process. In chapter 7, Averill suggests that anger is an account that people give to legitimize aggression. He views anger, like other emotions, as a social construction. Anger excuses aggression because it suggests that the person was not in full control of his or her behavior; thus, acts of passion are treated more leniently than are calculated actions. Anger also justifies aggression because it identifies the behavior as a response to the target's misdeeds. Thus, anger involves the claim that the individual has been treated unjustly by another person. The claim is likely to be accepted when the behavior is consistent with social norms (or "folk theories") that specify when a person should be angry. These community standards are used to determine whether anger is accepted as real or treated as illusory.

In chapter 8, Toch also examines the accounts that individuals give to legitimize violent behavior. In their self-portraits, violent actors must explain the disproportionality of their responses to provocations and their tendencies to lose control of themselves. Defensive accounts are likely to be used in official circumstances, but more assertive stories may be told to intimates, who share the actor's values. Defensive accounts are meant to deny, excuse, or justify the action in question and to avoid blame or retribution. For example, aggressors may cite intense pressures or other environmental factors to explain their violent behavior. In addition, they may attempt to increase the social distance between the victim and the listener with the goal of reducing empathy for the victim. In assertive self-portraits, actors boast about their violent behavior. In their "war stories," storytellers present themselves as heros in a "morality play" by emphasizing the victim's provocations and their own honorable motives and heroic struggle: They are only countering bad violence from nasty aggressors who pick on helpless victims.

The two contributions in part 4 focus on violence against women. In chapter 9, Baumgartner examines cross-cultural evidence on physical violence between husbands and wives. She argues that domestic violence cannot be understood without examining the larger social networks of both wives and husbands. Third parties play a role in the generation of domestic conflict by, for example, participating in adulterous relationships or encouraging a spouse's grievance. In addition, third parties play a critical role in determining how conflict is managed. Because of superior physical strength, husbands can assault their wives. However, the brothers and father of an abused woman may seek revenge against her husband. Kinship alliance structures, therefore, critically affect the incidence of wife abuse. The nearer their families of origin, the less apt are women to suffer physical beatings from their husbands. On the other hand, when the wife's kin live far away, the husband is less deterred by a threat of retaliation.

In chapter 10, Felson examines some fundamental issues related to sexual coercion. He identifies three outcomes in incidents of sexual coercion: sexual behavior, harm to the target, and domination of the target. He then examines evidence concerning which of these outcomes is the goal of the action and which outcomes are incidental. The review of evidence suggests that many acts of sexual coercion are sexually motivated. For example, research suggests that offenders have high sexual aspirations, that they also use noncoercive methods to encourage sexual relations, and that they almost always choose young women. However, in some instances of sexual coercion, the offender is probably motivated by a desire to punish the victim. In these instances, the offender feels aggrieved and tends to engage in gratuitous violence in addition to the sexual offense.

Conclusion

The chapters in this volume demonstrate the central themes suggested by a social interactionist approach. Underlying interpersonal aggression is social conflict, a ubiquitous aspect of human relations. When interests diverge, aggression is one method that individuals use to influence each other. Thus, Pruitt et al. examine when struggle tactics are likely to be used to resolve a conflict as opposed to more peaceful means; Stafford and Gibbs associate the use of violence with the efficacy of nonaggressive forms of control; Tedeschi and Nesler focus on the alternative ways in which grievances are expressed; and Felson examines the use of sexual coercion in relation to other forms of social influence. The decision to use aggressive means is then viewed as a rational choice in which both the rewards and costs of the action are considered. On the other hand, according to Gottfredson and Hirschi, people vary in the extent to which they consider the long-term consequences of their choices. Those people with low self-control are likely to make an impulsive choice—which may be an aggressive one.

The actor's definition of the situation is critical from a social interactionist point of view. Thus, Tedeschi and Nesler discuss the importance of the attribution of blame in the formation of grievances, whereas Mummendey and Otten examine dogmatism and other cognitive factors that affect whether the aggrieved is likely to be satisfied with the offender's account. Actors also attempt to legitimize their aggressive behavior by giving excuses and justifications. Thus, Averill describes anger as a legitimizing concept, and Toch describes the violent actor's accounts of his heroic acts.

Once individuals perceive that they have been attacked, they are likely to retaliate, leading to an escalatory cycle. Patchen describes these patterns of reciprocal attack, focusing on the balance of power and the effect of context on the evaluation of the seriousness of a provocation. Baumgartner, on the other hand, emphasizes the strategic role of third parties, particularly when one antagonist is more powerful than the other.

In sum, a social interactionist perspective, as represented by the chapters in this volume, is an integrative approach. By showing the connection between various forms of aggression usually studied in different disciplines, a parochial approach is avoided. In addition, the study of aggression is integrated with the study of human behavior generally, making a unique theory of aggressive behavior unnecessary. Simple and well-established processes in the social sciences—grievance expression, justice and reciprocity, attribution processes, conflict, and social influence—can be applied. If all harmdoing actions are interpreted as motivated to achieve interpersonal goals, a general social psychological theory can be developed to understand them.

References

Averill, J. R. (1982). *Anger and aggression: An essay on emotion.* New York: Springer-Verlag.

Baumgartner, M. P. (1984). Social control from below. In D. Black (Ed.), *Toward a general theory of social control* (pp. 303–345). New York: Academic Press.

Black, D. (1983). Crime as social control. *American Sociological Review, 48,* 34–35.

Borden, R. J. (1975). Witnessed aggression: Influence of an observer's sex and values on aggressive responding. *Journal of Personality and Social Psychology, 31,* 567–573.

Cohen, L. E., & Felson, M. (1979). Social change and crime rate trends: A routine activity approach. *American Sociological Review, 44,* 588–608.

Cornish, D. B., & Clarke, R. V. (1986). *The reasoning criminal.* New York: Springer-Verlag.

Donnerstein, E., & Hatfield, E. (1982). Aggression and inequity. In J. Greenberg & R. Cohen (Eds.), *Equity and justice in social behavior* (pp. 309–336). New York: Academic Press.

Felson, R. B. (1978). Aggression as impression management. *Social Psychology, 41*, 215–213.

Felson, R. B. (1982). Impression management and the escalation of aggression and violence. *Social Psychology Quarterly, 45*, 245–254.

Felson, R. B. (1984). Patterns of aggressive interaction. In A. Mummendey (Ed.), *Social psychology of aggression: From individual behavior to social interaction* (pp. 107–126). Berlin: Springer-Verlag.

Felson, R. B. (1992). "Kick'em when they're down": Explanations of the relationship between stress and interpersonal aggression and violence. *Sociology Quarterly, 33*, 1–16.

Goode, W. J. (1971). Force and violence in the family. *Journal of Marriage and the Family, 33*, 624–635.

Gouldner, A. (1960). The norm of reciprocity: A preliminary statement. *American Sociological Review, 25*, 161–178.

Hirschi, T. (1969). *Causes of delinquency.* Berkeley, CA: University of California Press.

Kadushin, A., & Martin, J. (1981). *Child abuse: An interactional event.* New York: Columbia University Press.

Luckenbill, D. F. (1977). Criminal homicide as a situated transaction. *Social Problems, 25*, 176–186.

Mummendey, A., Linneweber, V., & Löschper, G. (1984). Actor or victim of aggression: Divergent perspectives–divergent evaluations. *European Journal of Social Psychology, 14*, 297–311.

Patterson, G. R. (1982). *Coercive family processes.* Eugene, OR: Castalia.

Rule, B., & Nesdale, A. (1976). Moral judgment of aggressive behavior. In R. G. Geen & E. C. O'Neal (Eds.), *Perspectives on aggression* (pp. 37–60). New York: Academic Press.

Schonbach, P. (1990). *Account episodes: The management or escalation of conflict.* Cambridge, England: Cambridge University Press.

Tedeschi, J. T. (1983). Social influence theory and aggression. In R. Geen (Ed.), *Aggression: Theoretical and empirical reviews* (pp. 135–162). New York: Academic Press.

Tedeschi, J. T., Smith, R. B., III, & Brown, R. C., Jr. (1974). A reinterpretation of research on aggression. *Psychological Bulletin, 89*, 540–563.

Toch, H. (1969). *Violent men: An inquiry into the psychology of violence.* Chicago: Aldine.

Wolfe, D. A. (1985). Child-abusive parents: An empirical review and analysis. *Psychological Bulletin, 97*, 483–496.

PART ONE

Aggression and Control

CHAPTER 1

Grievances: Development and Reactions

James T. Tedeschi and Mitchell S. Nesler

A theory of grievances is first and foremost an explanation of the perceptions and responses of people to injustice. In this chapter, we review the research on perceptions of injustice and the factors associated with attributing responsibility and blame to other people. Perception of injustice typically arouses anger, so it is important to understand how anger affects the individual and subsequent social interactions. We begin by examining the conditions that lead to the formation of a grievance. Then, we elucidate the factors that the grievant considers in deciding how to respond to the unjust and blameworthy person and the factors that affect which response is chosen.

The term *grievance* has been typically defined as a judgment that one has been unjustly harmed by another person, a group, or an institution (see Felstiner, Abel, & Sarat, 1980–1981; Stafford & Gibbs, 1991). We think that the definition should be expanded to include unjust or unfair actions regardless of whether harm is actually done. A perception that another person engaged in an action with the intent to do harm would be a sufficient basis for a complaint. Heider (1958) suggested that people tend to respond to intentions as well as to the outcomes of actions. This hypothesis was substantiated by Horai (1977), who found that unharmed subjects responded with strong punitive actions as a direct function of the amount of harm they perceived another person as intending toward them, irrespective of whether they actually were harmed. Thus, the definition of grievance proffered here is not restricted to injury or harm but is based more generally on a judgment that another social agent has performed an unjust or unfair action—a norm-violating action. Although attributing blame to another person for a norm-violating action leads to a grievance, no grievance occurs unless the victim perceives options to redress or challenge the injustice (Fine, 1985).

Norms were described by DeRidder, Schruijer, and Tripathi (1992) as if–then statements. People have expectations about what actors should or should not do in particular situations. If a particular situation occurs, then the actor should (or should not) perform certain actions. When a person either does not perform the prescribed action or performs a proscribed action, the norm is being violated. Norm violations may or may not lead to grievances, but all grievances are based on norm violations.

The development of grievances and what people do about them is typically explained as a series of stages or transformations. Felstiner et al. (1980–1981) identified these stages as the perception of injury, the attribution of responsibility and blame, and the subsequent demand for some remedy. These stages are referred to as *naming, blaming,* and *claiming,* respectively. It is unclear whether naming and blaming are separate stages in information processing. A distinction between perception and cognitive interpretation appears false in that it suggests separation between naming and blaming. On the other hand, a consideration of types of harm and judgments of antinormative actions is useful for presenting aspects of a general theory of grievances. Also, the view that claiming is a final stage ignores the fact that there are other actions that a person may take following the formation of a grievance. We examine a number of action alternatives available to a grievant.

We will examine a sequence of processes beginning with a negative event experienced by a person. The person will attempt to explain the event by processes of attribution and access of available cognitive scripts. If through this process, blame is assigned to another person for the negative event, the attributor will experience anger and under certain conditions will form a grievance. The role of anger in the subsequent behavior of the attributor will be examined by separating the anger experience from angry behaviors. Once a grievance is formed, a number of action alternatives are available to a grievant. The nature of these alternatives and some factors that the grievant considers in deciding what to do will be discussed.

Types of Negative Events and Antinormative Actions

The conditions that lead people to perceive themselves as victims of unjust actions are rather complex. Any of a host of actions by others may produce a grievance. A newly purchased automobile may begin to display many symptoms of mechanical disorders immediately after the expiration of the warranty. Such autos are referred to as lemons, probably because of the sour disposition they produce in their owners. We may discover that someone we trust has been lying to us. These two examples indicate that grievances are based on a diverse range of events.

Types of Events Involved in Grievances

There are at least four types of events that can lead to grievances. In each case, the kind of event forms the basis for a grievance only if the person attributes responsibility and blame for the event to another person. First, injury, pain, or unpleasant sensations produced by physical stimuli or the perception of an intent to inflict physical harm may form the basis for grievances. The intensity and duration of pain, the permanence of injury, the degree of disability produced, and other such factors will be directly related to the amount of resentment by the injured person if they are blamed on another person. Many lawsuits involve a grievant suing for damages in cases in which they feel that they have been wrongfully caused to suffer physical harm by the defendant.

Second, loss of or damage to existing or expected goods or resources or the perception of an intention to impose deprivation of resources may form the basis for a grievance. For example, damage to an automobile or to other objects possessed by the person may lead to a perception of injustice. The degree of resentment experienced will vary directly with the subjective value of the material deprivation experienced by the person.

Third, perceived damage to desired social identities can also lead to resentment. Bies (1986) and Bies and Moag (1986) proposed that people are concerned about the quality of treatment that they receive from others in social interactions. They referred to the individual's sensitivity to respectful treatment and honesty as aspects of interaction justice. Tyler and Lind (1990) also emphasized that judgments of justice frequently involve the perception that others failed to show politeness and respect. Tyler (1988) found that people who had contact with police or courts perceived the procedures as more fair if they had been treated with respect. Messick, Bloom, Boldizar, and Samuelson (1985) asked subjects to write lists of fair and unfair things that other people did. Among the events listed were vicious gossip, rudeness, lack of punctuality, exploitative behavior, and selfishness. The list was overwhelmingly concerned with issues of interactional justice. We propose that the centrality, salience, or situational importance of the social identity that has been threatened or damaged will be directly related to the strength of any grievance formed by the person.

Fourth, political harm in the form of violation of rights, interference with opportunities, or constraints on freedoms may serve as the basis for grievances. For example, people may perceive that others prevent them from purchasing houses in particular neighborhoods or discriminate against them in hiring for jobs. The degree of legitimacy assigned to rights, the importance of opportunities, and the strength of constraints will directly affect the amount of resentment the person will experience if a grievance is formed.

Antinormative Actions and Forms of Injustice

The four types of negative actions just discussed tend to be perceived in terms of different types of injustice. In an international study involving samples from Austria, Bulgaria, Finland, and West Germany, subjects were asked to recall events in which they experienced emotions such as anger, fear, and shame (Mikula, Petri, & Tanzer, 1990). They were then asked to characterize the events as just or unjust. The unjust events were analyzed and found to be organized under three basic types of injustice: distributive, procedural, and interactional.

Distributive justice includes the fair distribution of goods and benefits, the impartiality of judges or referees, fair allocation of responsibilities, legitimacy of punishments, and recognition of performance or effort. *Procedural justice* involves issues such as the arbitrariness of rules and authorities and the construction and grading of examinations. *Interactional justice*, which was involved in a majority of events described by subjects, refers to regard for the feelings of others, keeping agreements, accusations or censure, selfishness, and hostility. Mikula et al. (1990) found that by far the greatest number of unjust incidents were aggregated around the norms of interaction and social identity.[1]

In a further study by Mikula et al. (1990), subjects were asked to rate 84 unjust situations on several scales, assessing the relationship between the two parties, the degree of injustice, and the magnitude of the consequences to the victim. These ratings

---

[1] *These results suggest that defensive self-presentations and concern for social justice may both be present in most instances of perceived injustice. In this chapter, the justice motive is conceptually separated from self-presentational motive (see Tedeschi & Felson, 1992, for a more complete theory of coercive justice).*

were then fit to a multidimensional scale. The first and most important dimension differentiated injustices that occur in task-related, unequal power situations from injustices that occur in long-term relationships between people who are equal in power.

The second dimension referred only to informal long-term relationships and differentiated between lack of loyalty and a variety of inconsiderate and annoying actions by one of the parties. The third dimension distinguished between commission of acts that inflict injustice and omission of acts that withhold deserved outcomes.

Comparison Level and Relative Deprivation

The level of dissatisfaction experienced by the individual may depend on expectations regarding acceptable outcomes. In social psychology, this expectation factor is referred to as *comparison level* (see Thibaut & Kelley, 1959). The simplest explanation of this concept is that people who have high aspirations will be disappointed with outcomes that people with lower aspirations would find satisfying. For example, it has been found that consumers from the middle class indicate a greater dissatisfaction with goods and services than do consumers from the lower class (Best & Andreasen, 1977).

An interesting aspect of comparison level is that a person can feel harmed and blame others after having been rewarded. Insufficient or inappropriate rewards can serve as the basis for a feeling of relative deprivation. A classic study found that air force personnel in the U.S. Army were more dissatisfied than were military police with the promotional system even though promotions were faster for air force personnel (Stouffer, Suchman, DeVinney, Star, & Williams, 1949). Apparently, the fact of more promotions created higher expectations among air force personnel and paradoxically created more dissatisfaction.

Runciman (1966) provided the following concise statement of relative deprivation theory: "A is relatively deprived of X when (1) he does not have X, (2) he sees some other person or persons . . . as having X . . . , (3) he wants X, and (4) he sees it as feasible that he should have X" (p. 11). Runciman distinguished between egoistical relative deprivation, which involves social comparisons with other individuals, and fraternal relative deprivation, which involves intergroup comparisons.

Serious shortcomings exist with regard to egoistical relative deprivation theory. It does not provide a basis for predicting who an individual will choose as a comparison other (Schruijer, 1990). Research has shown that the choice of a comparison group is dependent on the goals of the individual (D. M. Taylor, Moghaddam, & Bellerose, 1989). Also, egoistical relative deprivation theory is not adequate for understanding grievances because it does not consider the process of the attribution of blame for unsatisfactory outcomes.

However, relative deprivation theory does suggest the possibility of reducing the incidence of grievances by lowering expectations. For example, realistic job previews, which show both the negative and positive aspects of a job to prospective employees, increase job satisfaction and reduce turnover (Dugoni & Ilgen, 1981; Muchinsky, 1987; Wanous, 1977).

Changes in comparison levels in segments of the population can increase the level of grievances in a society without any change in the distribution of rewarding or punishing actions. For example, Adams and Dressler (1988) found that elderly people perceived less injustice than did young people in a Black community in the U.S. South. An explanation of the relations of age to perceived injustice is that older Black people were socialized to have lower expectations with regard to rights and opportunities than were younger people raised during the civil rights movement. Among political scientists, such changes in expectations are referred to as *rising expectations*, which can be a potent basis of revolution and social change.

Equity theory proposes that the experience of justice or injustice occurs in comparison with similar others. For example, workers who perceive peers as achieving higher rewards than themselves will experience relative deprivation (Olson, Herman, & Zanna, 1986). Negative events that affect a large segment of the population may be experienced as less unjust than when they happen to a single person. Although shared fate does not always prevent feelings of injustice, evidence indicates that people cope more successfully with normative events than with nonnormative ones (Filipp & Gräser, 1982).

Blaming

Negative actions by others do not always lead to grievances. People sometimes believe that they deserve to be punished or they may have fatalistic beliefs about negative events. Research by Fine (1979, 1983, 1985) indicated that the introduction of options activates a sense of injustice in observers. When no procedure exists for challenging injustice, grievances may not be formed. Prior to forming grievances, victims must analyze the behavior of the perpetrator. When harm is attributed to the action or inaction of another person, the harmed person seeks an explanation for the other's harm-doing action. The individual tries to determine whether the other person is responsible (i.e., accountable) for the harm-doing action. To hold a person responsible is to make that person liable for sanctions.

Norm Violations and Intent To Do Harm

The first stage in determining accountability and assigning blame is the judgment that another person performed an antinormative action. Ferguson and Rule (1981, p. 43) represented a norm violation as a discrepancy between what the perceiver believed should have occurred and what actually did occur. In several studies in which subjects read scenarios and provided ratings of depicted actors, DeRidder (1985) found that norm violation was a more important determinant of attributions of malevolent intentions than was degree of harm actually done by the actors. However, he cautioned that this strong impact of norm violations probably occurs only when the actor is perceived as a causal agent, the observer does not have information about prior actions of the actor, and there is a clearly distinguishable difference between what the actor did and what the actor should have done.

Either intent to do harm and violate norms or unjustified harm-doing can lead to attributions of responsibility and blame. In a study that provided information to children about incidents that took place in school settings, degree of norm violation, malevolent intent, and injury were manipulated (Löschper, Mummendey, Linneweber, & Bornewasser, 1984). All three factors contributed to attributions. There was a high degree of correlation between norm violation and intent, suggesting that forming a harmful intention is itself frequently considered to be antinormative. It is important to point out that norm violations and perceived intentions are in the eye of the beholder and are not objective features of events, although objective conditions may be identified as the bases for the occurrence of these subjective judgments. Indeed, quarrels often occur when each party believes that the other is acting in an antinormative manner.

R. C. Brown and Tedeschi (1976) demonstrated that a harmdoer may be perceived as less offensive and morally wrong than may a protagonist who intends to do harm but fails. In the example in their study, the protagonist initiated the use of force by throwing a punch but missing the target person. Subsequently, the target punched the protagonist in the stomach, doubling him over. This scene was performed on stage by actors. The audience was then asked to rate the two actors on a series of scales. The protagonist was perceived as offensive, bad, and aggressive, whereas the target was rated as defensive, good, and nonaggressive. This study indicates that the intention attributed to the protagonist and the judgment that the act was in violation of interaction norms was the basis for impressions formed of him rather than the degree of harm that he did.

The Attribution Process

People are apt to begin a cognitive search for the reasons for an actor's behavior when confronted with unexpected behavior, unwanted consequences, or stressful, puzzling, and important events (Wong & Weiner, 1981). Thus, the attribution process may be activated either when the individual experiences harm or perceives an antinormative or enigmatic action by another person. Responsibility and blame will be attributed when the actor's intent is perceived as malevolent.

The attribution process may be described as a decision tree. The perceiver makes a judgment as to whether the agent's action was intended or unintended. If the agent's action is perceived as intended, the perceiver makes a judgment as to whether the agent's motivation was malevolent. An agent who engages in an antinormative action with malevolent intent is perceived as responsible and blameworthy. If the initial decision was that the agent's antinormative behavior was unintentional, the perceiver then makes a judgment as to whether the consequences of the action were foreseeable. If the consequences are viewed as foreseeable, then they are avoidable, and the agent may be judged to be responsible and blameworthy for not avoiding the consequences.

Among the conditions that contribute to the attribution that an actor intended the harmful consequences of behavior are perceptions that the actor had the ability to bring about the observed harm, knew before the act that the harmful consequences would occur, and was free to engage in some alternative behavior (Heider, 1958; Jones & Davis, 1965). It is beyond the scope of this chapter to review the attribution literature to establish the bases for perceptions of ability, knowledge, and freedom (but see Frieze, 1976; Hewstone, 1989; Shaver, 1985).

Actors and victims frequently make different attributions about an actor's malevolent intentions. In one study of divergent attributions, each of two marital partners was asked to report instances of unfair behavior by the other partner, and each was also asked to respond to questions about the events that the other partner thought were unfair (Mikula & Heimgartner, 1992). Perpetrators rated the events as less serious and unjust, their causal contribution to the event as smaller, and their actions as more justified than did victims. A similar finding was obtained in a role-playing study of aggressive interactions (Mummendey, Linneweber, & Löschper, 1984).

Caution must be used in interpreting these results as due only to cognitive processes. Mikula and Heimgartner (1992) found that victims' perceptions of injustice were based on causality, intention, and lack of justification for a perpetrator's action, but these factors did not predict the assessment of injustice by the perpetrator. Actors have a vested interest in minimizing injustices that they perpetrate, and victims often have a vested interest in exaggerating the degree of harm done and the responsibility of the actors. These divergent interests and attributional biases contribute to a widening of differences and the intensification of conflict between individuals (Mikula, 1984; Orvis, Kelley, & Butler, 1976; Reis, 1984).

Individual Differences in Attribution

Some individuals are prone to assign blame without considering extenuating circumstances or attributing intentionality or motivation to the actor. There are instances of strict liability in the law and no doubt also in everyday interactions, but typically the attribution process occurs in assigning responsibility and blame for antinormative actions. Heider (1958), Piaget (1932), and Kohlberg (1981) each suggested that strict liability is a primitive or immature level of moral reasoning. Horan and Kaplan (1983) found that subjects who were identified by a paper-and-pencil scale as having high levels of moral reasoning assigned greater punishments to an agent who intended to do severe harm than to an agent who intended to do mild harm (with the actual harm held constant). Subjects identified as having a low level of moral reasoning did not distinguish between mild and severe intentions but instead assigned severe punishment in all cases. Some adults who reason in terms of strict liability may react in ways that may appear irrational to other people. A desire to avoid responsibility and self-blame may also be associated with blaming others for unwanted consequences of social interactions. A 30-year longitudinal study by Vaillant (1977) indicated that there are individual differences in the tendency to blame others for injustices.

Some people may have a disposition to distrust others and may be suspicious of the intentions of others. Although there is a tendency by most people to assign more weight to negatively valenced information than to positively valued information—a phenomenon referred to as *negativity bias* (Kanouse & Hansen, 1972)—some people may have a stronger disposition to do so. Buss and Durkee (1957) measured individual differences in hostility and related them to aggressive behavior (Buss, 1961). Dodge and Coie (1987) reported that a bias in making hostile attributions was related to displays of anger by schoolchildren. Field observations led Toch (1969) to propose that violent men tend to view movements or cues emitted by others as threatening and dangerous and that their violent reactions are often perceived by themselves as preemptive strikes. This link between attributional biases, anger, and aggression was further supported in a study of male adolescents who were being held in a maximum security prison. It was found that scores on a paper-and-pencil measure of hostile attribution bias were significantly related to the number of violent (but not nonviolent) crimes committed by them (Dodge, Price, Bachorowski, & Newman, 1990).

Responsibility and Blame

When harm to a victim is severe, it is more likely that perceivers will attribute blame to the agent (Affleck, Allen, Tennen, McGrade, & Ratzan, 1985; Affleck, Pfeiffer, Tennen, & Fifield, 1987; Rosen & Jerdee, 1974; Shaver, 1970; Vidmar & Crinklaw, 1974; Walster, 1966). Perhaps people believe that severe consequences should be more foreseeable than less harmful outcomes. According to a review of the literature on self-blame and blame of others (Tennen & Affleck, 1991), there is a distinct tendency to blame others for unwanted consequences of an acute or identifiable event. For example, a high percentage of women blamed a particular man for unwanted pregnancy (Major, Mueller, & Hildebrandt, 1985). When subjects in another study were asked to assign a level of punishment to an agent who harmed a victim, more severe punishments were given the greater the harm done (Horai & Bartek, 1978; Landy & Aronson, 1969; Vidmar & Miller, 1980). Substantial evidence has also been garnered to show that the actor's intention to harm is sanctioned in the same way regardless of whether the actor is successful in meting out the harm (Epstein & Taylor, 1967; Geen, 1968; Gentry, 1970; Nickel, 1974; S. P. Taylor & Pisano, 1971).

Although moral responsibility is typically attributed to an actor when he or she is a causal agent in intentionally producing negatively valenced events, blame may also be attributed when the actor did not cause the harm or when an act is perceived as unintentional. An agent does not have to be the cause of harm to be held responsible for its occurrence. For example, a lifeguard may be blamed when a swimmer drowns. A person perceived as having authority in a situation is more apt to be blamed for harm that is done, regardless of whether he or she is at the scene when the event occurs. A police officer may be blamed for not preventing harm, or a corporate executive may be blamed for an action performed by a subordinate.[2]

If an agent is perceived as negligent in causing harm, responsibility and blame will be attributed (Walster, 1966). Negligence occurs when an agent does not take sufficient care for the interests of others when performing an act. Schultz and Wright (1985) found that workers were considered equally blameworthy for harm done through thoughtless acts as they were for harm done through intentional acts. A type of negativity bias was also found. Subjects attributed more responsibility to actors for negligent harm-doing than for negligent bestowing of benefits. Blaming people for negligent acts is reasonable because it may induce them (and others) to act with greater care in the future (Hart, 1968).

A person who acts recklessly may also be held responsible for any negative consequences that occur. Hart (1968) defined a reckless action as "wittingly flying in the face of a substantial, unjustified risk, or the conscious creation of such a risk" (p. 137). Risky actions may be justified by their social utility. Melburg and Tedeschi (1981) found that an ambulance driver who was driving at high speed toward a hospital with a critically ill patient was not perceived as responsible for hitting a child who darted across the highway. However, when the driver was speeding and the ambulance had a passenger with only a slight injury, the driver was judged as reckless, responsible, and blameworthy for hitting the child.

If the harmdoer has an acceptable excuse or can adequately justify the harmdoing action, either no blame will be ascribed and no grievance will occur or the degree of blame will be mitigated and the grievance will be of a lesser magnitude (Heider, 1958; Horai, 1977). However, if the harmdoer's action is perceived as unjustified or illegitimate (i.e., as norm violating), then the individual will assign responsibility and blame and will feel resentment toward the harmdoer.

Social Knowledge and Social Explanations

The attribution process described here is conceived as occurring in discrete steps, involving a series of inferences. Another view is that the individual constructs an account of an action by drawing from a knowledge base (Abelson & Lalljee, 1988). A human explainer

---

[2]A person who incites or initiates actions by others that eventuate in foreseeable harm may also be held responsible and blameworthy even though no direct action by that person produced harm. For example, a person who hires another to murder a designated victim will be treated as a murderer.

has a storehouse of information about the nature of plans and the kinds of goals that people strive to attain. In any given instance, the individual's task is to identify the operative goal of the actor and the plan that the actor used to attain the goal. When acts are connected to goals and plans, the explainer has an adequate account of what happened. Social context and the rules that govern conduct are important in providing clues to such accounts.

The impact of social context on observers' evaluations of actions by police officers was demonstrated by Lincoln and Levinger (1972). In all cases, a White police officer was shown in a photograph as grabbing the shirt of a young Black man. When the scene was described as a peaceful civil rights demonstration, the police officer was evaluated negatively. However, when no cues were presented that indicated that the officer's action was antinormative, the officer's action was rated as legitimate and he received positive evaluations. The raters were young college students attending a liberal New England university. Segregationists might not have accepted the Black man's right to demonstrate in the streets and might have rated the policeman positively in both conditions of the experiment. There is ample evidence that whether a particular action is considered justified depends on the values and norms of the observer (e.g., Blumenthal, Kahn, Andrews, & Head, 1972).

Primacy Effects

The observer's prior impression of an actor may also affect attributions for a current action. Fauconnet (quoted in Heider, 1944) emphasized the primacy effect of prior impressions of the evaluation of a person:

> Persons dreaded for their brutality are the first ones to be suspected of a violent crime; despised persons of a mean act; and those who arouse disgust of an unclean act. People with bad reputations are accused and convicted on the basis of evidence which one would consider insufficient if an unfavorable prejudice did not relate them to the crime in advance. On the contrary, if the accused has won our favor we demand irrefutable proof before we impute to him the crime. (p. 363)

Self-Blame

Often, victims blame themselves because they believe that they could have done something to avoid the harmful event. Studies of parents who have lost a child (Chodhoff, Friedman, & Hamburg, 1964), relatives of victims of Nazi concentration camps (Rappaport, 1971), rape victims (Burgess & Holmstrom, 1979; Medea & Thompson, 1974), and battered women (Ferraro & Johnson, 1983; Frieze, 1979; Martin, 1978) indicate that victims often blame themselves when there is no objective reason to do so. Because self-blame is associated with depression and poor adjustment (e.g., Meyer & Taylor, 1986), counselors, clergy, and psychologists may be motivated to persuade the individual to shift the perception of blame onto some other person, group, or institution.

Interpersonal Processes and Blame

The attribution process leading to a judgment of exculpation or blame is obviously a complicated one. It is not a purely cognitive information-processing exercise or a search of one's store of social knowledge but typically is also an interpersonal process. Decision-makers in organizations attempt to focus blame as far down the authority hierarchy as they can. Friends, relatives, clerics, psychologists, counselors, union stewards, and attorneys are only some of the people whose consultation and advice may affect perceptions of harm, decisions concerning whom to blame, and courses of action to satisfy grievances. The influence of third parties may be crucial for redirecting self-blame for aversive consequences to another person.

The attribution process may be affected by the social identities, personal relationships, and group affiliations of the two parties. Friends are likely to make allowances for one another and to look for justifying reasons for harmdoing, whereas people who dislike one another may have the opposite bias. Jones and Nisbett (1971) proposed that

> the tendency to infer dispositional causes is undoubtedly also enhanced when the observer disliked the actor who performs a blameworthy act . . . however, the observer's bias can just as easily be reversed when the observer likes the perpetrator of bad acts. (p. 15)

The relation of attraction to attributions of blame was illustrated in a study by Dion (1972). College students were given a description of a child's action, which was accompanied by a picture of an attractive or unattractive child. The child was said to have attacked a dog or another child. In the mild harm condition, the child stepped on the tail of a sleeping dog or hit another child on the leg with a snowball, producing only a stinging sensation. In the severe harm condition, the child threw stones at the dog, cutting it on the leg, or put a piece of ice in a snowball, threw it, and cut another child's scalp.

Severe harm was rated as more antinormative than was mild harm, and harming the dog was considered just as blameworthy as was harming the other child. However, the unattractive child in the severe harm condition was perceived as acting in a more antisocial way, as more likely to engage in a similar action in the future, and as more unpleasant than was the attractive child.

In a retrospective study of the criminal court system, Kalven and Zeisel (1966) asked judges to complete questionnaires about criminal jury trials over which they had presided. Each judge recounted the decision made by the jury, the decision he or she would have made in the absence of a jury, and the reasons for disagreements between the two verdicts. Of the 962 cases in which the judges disagreed with the juries' decisions, 11% were attributed to positive or negative impressions formed by the jury of the defendant.

Byrne (1971) manipulated differences in attraction for a stranger by establishing attitude similarity or dissimilarity. Many studies have established that observers perceive harmdoers who have similar attitudes as more well intentioned and as more justified than they do harmdoers who have dissimilar attitudes (e.g., Nesdale, Rule, & Hill, 1978; Turkat & Dawson, 1976; Veitch & Piccione, 1978). Caution must be exercised in generalizing from these findings because attraction in these studies was shallow, and the subjects were observers rather than victims.

One of the reasons for the frequent grievances that occur between intimates is that the norms that govern behavior depend to some degree on the nature of the relationship between interacting parties. Relationships that are limited to economic exchange or formal settings have elaborate rules of politeness and demeanor that must be maintained in the context of specific sets of rules and sanctions (Blau, 1964; P. Brown & Levinson, 1987; Goffman, 1971). Intimate relationships, such as those that occur in courtship and marriage or families, may involve expectations that are different from more casual associations. Among the characteristics of relationships with friends, lovers, spouses, and children are stronger intensity of feelings, greater depth and breadth of exchange of information, commitment to each other, greater variety and value of material and emotional resources that are exchanged, and tendency to view the relationship in terms of "we" rather than independent units (Hatfield, Utne, & Traupmann, 1979). In the context of these characteristics of intimate relationships, a wide variety of actions may be perceived as harmful and antinormative. For example, a conflict about the allocation of role responsibilities, particularly when outside pressures require changes, may lead to perceptions of unfairness.

People who are dissatisfied with their close relationships tend to make more malevolent attributions to their partners than do people in more satisfactory relationships

(Bradbury & Fincham, 1990). Furthermore, the more dissatisfied actors are, the more willing they are to admit committing injustices (Mikula & Heimgartner, 1992).

Compared with people in casual relationships, who often accept an equity principle of resource allocations, people in intimate relationships prefer an equality principle of distributive justice. Austin (1980) found that strangers in a laboratory study divided rewards in a manner that was commensurate with performance on a task, whereas college roommates were more likely to divide the reward equally and to ignore task performance as a criterion for distribution.

Parents who abuse their children tend to view the children as engaging in abrasive behaviors not performed by their siblings (Gelles, 1980). Kempe and Kempe (1978) suggested that the perception that children intentionally defy their wishes leads parents to judgments of unfairness, which result in harsh punishments (i.e., child abuse). The abuse may not be based on a single event but may be the culmination of many annoying acts.

When people perceive each other in terms of group categories, there is a distinct ethnocentric bias. For example, D. M. Taylor and Jaggi (1974) found that Hindu subjects attributed undesirable behavior by ingroup members to external factors but made internal attributions for identical behavior by Muslims.

Anger, Resentment, and Grievances

Once blame is focused on an outside party, the individual is likely to experience resentment and anger. These emotions may create a desire in the individual to restore justice; if the individual believes that some remedial action *should* be carried out, one would say he or she has formed a grievance. Grievants must believe that remedial actions are available. The belief is that justice would be restored if the remedial action were successfully performed, independently of who performs it.

Anger Arousal

Undoubtedly, emotions are complex events, consisting of cognitive, affective, and behavioral components (Mandler, 1979).[3] A cognitive judgment is implicated in the arousal of angry feelings. In a study that asked college students to recall incidents that made them

---

[3]Mandler also referred to physiological aspects of emotion, whereas Kemper (1978) referred to links to the social system. We ignore those aspects of emotion in this exposition.

feel angry, subjects mostly recalled events that were described as voluntary and unjustified or as harmful and avoidable (Averill, 1983). Angry feelings apparently result from the cognitive process of attributing responsibility and blame to others. Averill (1983, p. 1150) stated that the most important fact about anger is that it is a reaction to some perceived misdeed.

The importance of the judgment of injustice for the arousal of anger was demonstrated by Klein and Bierhoff (1991), who manipulated distributive (pay) and procedural (selfish interest of supervisor) factors in a relationship between a subordinate and a supervisor in three scenario studies. Subjects were asked to take the viewpoint of the subordinate and to assess the fairness of the situation and how angry they would feel, to evaluate the relevant activity, and to indicate how motivated they would be to succeed in the future. The main finding of interest here is that when perceived fairness was controlled, the effects of distributive and procedural justice on anger, devaluation of the activity, and achievement motivation were no longer significant. In other words, anger was not aroused and reactions associated with anger were not performed unless a prior judgment was made that injustice had occurred.

If anger feelings are aroused by judgments of injustice, then the divergences of attribution between actor and victim, noted in the prior section, should be reflected in the intensity of the anger experienced by the two parties. Some evidence for divergences in anger has been provided by Baumeister, Stillwell, and Wotman (1990). Respondents who had been asked to provide a story of an incident in which they were perpetrators of an anger-provoking incident and a story in which they were the victims, provided indications of role bias. Victim accounts contained references to lasting negative consequences and continuing anger, whereas perpetrator accounts more frequently denied the significance of negative consequences and referred to happy endings for the incidents described.[4]

Functions of Anger

The behavioral expression of anger is not automatic or reactive, nor does it have a single goal such as inflicting injury or harm on others. The conflation of expressions of anger with reactive aggression by some theorists (e.g., Berkowitz, 1989) has obscured the multiple functions of anger in social interactions. It is our view that the cognitive and affective

---

[4]These divergences of perpetrators and victims may partially be due to vested interests of perpetrators to close the issue as no longer relevant to the relationship, whereas the victim may find it worthwhile to keep the issue open as having implications for currect interactions.

components of anger should be theoretically separated from the behavioral expression of anger.[5] One reason for this theoretical choice is that the conditions for the experience of anger appear to be distinguishable from the kinds of responses that the person is likely to perform following an experience of anger. Also, the effects of experienced anger appear to be different from anger expressions. Among the functions of anger noted by Novaco (1976) are energizing, disruptive, expressive, self-presentational, defensive, and potentiating functions.

The energizing function of anger is indicated by the increase in volume of one's voice, the slamming of doors, or other vigorous motor responses. However, anger arousal also tends to disrupt and disorganize cognitive processes. The tendency in angry people is to simplify information processing and to make judgments that are more black and white than in calmer circumstances (White, 1968). The energizing and disruptive functions may cause reactions to become more impulsive; thus, the admonition to count to 10 when angry (cf. Tavris, 1982).

Attributions of blame and injustice frequently lead to expressions of anger. Communications of anger are typically accusatory, and because of cognitive disruptions, they may be inadequately or crudely expressed. Problems that exist between people, particularly in intimate relationships, may not be fully expressed until one or both parties become angry. In Averill's (1983) study of college students, 76% who had been targets of anger said that they better understood their own faults following the other person's expression of anger. Students reported that the relationship with the other person was frequently strengthened following an angry episode. Although anger may sometimes lead to impulsive and destructive actions, as we show, it more often has the constructive function of instigating solutions to interpersonal problems.

Anger also has a self-presentational function of establishing one's identity as a strong and determined person who demands respect and will not tolerate being treated unjustly by others. The expression of anger, among other things, is also a claim that the person has socially valued attributes and is deserving of respectful behavior by the blameworthy individual. The accusatory aspect of anger expressions is not separate from its self-justification aspect. As Warner (1986) stated, "our exoneration is their culpability" (p. 145). By accusing the other person of persecution, the angry individual simultaneously makes himself or herself a victim. If the victim attributes blame to himself or herself,

---

[5]*Facial expressions may be a rather automatic accompaniment to the experience of anger, but even they can be controlled by the individual.*

anger might be directed inward and the perpetrator exonerated. The question raised by the direction of anger (outward or inward) is one of innocence and guilt.

Jones and Pittman (1982) referred to intimidation as consisting of self-presentation tactics that actors sometimes use to induce fear in and behavioral compliance from target people. The expression of anger, especially when intense and eruptive, may have such an intimidation effect and can serve to increase the believability of threats issued by the angry person.

The expression of anger may reduce anxiety because anger externalizes problems, whereas anxiety internalizes problems. As Novaco (1976) stated, "There is nothing wrong with me; there is something wrong with you" (p. 1125). Thus, anger reduces feelings of insecurity. When a person experiences injustice, there is a corresponding perception of disrespect, lowering of status, and loss of power or control. Content analyses of interviews of college students revealed that anger was characteristically associated with reports of anxiety and sadness (Wickless & Kirsch, 1988). Anger expressions potentiate an experience of power and control over a situation. It is worth noting that Type A personalities, who are obsessed with time and control over events, are also characterized by short tempers and explosions of hostility and anger (Diamond, 1982).

Anger may activate motives for self-presentation, control, modifying social relationships, and/or justice. Which of these motives is activated will be guided by the victim's interpretation of the nature of the actor's antinormative behavior identified in the naming phase of grievance formation. If the antinormative action consisted of disrespect, insult, or another form of identity attack, the major concern of the target person will be to restore face. If the antinormative action was one that produced relative deprivation for the grievant, the major concern will be to restore justice. In this chapter, we are primarily interested in the justice motive that directs the victim to consider alternative means of restoring justice in the relationship with the blameworthy person (Lerner, 1980).

Grievance-Related Actions

Once people form grievances and a justice motive is activated, what they will actually do depends on the type and magnitude of harm experienced, the importance and salience of the rule that has been violated, the relationship to the other party, the remediability of the harmful consequences, and the expected reactions of the harmdoer or third parties. Figure 1 indicates the alternatives that an aggrieved party may consider following the formation of a grievance.

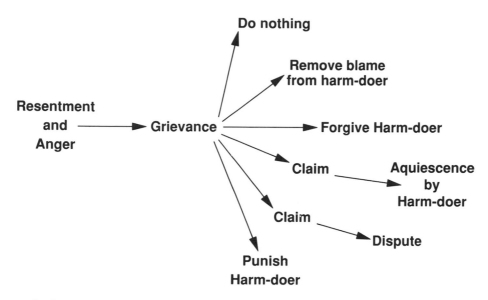

FIGURE 1 Possible reactions by grievant.

Do Nothing

One possibility is to do nothing. Inaction may occur because of a lack of confidence that any action will restore justice or an expectation that punitive actions will bring unacceptable costs. Lack of confidence may be due to past experiences of failure by the individual, represented by low self-efficacy, or by current circumstances. Among the situational factors are the status of the harmdoer, the control that the harmdoer has over future reinforcements, the probability of resistance and retaliation by the harmdoer, and expected reactions of significant third parties. All of these factors relate to the probable costs of carrying out a justice-restoring action. The greater the expected costs of carrying out any action, the less likely it is that the person will carry out the action. If the expected gains are believed to exceed the expected costs and if the net gain for a decision alternative is greater than other actions that are considered, the person will accept the costs and will engage in the action. These predictions, derived from a rational choice perspective, must incorporate material, social, and psychic factors in calculating costs and gains. For example, respondents reported that they frequently did not express their anger because they did not want to induce conflict or damage the relationship with the perpetrator (Deshields, Jenkins, & Tait, 1989).

Whereas others may take action to restore justice, frequently the choice by the victim to do nothing lets the injustice stand unrectified. The victim may ruminate about the precipitating incident, interpret subsequent negative events as connected to it, and experience increasing resentment toward the perpetrator. These subjective reactions to the original unjust incident may last for years afterward (Silver, Boon, & Stones, 1983).

The perpetuation of perceived injustice may be associated with increasing depression and learned helplessness (cf. Tennen & Affleck, 1991), which frequently interfere with adaptive behavior or coping responses. On the other hand, the "straw that broke the camel's back" phenomenon may occur. An accumulation of injustices that are experienced by the victim without response may suddenly evoke a strong response. This process is sometimes interpreted as built-up frustrations that lead to aggressive behavior (Dollard, Doob, Miller, Mowrer, & Sears, 1939).

Remove Blame and Withdraw Grievance

A second possible reaction following a grievance is for the harmed person to reevaluate the basis for blame and decide that the harmdoer is not blameworthy. The most common cause of a removal of blame is some account provided by the harmdoer or by a third party that excuses or justifies the negative event (Scott & Lyman, 1968). An excuse is an explanation that denies (at least partially) responsibility for the negative event. There are many types of excuses, including assertions that the event was an accident, the consequences were unforeseen and thus unintended, or the harmdoer could not control behavior because of temporary states induced by alcohol, drugs, illness, insanity, or coercion (Tedeschi & Reiss, 1981).

A justification is an explanation that accepts responsibility for the negative event but provides reasons why the harmdoer's action was the correct or at least the necessary thing to do in that situation. According to Hewitt and Stokes (1976), justifications align actions to social norms and make the actions both intelligible and acceptable. Among the types of justifications that might be offered are that the good accomplished outweighed the negative consequences, that some higher-order principle or authority required the action, or that the harmed person deserved the negative consequences. In a study by Sykes and Matza (1957), the latter type of justification was frequently used by juvenile delinquents. If the harmed person accepts the account offered, blame may be removed, or the degree of responsibility may be mitigated.

Schönbach (1990) provided a model of accounting episodes, which begin with the perception of a norm violation and evolve to a second stage in which the victim may express some form of reproach involving an accusation or perhaps a more neutral *why* question. The perpetrator may refuse to acknowledge the reproach (by denying guilt or the other's right to reproach or denying that the event occurred) or may offer an excuse or justification for the action in question. Successful accounts terminate the episode. Reproaches may lead to conflict and possible escalation of hostilities between the two parties. In Schönbach's view, the victim's decision to attribute blame leads to actions intended to regain control over the interaction with the perpetrator. Although this model is similar in some respects to the view presented here, it appears to be restricted to identity attacks rather than more general bases of grievances and is much less detailed with respect to the antecedent conditions for starting an episode and the kinds of choices that a victim may make in response to unjust situations.

The effectiveness of accounts in removing or mitigating a grievance may depend on the characteristics of the perpetrator, his or her social relationship with the victim, the type of account provided, and the nature of the precipitating incident. Melburg, Lesser, and Tedeschi (1983) found that the excuses of a low-status nurse were more believed than were identical excuses from a higher status physician. Apparently, it is more difficult to absolve oneself from responsibility when one has higher status. In an experiment by Riordan, Marlin, and Kellogg (1983), both the believability of the account and its normativeness were found to be related to its acceptability. Believability was related to the credibility of the source (cf. Tedeschi, Lindskold, & Rosenfeld, 1985) and to the social knowledge possessed by the target audience (Scott & Lyman, 1968).

Some research has found excuses not to be very effective in mitigating responsibility. For example, defendants in traffic court who denied guilt and provided evidence against the charges of speeding were much more effective in gaining desired verdicts than were those who offered excuses or justifications for speeding (McLaughlin, Cody, & French, 1990). Of course, excuses and justifications effectively confess to the charge, and in such circumstances there are few accounts other than some form of life-and-death emergency that would remove guilt. Thus, in terms of acceptability, the type of account must be examined in the context of the incident for which the perpetrator stands accused.

When excuses and justifications are accepted by the victim, they may only lessen the magnitude of the grievance and not remove the motivation to restore justice. Presumably, the magnitudes of blame, anger, grievance, and justice motivation are directly related to one another. There are factors that disrupt these direct relationships. For example, anger may not lead to the formation of a grievance if the victim cannot foresee any action that could restore justice. Whatever residue of blame is left after the issuance and receipt of an account will continue to work through anger, grievance, and justice motivation to affect the judgments and behavior of the victim.

From the point of view of the perpetrator, it can be asked what the conditions are for using accounts and for preferring one kind of account over another. Presumably, the use of accounts will be more frequent when the prospective reactions of target audiences arc likely to be more negative in their consequences. One such condition is the amount of harm done in the precipitating incident. Schlenker (1980) proposed that perpetrators are more apt to proffer accounts as the relevant incident increases in severity. Hupka, Jung, and Silverthorn (1987) found that subjects rated the use of justifications as more acceptable in severe than in mildly harmful incidents, but the reverse relationship was found with excuses.

Forgive the Harmdoer

A third possible reaction of the harmed person is to forgive the harmdoer. According to *Webster's Dictionary*, to forgive is "to cease to feel resentment against, on accord of wrong committed, to give up claims to requital from or retribution upon an offender, to absolve; pardon." But how can a victim forgive humiliation, injustice, or assault from another person? It is particularly difficult when the perpetrator is unrepentant and domineering.

There are social and psychic costs for maintaining resentment. One important social cost is the deterioration of intimate relationships. Probably most incidents of disappointment, omission, failure to act, and other forms of neglect and failed expectations are the bases for grievances in intimate relationships. A desire for remedial justice may have a negative impact on intimate relationships. Yet, a refusal to forgive an insult or to resume the relationship can be a conservative, defensive tactic that prevents the victim from further humiliations from the other person. Such a defensive strategy is particularly likely when the perpetrator is perceived to be more powerful and unrepentant and can lead to the withdrawal from an intimate relationship. In a series of case studies from marital therapy, Vogel and Lazare (1990) found this mechanism to be central to divorce actions.

Failure to forgive coupled with failure to act to restore justice may be associated with depression and feelings of powerlessness. According to Hope (1987, p. 241), a central feature of psychotherapy is the experience of injustice, abuse of the weak by the strong, betrayals of trust, and feelings of rage. Forgiveness allows the grievant to let go of the resentment, bitterness, or anger associated with an injustice (Fitzgibbons, 1986). Forgiveness also removes the need to engage in justice-restoring actions, which may be dangerous and costly. On the other hand, to forgive the perpetrator may mean admitting the effectiveness of the other person's criticisms or insults—to confess to the other's power to hurt.

Forgiveness may follow an apology offered by the harmdoer. The most complete form of apology contains at least three components: (a) an acceptance of responsibility and blame for the negative event; (b) an expression of remorse, indicating an acceptance of the norm that was violated and a promise not to violate the norm again; and (c) an expression of unhappiness about the harm that was done and an offer to engage in some form of restitution (Goffman, 1971; Schlenker, 1980). Any apology may consist of one or more of these three aspects.

An acceptance of an apology constitutes forgiveness and removes the resentment underlying a grievance. However, forgiveness is not the same as removing blame. Whereas the removal of blame means to reestablish the relationship as if no untoward event had occurred, the removal of blame is provisional. Although an aggrieved person may forgive a perpetrator, the incident will not be forgotten. Should the harmdoer engage in some further blameworthy action, particularly if it violates the same norm as the forgiven action, the intensity of the grievance brought about by the new transgression will be higher than would have been the case if the forgiven action had never occurred. This is so because the recidivism implies the insincerity of the perpetrator on the prior occasion and because an apology typically carries with it a promise not to repeat the transgression. Thus, the next offense is both an antinormative action and a betrayal of the offender's prior promise.

Several studies have shown that apologies can be quite effective in ameliorating negative impressions, mitigating blame, and reducing punitive actions toward the perpetrator (Riordan et al., 1983; Schlenker & Darby, 1981; Schwartz, Kane, Joseph, & Tedeschi, 1978). In a study in which apologies were shown to ameliorate negative impressions of an inept experimenter, a regression analysis showed that the effects of apology were mediated by improvement in the impression of the responsibility and sincerity of the harmdoer and the reduction of blame (Ohbuchi, Kameda, & Agarie, 1989).

Assert Claims, Disputes, and Conflict

A fourth possible reaction of the harmed person is to make a claim for some action by the harmdoer. The harmed person must believe that there is a remedy or some form of restitution that can be obtained by making a claim. The specific content of claims may depend on the type of harm that was experienced. Imposition of constraints may lead to a demand for their removal, destruction or removal of goods may lead to a demand for replacement, and aspersions on one's social identity may lead to a demand for a retraction or a public apology.

The course of events following a claim depends on what the harmdoer does. Acquiescence by the harmdoer to the claim resolves the grievance. The episode may permanently affect the relationship (negatively or positively) between the two parties, but the resentment that had followed the negative event will be dissipated. The harmdoer may refuse the claim in whole or in part and may make a counteroffer. This refusal moves the interaction into a dispute phase. The harmed person may perceive the refusal as at least a partial denial of responsibility for the harm that was done or a minimization of the degree of harm done. A refusal may expand the scope or intensity of a grievance if the harmed person perceives it as a further norm violation. The grievant may believe that people should accept responsibility for what they do or that the harmdoer is lying about the negative event. The harmdoer, on the other hand, may believe that the grievant is exaggerating the degree of harm, is misinterpreting what happened, or is seeking some advantage by pressing the claim. The harmdoer may feel victimized, attribute blame to the original grievant, develop a resentment, and make a countergrievance. This type of situation is ripe for an escalation of hostilities between the two parties.

A dispute is a form of social conflict. The two parties may arrive at an informal bargaining agreement either directly or through third-party mediation. Either or both parties may resort to coercion as a means of compelling the other party to make concessions in the bargaining process. The intensity of anger conveys the degree of unjust harm experienced by the angered party. Anger has the function of drawing the other person's attention to the issues of concern to the angered party. Anger also shows a commitment to resolving the grievance. And, of course, anger is a type of threat given that it is frequently associated with aggression. When both parties to the dispute display strong anger, an escalation of hostilities is the most probable outcome.

There is a rather sizable literature on the structure, causes, strategies, and outcomes of interpersonal conflicts (cf. Pruitt & Rubin, 1986). There is not enough space here to delve into such a complex topic. It is sufficient to point to the connection between perceived injustice and grievances and processes involved in social conflicts.

Punish the Harmdoer

There is one other way in which a harmed person may react to a harmdoer. A grievant may directly punish the harmdoer as a means of administering justice. One of the justifications for the use of punishment is to inflict suffering on blameworthy people. In general, the rule of justice is that the amount of suffering inflicted by a punishing action should be proportional to the amount of harm done by the blameworthy person. The punishment may be intended not only to restore justice but also to reform the harmdoer and to deter further offenses. These additional goals for the use of punishment may lead the actor to inflict more harm on the blameworthy person than when the only motive is restoring justice.

The motive to restore justice and settle a grievance may lead people to take the law into their own hands (Black, 1983). Illegal "self-help" actions are frequently taken by grievants who believe that they have no recourse to legal agencies to achieve justice. Thus, self-help is a means of informal social control. Actions may take myriad forms, such as arson, robbery, assault, killing livestock, and defacing property.

Of course, the recipient of punishment may perceive the punishing action as unjustified or excessive, blame the grievant, form a grievance of his or her own, and retaliate. The retaliation may be intended to punish the first person's punishing action, to deter future punishing actions, or to reform the first person. A study by Felson and Steadman (1983) found that one extreme result of this type of escalatory interaction is physical assault and even homicide. A key to the explosiveness of a spiral of this type may be the magnitude of overretaliation by one of the parties in the early stages of a dispute. On the other hand, parties to conflict may be more willing to negotiate a solution under more intense levels of threats and punishments (Youngs, 1987).

Organizations and institutions provide mechanisms for resolving grievances to avoid the destructive conflicts that often result from individuals trying to resolve the issues on a face-to-face basis. Legal structures, union–management agreements, counselors, and insurance are only some of the avenues through which grievances can be channeled for resolution.

Grievances and Aggression

The inability of the aggrieved party to restore justice, either because of inaction or because of a failure of some course of action, will be represented by unresolved resentment. The assumption here is that grievances do not just go away or dissipate. Indeed, the lack of settlement of a grievance may act like an aggressive drive, maintaining a certain level of readiness to do something until a viable opportunity occurs. The process is similar to Berkowitz's (1989) cue-arousal theory of aggression, except that it is not blind mechanistic drive that causes the behavior but a social motive for personal justice.

People who have not resolved grievances remain ready for a triggering event to release some justice-restoring behavior. A woman on the Phil Donahue show reported that she had her father arrested and tried for childhood sexual abuse 30 years after the events took place. Afro-Americans living in the inner cities harbored grievances against a discriminatory system imposed by Whites, and when Martin Luther King, Jr., was assassinated, there ensued a series of property riots in the major cities in the United States. The role of television was central in directing the behavior of grievants, which was similar in a number of cities.

The grievance process can account for a substantial portion of the laboratory research on aggression. Donnerstein and Hatfield (1982) reinterpreted much of this research in terms of the distributive principle of equity. Much of the aggression research findings that could not be interpreted as responses to inequity could be reinterpreted in terms of reactions to violations of procedural and interaction norms or as forms of social influence (see Tedeschi & Felson, 1993). The time appears right to develop a general theory linking questions of injustice, identity, and influence with the literatures on social conflict, social control, and human aggression.

References

Abelson, R. P., & Lalljee, M. (1988). Knowledge structures and causal explanation. In D. Hilton (Ed.), *Knowledge structures* (pp. 175–203). Hillsdale, NJ: Erlbaum.

Adams, J. P., Jr., & Dressler, W. W. (1988). Perceptions of injustice in a Black community: Dimensions and variation. *Human Relations, 41,* 753–767.

Affleck, G., Allen, D. A., Tennen, H., McGrade, B. J., & Ratzan, S. (1985). Causal and control cognitions in parent coping with a chronically ill child. *Journal of Social and Clinical Psychology, 3,* 369–379.

Affleck, G., Pfeiffer, C., Tennen, H., & Fifield, J. (1987). Attributional processes in rheumatoid arthritis. *Arthritis and Rheumatism, 30,* 927–931.

Austin, W. (1980). Friendship and fairness: Effects of type of relationship and task performance on choice of distribution rules. *Personality and Social Psychology Bulletin, 6,* 401–408.

Averill, J. R. (1983). Studies on anger and aggression: Implications for theories of emotion. *American Psychologist, 38*, 1145–1160.

Baumeister, R. F., Stillwell, A., & Wotman, S. R. (1990). Victim and perpetrator accounts of interpersonal conflict: Autobiographical narratives about anger. *Journal of Personality and Social Psychology, 59* (5), 994–1005.

Berkowitz, L. (1989). The frustration–aggression hypothesis: An examination and reformulation. *Psychological Bulletin, 106*, 59–73.

Best, A., & Andreasen, A. R. (1977). Consumer responses to unsatisfactory purchases: A survey of perceiving defects, voicing complaints, and obtaining redress. *Law and Society Review, 11*, 701–742.

Bies, R. J. (1986, August). *Identifying principles of interactional justice: The case of corporate recruiting.* Paper presented at meeting of the National Academy of Management, Chicago, IL.

Bies, R. J., & Moag, J. S. (1986). Interactional justice: Communications criteria of fairness. In R. Lewitzki, M. Bazerman, & B. Sheppard (Eds.), *Research on negotiation in organizations* (Vol. 1, pp. 43–55). Greenwich, CT: JAI Press.

Black, D. (1983). Crime as social control. *American Sociological Review, 48*, 34–45.

Blau, P. M. (1964). *Exchange and power in social life.* New York: Wiley.

Blumenthal, M., Kahn, R. L., Andrews, F. M., & Head, K. B. (1972). *Justifying violence: Attitudes of American men.* Ann Arbor, MI: Institute for Social Research.

Bradbury, T. N., & Fincham, F. D. (1990). Attributions in marriage: Review and critique. *Psychological Bulletin, 107*(1), 3–33.

Brown, P., & Levinson, S. C. (1987). *Politeness: Some universals in language usage.* Cambridge, England: Cambridge University Press.

Brown, R. C., Jr., & Tedeschi, J. T. (1976). Determinants of perceived aggression. *Journal of Social Psychology, 100*, 77–87.

Burgess, A. W., & Holmstrom, L. L. (1979). Adaptive strategies and recovery from rape. *American Journal of Psychiatry, 136*, 1278–1282.

Buss, A. H. (1961). *The psychology of aggression.* New York: Wiley.

Buss, A. H., & Durkee, A. (1957). An inventory for assessing different kinds of hostility. *Journal of Consulting Psychology, 21*, 343–349.

Byrne, D. (1971). *The attraction paradigm.* San Diego, CA: Academic Press.

Chodhoff, P., Friedman, S. B., & Hamburg, D. A. (1964). Stress, defense, and coping behavior: Observations in parents of children with malignant diseases. *American Journal of Psychiatry, 120*, 743–749.

DeRidder, R. (1985). Normative considerations in the labeling of harmful behavior as aggressive. *Journal of Social Psychology, 125*, 659–666.

DeRidder, R., Schruijer, S. G. L., & Tripathi, R. C. (1992). Norm violation as a precipitating factor of negative intergroup relations. In R. DeRidder & R. C. Tripathi (Eds.), *Norm violation and intergroup relations* (pp. 3–37). New York: Oxford University Press.

Deshields, T. L., Jenkins, J. O., & Tait, R. C. (1989). The experience of anger in chronic illness: A preliminary investigation. *International Journal of Psychiatry in Medicine, 19*, 299–309.

Diamond, E. L. (1982). The role of anger and hostility in essential hypertension and coronary heart diseases. *Psychological Bulletin, 92*, 410–433.

Dion, K. K. (1972). Physical attractiveness and evaluation of children's transgressions. *Journal of Personality and Social Psychology, 24*, 207–213.

Dodge, K. A., & Coie, J. D. (1987). Social information processing factors in reactive and proactive aggression in children's peer groups. *Journal of Personality and Social Psychology, 53*, 1146–1158.

Dodge, K. A., Price, J. M., Bachorowski, J., & Newman, J. P. (1990). Hostile attributional biases in severely aggressive adolescents. *Journal of Abnormal Psychology, 99*, 385–392.

Dollard, J., Doob, L. W., Miller, N. E., Mowrer, O. H., & Sears, R. R. (1939). *Frustration and aggression.* New Haven: Yale University Press.

Donnerstein, E., & Hatfield, E. (1982). Aggression and inequity. In J. Greenberg & R. Cohen (Eds.), *Equity and justice in social behavior* (pp. 309–336). San Diego, CA: Academic Press.

Dugoni, B. L., & Ilgen, D. R. (1981). Realistic job previews and the adjustment of new employees. *Academy of Management Journal, 24*, 579–591.

Epstein, S., & Taylor, S. P. (1967). Instigation to aggression as a function of degree of defeat and perceived aggressive intent of the opponent. *Journal of Personality, 35*, 265–289.

Felson, R. B., & Steadman, H. S. (1983). Situations and processes leading to criminal violence. *Criminology, 21*, 59–74.

Felstiner, W. L. F., Abel, R. L., & Sarat, A. (1980–1981). The emergence and transformation of disputes: Naming, blaming, claiming . . . *Law and Society Review, 15*, 631–654.

Ferguson, T. J., & Rule, B. G. (1981). An attributional perspective on anger and aggression. In R. Geen & R. E. Donnerstein (Eds.), *Perspectives on aggression: Theoretical and empirical reviews* (pp. 41–74). San Diego, CA: Academic Press.

Ferraro, K. J., & Johnson, J. M. (1983). How women experience battering: The process of victimization. *Social Problems, 30*, 325–339.

Filipp, S. H., & Gräser, H. (1982). Psychologische prävention im umfeld kritischer lenbensereignisse. In J. Brandstädter & A. von Eye (Eds.), *Psychologische prävention* (pp. 155–195). Bern, Switzerland: Huber.

Fine, M. (1979). Options to injustice: Seeing other lights. *Representative Research in Social Psychology, 10*, 61–76.

Fine, M. (1983). The social context and a sense of injustice: The option to challenge. *Representative Research in Social Psychology, 13*, 15–33.

Fine, M. (1985). The social construction of "what's fair" at work. *Journal of Applied Social Psychology, 15*, 166–177.

Frieze, I. H. (1976). The role of information processing in making causal attributions for success and failure. In J. S. Carroll & J. W. Payne (Eds.), *Cognition and social behavior* (pp. 95–112). Hillsdale, NJ: Erlbaum.

Frieze, I. H. (1979). Perceptions of battered wives. In I. H. Frieze, D. Bar-Tal, & J. S. Carroll (Eds.), *New approaches to social problems: Applications of attribution theory* (pp. 79–108). San Francisco: Jossey-Bass.

Geen, R. G. (1968). Effects of frustration, attack, and prior training in aggressiveness upon aggressive behavior. *Journal of Personality and Social Psychology, 9,* 316–321.

Gelles, R. J. (1980). A profile of violence toward children in the United States. In G. Gerbner, C. Ross, & E. Zigler (Eds.), *Child abuse* (pp. 82–105). New York: Oxford University Press.

Gentry, W. D. (1970). Effects of frustration, attack, and prior aggressive training on overt aggression and vascular processes. *Journal of Personality and Social Psychology, 16,* 718–725.

Goffman, E. (1971). *Relations in public.* New York: Basic Books.

Hart, H. L. A. (1968). *Punishment and responsibility.* New York: Oxford University Press.

Hatfield, E., Utne, M. K., & Traupmann, J. (1979). Equity theory and intimate relationships. In R. Burgess & T. L. Huston (Eds.), *Social exchange in developing relationships* (pp. 99–133). San Diego, CA: Academic Press.

Heider, F. (1944). Social perceptual and phenomenal causality. *Psychological Review, 51,* 358–374.

Heider, F. (1958). *The psychology of interpersonal relations.* New York: Wiley.

Hewitt, J. P., & Stokes, R. (1976). Disclaimers. *American Sociological Review, 40,* 1–11.

Hewstone, M. (1989). *Causal attribution: From cognitive processes to collective beliefs.* Cambridge, MA: Basil Blackwell.

Hope, D. (1987). The healing paradox of forgiveness. *Psychotherapy, 24,* 240–244.

Horai, J. (1977). Attributional conflict. *Journal of Social Issues, 33,* 88–100.

Horai, J., & Bartek, M. (1978). Recommended punishment as a function of injurious intent, actual harm done, and intended consequences. *Personality and Social Psychology Bulletin, 4,* 575–578.

Horan, H. D., & Kaplan, M. F. (1983). Criminal intent and consequence severity: Effects of moral reasoning on punishment. *Personality and Social Psychology Bulletin, 9,* 638–645.

Hupka, R. B., Jung, J., & Silverthorn, K. (1987). Perceived acceptability of apologies, excuses, and justifications in jealousy predicaments. *Journal of Social Behavior and Personality, 2,* 303–313.

Jones, E. E., & Davis, K. E. (1965). From acts to dispositions: The attribution process in person perception. In L. Berkowitz (Ed.), *Advances in experimental social psychology* (Vol. 2, pp. 220–266). San Diego, CA: Academic Press.

Jones, E. E., & Nisbett, R. E. (1971). *The actor and the observer: Divergent perceptions of the causes of behavior.* New York: General Learning Press.

Jones, E. E., & Pittman, T. S. (1982). Toward a general theory of strategic self-presentation. In J. Suls (Ed.), *Psychological perspectives on the self* (Vol. 1, pp. 231–262). Hillsdale, NJ: Erlbaum.

Kalven, H., Jr., & Zeisel, H. (1966). *The American jury.* Boston: Little, Brown.

Kanouse, D. E., & Hansen, L. R., Jr. (1972). Negativity in evaluations. In E. E. Jones, D. E. Kanouse, H. H. Kelley, R. E. Nisbett, S. Valins, & B. Weiner (Eds.), *Attribution: Perceiving the causes of behavior* (pp. 47–62). Morristown, NJ: General Learning Press.

Kempe, R. S., & Kempe, C. H. (1978). *Child abuse.* Cambridge, MA: Harvard University Press.

Kemper, T. D. (1978). *A social interactional theory of emotions.* New York: Wiley.

Klein, R., & Bierhoff, H. W. (1991). *Responses to achievement situations: The mediating function of perceived fairness.* Unpublished manuscript.

Kohlberg, L. (1981). *The philosophy of moral development.* New York: Harper & Row.

Landy, D., & Aronson, E. (1969). The influence of the character of the criminal and his victim on the decisions of simulated jurors. *Journal of Experimental Social Psychology, 5,* 141–152.

Lerner, M. J. (1980). *The belief in a just world.* New York: Plenum.

Lincoln, A., & Levinger, G. (1972). Observers' evaluations of the victim and the attacker in an aggressive incident. *Journal of Personality and Social Psychology, 22,* 202–210.

Löschper, G., Mummendey, A., Linneweber, V., & Bornewasser, M. (1984). The judgment of behavior as aggressive and sanctionable. *European Journal of Social Psychology, 14,* 391–404.

Major, B., Mueller, P., & Hildebrandt, K. (1985). Attributions, expectations, and coping with abortion. *Journal of Personality and Social Psychology, 48,* 585–599.

Mandler, G. (1979). Emotion. In E. Hearst (Ed.), *The first century of experimental psychology* (pp. 275–321). Hillsdale, NJ: Erlbaum.

Martin, J. (1978). The tolerance of injustice. In J. Olson & M. Zanna (Eds.), *Relative deprivation and assertive action: The Ontario Symposium* (pp. 217–242). Hillsdale, NJ: Erlbaum.

McLaughlin, M. L., Cody, M. J., & French, K. (1990). Account-giving and the attribution of responsibility: Impressions of traffic offenders. In M. J. Cody & M. L. McLaughlin (Eds.), *The psychology of tactical communication* (pp. 244–267). Philadelphia, PA: Multilingual Matters.

Medea, A., & Thompson, K. (1974). *Against rape.* New York: Farrar, Straus & Giroux.

Melburg, V., Lesser, J., & Tedeschi, J. T. (1983, April). *Status, reasons, and person perception.* Paper presented at poster session at the 54th Annual Meeting of the Eastern Psychological Association, Philadelphia.

Melburg, V., & Tedeschi, J. T. (1981). Risk-taking, justifiability, recklessness, and responsibility. *Personality and Social Psychology Bulletin, 7,* 509–515.

Messick, D. M., Bloom, S., Boldizar, J. P., & Samuelson, C. D. (1985). Why we are fairer than others. *Journal of Experimental Social Psychology, 21,* 480–500.

Meyer, C. B., & Taylor, S. E. (1986). Adjustment to rape. *Journal of Personality and Social Psychology, 50,* 1226–1234.

Mikula, G. (1984). Personal relationships: Remarks on the current state of research. *European Journal of Social Psychology, 14,* 339–352.

Mikula, G., & Heimgartner, A. (1992). *Experiences of injustice in intimate relationships.* Unpublished manuscript, University of Graz, Austria.

Mikula, G., Petri, B., & Tanzer, N. (1989). What people regard as unjust: Types and structures of everyday experiences of injustice. *European Journal of Social Psychology, 20,* 133–149.

Mikula, G., Petri, B., & Tanzer, N. (1990). What people regard as unjust: Types and structures of everyday experiences of injustice. *European Journal of Social Psychology, 20,* 133–149.

Muchinsky, P. M. (1987). *Psychology applied to work: An introduction to organizational psychology.* Chicago: Dorsey Press.

Mummendey, A., Linneweber, V., & Löschper, G. (1984). Actor or victim of aggression. Divergent perspectives—divergent evaluations. *European Journal of Social Psychology, 14*, 291–311.

Nesdale, A. R., Rule, B. G., & Hill, K. A. (1978). The effect of attraction on causal attributions and retaliation. *Personality and Social Psychology Bulletin, 4*, 231–234.

Nickel, T. W. (1974). The attribution of intention as a critical factor in the relation between frustration and aggression. *Journal of Personality, 42*, 482–492.

Novaco, R. W. (1976). The functions and regulation of the arousal of anger. *American Journal of Psychiatry, 133*, 1124–1128.

Ohbuchi, K., Kameda, M., & Agarie, N. (1989). Apology as aggression control: Its role in mediating appraisal of and response to harm. *Journal of Personality and Social Psychology, 56*, 219–227.

Olson, J. M., Herman, C. P., & Zanna, M. P. (1986). *Relative deprivation and social comparison: The Ontario Symposium* (Vol. 4). Hillsdale, NJ: Erlbaum.

Orvis, B. R., Kelley, H. H., & Butler, D. (1976). Attributional conflict in young couples. In J. H. Harvey, W. J. Ickes, & R. F. Kidd (Eds.), *New directions in attribution research* (Vol. 1, pp. 353–386). Hillsdale, NJ: Erlbaum.

Piaget, J. (1932). *The moral judgment of the child.* New York: Harcourt, Brace.

Piaget, J. (1966). *The moral judgment of the child.* New York: Free Press. (Original work published 1932)

Pisano, R., & Taylor, S. P. (1971). Reduction in physical aggression: The effects of four different strategies. *Journal of Personality and Social Psychology, 19*, 237–242.

Pruitt, D. G., & Rubin, J. Z. (1986). *Social conflict: Escalation, stalemate, and settlement.* New York: Random House.

Rappaport, E. A. (1971). Survivor guilt. In I. H. Frieze, D. Bar-Tal, & J. S. Carroll (Eds.), *New approaches to social problems: Applications of attribution theory* (pp. 21–52). San Francisco: Jossey-Bass.

Reis, H. T. (1984). The multidimensionality of justice. In R. Folger (Ed.), *The sense of injustice: Social psychological perspectives* (pp. 25–61). New York: Plenum.

Riordan, C. A., Marlin, N. A., & Kellogg, R. T. (1983). The effectiveness of accounts following transgression. *Social Psychology Quarterly, 46*, 213–219.

Rosen, B., & Jerdee, T. H. (1974). Factors influencing disciplinary judgments. *Journal of Applied Psychology, 59*, 327–331.

Runciman, W. G. (1966). *Relative deprivation and social justice.* London: Routledge & Kegan Paul.

Schlenker, B. R. (1980). *Impression management: The self-concept, social identity and interpersonal relations.* Pacific Grove, CA: Brooks/Cole.

Schlenker, B. R., & Darby, B. W. (1981). The use of apologies in social predicaments. *Social Psychology Quarterly, 44*, 271–278.

Schönback, P. (1990). *Account episodes: The management or escalation of conflict.* New York: Cambridge University Press.

Schruijer, S. G. L. (1990). *Norm violation, attribution and attitudes in intergroup relations.* Tilburg, The Netherlands: Tilburg University Press.

Schultz, T. R., & Wright, K. (1985). Concepts of negligence and intention in the assignment of moral responsibility. *Canadian Journal of Behavioral Science, 17*, 97–108.

Schwartz, G. S., Kane, T. R., Joseph, J. M., & Tedeschi, J. T. (1978). The effects of post-transgression remorse on perceived aggression, attribution of intent, and level of punishment. *British Journal of Social and Clinical Psychology, 17,* 293–297.

Scott, M. B., & Lyman, S. M. (1968). Accounts. *American Sociological Review, 33,* 46–62.

Shaver, K. G. (1970). Defensive attribution: Effects of severity and relevance on the responsibility assigned for an accident. *Journal of Personality and Social Psychology, 14,* 101–113.

Shaver, K. G. (1985). *The attribution of blame: Causality, responsibility and blameworthiness.* New York: Springer-Verlag.

Silver, R. L., Boon, C., & Stones, M. H. (1983). Searching for meaning in misfortune: Making sense of incest. *Journal of Social Issues, 39,* 81–101.

Stafford, M. C., & Gibbs, J. P. (1991, April). *Disputes and the efficacy of control.* Paper presented at the Albany Conference on Social Interactionist Approaches to Aggression and Violence, State University of New York at Albany.

Stouffer, S. A., Suchman, E. A., DeVinney, L. C., Star, S. A., & Williams, R. M., Jr. (1949). *The American soldier: Adjustment during army life* (Vol. 1, pp. 97–125). Hillsdale, NJ: Erlbaum.

Sykes, G. M., & Matza, D. (1957). Techniques of neutralization: A theory of delinquency. *American Journal of Sociology, 22,* 664–670.

Tavris, C. (1982). *Anger: The misunderstood emotion.* New York: Simon & Schuster.

Taylor, D. M., & Jaggi, V. (1974). Ethnocentrism and causal attribution in a South Indian context. *Journal of Cross-Cultural Psychology, 5,* 162–171.

Taylor, D. M., Moghaddam, F. M., & Bellerose, J. (1989). Social comparison in a group context. *Journal of Social Psychology, 129,* 499–515

Taylor, S. P., & Pisono, R. (1971). Physical aggression as a function of frustration and physical attack. *Journal of Social Psychology, 84,* 261–267.

Tedeschi, J. T., & Felson, R. (1993). *Aggression and coercive actions: A social interactionist view.* Manuscript in preparation.

Tedeschi, J. T., Lindskold, S., & Rosenfeld, P. (1985). *An introduction to social psychology.* St. Paul, MN: West

Tedeschi, J. T., & Reiss, M. (1981). Predicaments and verbal tactics of impression management. In C. Antaki (Ed.), *Ordinary language explanations of social behaviour* (pp. 271–309). San Diego, CA: Academic Press.

Tennen, H., & Affleck, G. (1991). Blaming others for threatening events. *Psychological Bulletin, 108,* 209–232.

Thibaut, J. W., & Kelley, H. H. (1959). *The social psychology of groups.* New York: Wiley.

Toch, H. (1969). *Violent men: An inquiry into the psychology of violence.* Chicago: Aldine.

Turkat, D., & Dawson, J. (1976). Attributions of responsibility for a chance event as a function of sex and physical attractiveness of target individual. *Psychological Reports, 39,* 275–279.

Tyler, T. R. (1988). What is procedural justice? Criteria used by citizens to assess the fairness of legal procedures. *Law and Society Review, 22,* 103–135.

Tyler, T. R., & Lind, E. A. (1990). Intrinsic versus community-based justice models: When does group membership matter? *Journal of Social Issues, 46*(1), 83–94.

Vaillant, G. E. (1977). Adaptation to life. Boston: Little, Brown.

Veitch, R., & Piccione, A. (1978). The role of attitude similarity in the attribution process. *Social Psychology Quarterly, 41*, 165–169.

Vidmar, N., & Crinklaw, L. D. (1974). Attributing responsibility for an accident: A methodological and conceptual critique. *Canadian Journal of Behavioural Science, 6*, 112–130.

Vidmar, N., & Miller, D. T. (1980). Social psychological processes underlying attitudes toward legal punishment. *Law and Society Review, 14*, 565–602.

Vogel, W., & Lazare, A. (1990). The unforgivable humiliation: A dilemma in couples' treatment. *Contemporary Family Therapy, 12*, 139–151.

Walster, E. (1966). Assignment of responsibility for an accident. *Journal of Personality and Social Psychology, 3*, 73–79.

Wanous, J. P. (1977). Organizational entry: Newcomers moving from outside to inside. *Psychological Bulletin, 84*, 601–618.

Warner, C. T. (1986). Anger and similar delusions. In R. Harre (Ed.), *Social construction of emotions* (pp. 135–166). New York: Blackwell.

White, R. K. (1968). *Nobody wanted war: Misperception in Vietnam and other wars.* Garden City, NY: Doubleday.

Wickless, C., & Kirsch, I. (1988). Cognitive correlates of anger, anxiety, and sadness. *Cognitive Therapy and Research, 12*, 367–377.

Wong, W. P. T., & Weiner, B. (1981). When people ask "why" questions, and the heuristics of attributional search. *Journal of Personality and Social Psychology, 40*, 650–660.

Youngs, G. A. Jr. (1986). Patterns of threat and punishment reciprocity in a conflict setting. *Journal of Personality and Social Psychology, 51*(3), 541–546.

CHAPTER 2

A Control Theory Interpretation of Psychological Research on Aggression

Michael R. Gottfredson and Travis Hirschi

B ehavior determined by inner drives poses problems for rational choice or social control theories. In everyday life and in psychology and law, such behavior is taken to be commonplace. In these domains, acts are frequently characterized as compulsive, expressive, passionate, or violent, with the clear intention of distinguishing them from acts governed by their social consequences, the acts with which control theories are concerned. Although terms denoting strong drives or motives implicitly acknowledge that some behavior may be explicable because it is rational, they simultaneously suggest that much important and interesting behavior is beyond the reach of control theories. Nowhere is the challenge to control theory more conspicuous than in the concept of aggression.

In the late 1930s, the frustration–aggression hypothesis emerged as an important theoretical construct in psychology and sociology. In psychology, Dollard, Doob, Miller, Mowrer, and Sears (1939) advanced the view that aggression is a consequence of frustration. With important qualifications and modifications, this tradition flourished in psychology for the next 50 years (Berkowitz, 1989). At about the same time in sociology, Merton (1938) advanced the view that crime is a consequence of the frustration that flows from failure to achieve culturally prescribed goals. With important qualifications and modifications, this version of the frustration–aggression hypothesis, often called *strain theory*, has flourished in sociology as well (Bernard, 1990; Blau & Blau, 1982; Cloward & Ohlin, 1960).

Scholarly interest in aggression remains high. Recent studies of this concept include investigations of the link of television to violence and aggression (Cook, Kendzierski, & Thomas, 1983; Eron, 1987), the role of temperature in the causation of aggression (Anderson, 1989), the stability of aggression over time (Olweus, 1979), and individual differences in aggression (Bandura, 1973; Berkowitz, 1989; Buss, 1961).

In criminology, the related concepts of violence and serious offending continue to maintain an important position in research and public policy (Gelles, 1980; Monahan, 1981; Straus, Gelles, & Steinmetz, 1980; Widom, 1989a). Two prominent reviews of the field, one on behalf of the National Academy of Sciences (Blumstein, Cohen, Roth, & Visher, 1986) and the other on behalf of the MacArthur Foundation (Farrington, Ohlin, & Wilson, 1986), urged that attention be focused on violent and serious offenses and offenders. A large literature also focuses on family violence or child and spouse abuse, with the underlying theme that these various forms of abuse are connected through a cycle of aggression (Widom, 1989b). And the strain model continues to trace such nonviolent offenses as theft and drug use to the frustration of legitimate aspirations or expectations (Elliott, Huizinga, & Ageton, 1985; Wilson & Herrnstein, 1985).

Much of the popularity of the concept of aggression may be traced to its compatibility with the basic assumptions of the behavioral science disciplines (Hirschi & Gottfredson, 1990). These disciplines assume that events are caused by prior states or events, that the actor is at the mercy of forces beyond the immediate situation over which he or she has no control, and that the nature of these forces or motives is not immediately evident in the behavior they produce. These assumptions are especially obvious in studies of aggression regardless of whether the theorist's orientation is frustration–aggression (Berkowitz, 1989) or learning theory (Bandura, 1973).

Such ideas may be contrasted to a social control model wherein the actor seeks to satisfy general needs and desires while attending to the relative social costs and benefits of alternative lines of action. In sociological control theories (Gottfredson & Hirschi, 1990; Heckathorn, 1990; Hirschi, 1969), individuals differ in the extent to which they attend to short-term as opposed to the long-term or social consequences of their actions. In this view, aggressive or violent acts are merely attempts to pursue some immediate self-interest through the use of force: The robber shoots the clerk to expedite the theft; the bully assaults the playmate to improve his position in the lunch line; the husband kills the wife to end an annoying argument. Such acts may seem irrational, impulsive, or inexplicable—the product of some deep-seated psychological need—even to the actor. After all, it appears to make little sense to risk the death penalty for a few dollars, to risk losing a friend for a momentary advantage, or to risk losing a wife for the sake of an argument. But this judgment compares the act's immediate benefits with its long-term costs. When immediate benefits are compared with immediate costs, the impression of irrationality is dispelled.

A social control perspective assumes that comparison of immediate benefits with immediate costs governs the behavior of some people in some situations, whereas comparison of immediate benefits with long-term costs governs the behavior of most people most of the time. Whichever comparison is operative, the ultimate decision is consistent with control principles.

The social control explanation is consistent with the long-established fact that most criminal acts are nonviolent, that the majority involve theft without confrontation between victim and offender. In these acts, too, the offender ignores long-term social costs in favor of the benefits of the moment. Although theft may seem more rational than violence because it produces immediate tangible benefits, social control theory explains it in the same way. The control model is thus consistent with the observation that violence and theft are typically found in the same offender (i.e., there is very little tendency to specialize in one of these types of offense to the exclusion of the other; Osgood, 1990; Osgood, Johnston, O'Malley, & Bachman, 1988; Rowe, Osgood, & Nicewander, 1990).

The psychological aggression model is inconsistent with the versatility of offenders: The frustration–aggression version (Berkowitz, 1989; Dollard et al., 1939) predicts behavior that is consistent with the frustration encountered; the learning version (Bandura, 1973) predicts behavior that is consistent with the role model imitated. Both versions thus tend to be act-specific or behavior-specific and as such overlook good evidence for a general tendency to engage in or to avoid criminal acts.

Similar problems emerge from policy-oriented research on the origins of aggressive behavior. Most such research assumes that particular experiences (e.g., watching violent television programs, reading violent pornography) are causes of particular violent acts. Policies aimed at violence control through content restrictions would be seen in a new light were it established that exposure to such content is itself a product of a latent trait that is consistent with aggressive behavior but that cannot reasonably be called aggressiveness (see e.g., National Institute of Mental Health, 1982).

All this would seem to raise sufficient question about the usefulness of the concept of aggression to justify further inquiry. In the analyses that follow, we assess the validity of the concept as it is used in experimental and nonexperimental research in psychology, using social control as the rival concept.

Although the predictive and convergent validity of aggression in nonexperimental research seems well established (Eron, 1987; Olweus 1980), strong convergent validity is a double-edged sword: It may suggest problems with discriminant validity. In this study, we therefore apply the principles of convergent and discriminant validity (Campbell & Fiske, 1959) to measures of the cognate concepts of aggression and social control to determine whether they are separable.

Operational Definitions of Aggression

Studies of aggression in psychology take place in both field and laboratory settings. In field studies, aggression is measured by interviews, questionnaires, or observation. Operational definitions of the concept typically include such acts as hitting and hurting, pushing and shoving, injuring and irritating (Eron, 1987), unprovoked physical aggression (e.g., starting a fight), and mildly provoked verbal aggression (e.g., sassing a teacher; Olweus, 1979). But they also often include stealing and vandalism (sometimes referred to as *property aggression*), lying, insulting, auto theft, and robbery (Eron, 1987; Milavsky, Kessler, Stipp, & Rubens 1982; Tedeschi, Smith, & Brown, 1974).

Such behavior can be measured with a high degree of reliability (Eron, 1987; Huesmann, Eron, Lefkowitz, & Walder 1984), and differences among individuals are highly stable over time. Olweus (1979) reported that aggression scores and intelligence scores are about equally stable: "The difference between the estimated coefficients would be only .10 for an interval of 10 years (.70 for intelligence and .60 for aggression)" (p. 866). Huesmann et al. (1984) showed that aggression scores remained reasonably stable over a 22-year period. In fact, they concluded that "what is not arguable is that aggressive behavior, however engendered, once established, remains remarkably stable across time, situation, and even generations within a family" (p. 1133).

Such naturalistic measures of aggression predict criminal behavior and do so well enough that those studying the stability of aggression over the life course often use standard crime counts (e.g., "criminal justice convictions," "seriousness of criminal acts," "driving while intoxicated") as measures of aggression during the later or adult years (Farrington 1978; Huesmann et al., 1984, p. 1124). Given such long-term predictability, short-term predictability would be expected to be excellent: Eron (1987) reported that his aggression scale had a "one-month test–retest reliability [of] .91" (p. 436).

Studying infrequent phenomena like aggression (infrequent at least among adults) is difficult in laboratory settings. Investigators interested in aggression cannot sit back and wait for it to occur but must generate it in sufficient quantities to allow reliable analysis. The problem may be further complicated by the standard practice of relying on university undergraduates, a population with especially low rates of aggression as it is typically measured in natural settings.

A few protocols seem to be standard. Subjects are asked to participate in a learning experiment in which deception is used about the true purpose of the study. The subject works with another subject on the learning task, and the subject's grade, score, or reward is partially dependent on the behavior of the second subject. The second subject is a confederate of the experimenter, instructed to interfere with performance of the task. The subject has the opportunity to punish the confederate (often with electrical shock) for his or her failure to perform adequately. Manipulations involve the setting (e.g., temperature), characteristics of the confederate, level of insult, and the legitimacy of the frustrated expectation (e.g., Baron, 1976; Gaebelein & Taylor, 1971; Geen, 1968; Gentry, 1970; Hynan & Grush, 1986; Kulik & Brown, 1979). These studies generally demonstrate that subjects can be induced to punish (behave aggressively toward) the confederate and that the degree of punishment (aggression) varies by setting, characteristics of the confederate, level of insult, and legitimacy of the frustration.

Authors of laboratory studies often suggest that a major purpose in studying aggression is to better understand criminal violence, spouse abuse, civil disorder, or war (e.g., Anderson, 1989; Baron, 1976; Berkowitz, 1989). Both laboratory and field research traditions therefore seek justification for the study of aggression in the real-world problem of criminal behavior. (The connection between aggressive acts in the laboratory and stable aggressive inclinations is thought to be straightforward. Because stable aggression accumulates "over repeated instances of unsatisfied expectation" [Berkowitz, 1989, p. 61], aggression observed in the laboratory may be assumed to reflect prior and subsequent states of the individual as well.)

Given the explanatory benefits that derive from equating aggressive acts with aggressive tendencies, the scientific community has not been particularly sensitive to the question of validity.[1] In our view, field research in psychology has been insufficiently sensitive to the problem of discriminant validity between aggression and crime, and laboratory research in psychology has not attended sufficiently to the prior question of convergent validity of its operational indicators with measures of aggression produced by other means.

Convergent Validity and Laboratory Measures of Aggression

In criminal law, as in common usage, the idea of aggression connotes unprovoked, senseless, or unjustifiable violence or threat of violence. The criminal law justifies the use of force under conditions of duress and in defense of self or others. Following similar logic, the *Oxford Dictionary* (3rd. ed.; Oxford University Press, 1955) defined aggression as "an unprovoked attack; the first attack in a quarrel; an assault."

Laboratory research in psychology seems little concerned with these standard definitions of aggression and not particularly concerned with maintaining consistency of meaning from one experiment to another. If, as Kulik and Brown (1979) noted, "recent experimental studies of human aggression have generally employed electric shock as the primary, if not sole, measure of aggression" (p. 183), the meaning of this operational definition is not obvious. In fact, Anderson (1989) gave as a "partial listing" five types of aggression, several of which would not qualify as aggression as it is generally understood: "predatory, pain elicited, defensive, offensive, and instrumental" (p. 74). Unprovoked electric shock of a colleague would clearly qualify as aggression under common understandings of the concept. But the electric shock administered in the psychology experiment on aggression is not unprovoked. On the contrary, it is carefully orchestrated. The experimenter's confederates insult the subject, fail to collaborate on an assigned task, or frustrate the achievement of some common goal—earning, it could be said, the hostility shown toward them. Nor do subjects come up with the idea of aggression on their own.

---

[1] *The response of some psychologists to our arguments suggests considerable sensitivity to the issue of the meaning of measures of aggression. In fact, our ignorance of "what psychologists know" about aggression has more than once been characterized as so colossal that our arguments need not be taken seriously. Fortunately for us, "what psychologists know" about aggression is not itself particularly reliable or stable. Fortunately, too, we are not the first to suggest that much laboratory research on aggression is, in fact, research on "defensive coercion" compelled by norms of reciprocity (see Tedeschi, Gaes, & Rivera, 1977; Tedeschi, Smith, & Brown, 1974).*

On the contrary, they are instructed to administer punishment, typically electric shock, to fellow experimental subjects who have agreed to accept it as punishment for their mistakes, all in the name of some lofty moral or scientific purpose (i.e., good reasons are given to support the experimenter's instructions to shock the confederate).

On their face, then, hostile acts in the laboratory are not necessarily aggressive behavior as traditionally defined. One could substitute for *aggression* words like *retribution, reciprocity,* or even *punishment* (and the latter is, in fact, common in the literature) and could easily justify the behavior as defense, as reasonable response to duress, or as simply following the instructions of a credible authority. (Tedeschi, Gaes, & Rivera, 1977, make precisely this point.)

Supporting this interpretation is the fact that physical punishment of confederates has also been used to study obedience to authority. In these studies, the subject is paid to participate in a scientific experiment devoted to understanding the learning process, is told that the confederate has volunteered to accept the electric shock that the subject is instructed to administer, is repeatedly prodded to continue by the scientist in charge, and is told if necessary that his or her actions will produce no permanent damage to the confederate (Milgram 1974, pp. 19–21).

Commenting on the most famous of these obedience experiments, Milgram (1974) said that the subject's shocking behavior has nothing to do with aggression (pp. 165–168) and points out that the increase in voltage produced by the experimenter's instructions greatly exceeds the effects obtained from frustration. So, an alternative interpretation of laboratory studies of aggression is that they in fact measure compliance, obedience, or, as it is usually called in survey research, acquiescence (the tendency to agree with whatever the interviewer says). If, in support of scientific progress, subjects find it easier to shock others when they "deserve it," this tendency may reflect nothing more than the fact that it is easier to go along with instructions when they are consistent with the respondent's beliefs about appropriate behavior.

On the other hand, these experiments may indeed be relevant to the concept of unprovoked aggression. Provoked and unprovoked aggression may be part of the same underlying construct. Addressing the question of the meaning of the behavior provoked in the laboratory, we undertook to identify analogous behavior in natural settings in which its meaning could be clarified.

On its face, the behavior studied in psychological laboratory research on aggression involves punishment of clear violations of rules or normative expectations. It may be that this form of aggression reflects tendencies to engage in assaultive or violent behavior outside these contrived settings. If so, such a measure would be said to possess convergent validity. Such a hypothesis seems to us highly implausible. In the absence of empirical evidence, evidence not available in the psychological literature, sociological control theories would predict the reverse—that people who are unusually sensitive to normative expectations (or the dictates of authorities) would be unlikely to engage in assaultive and violent acts. Available survey research allows a simple test of these competing hypotheses.

The data in Table 1 are from a large survey commonly used in the study of delinquency (Hirschi, 1969; Jensen & Eve, 1976; Matsueda, 1982; Matsueda & Heimer, 1987) that has not been previously used to study aggression. (Indexes and items used in this and the following tables are described in the Appendix.) The results of the survey, which was administered to junior and senior high school students, have often been shown to parallel results from other large surveys, including national surveys (cf. Dornbusch et al.,

TABLE 1

Correlations Among Measures of Aggression, Theft, Drug Use, and Exogenous Variables

Variable	Theft	Violence	Drug use	Laboratory aggression
Laboratory aggression	−.23	−.19	−.18	.—
Parental supervision	−.27	−.26	−.30	.18
Likes school	−.21	−.24	−.21	.20
English grade point average	−.14	−.14	−.28	.11
Verbal Aptitude Test (DAT)	−.10	−.04*	−.18	.12
Dropout	−.44	−.34	−.48	−.17
Fatalism	.15	.15	.17	−.17
Ambition	−.24	−.19	−.21	.18
Theft	—	.43	.43	−.23
Violence	—	—	.31	−.19
Official offenses	.31	.18	.31	−.15

Note. These data represent original analysis from the Richmond (California) Youth Project described in Hirschi (1969). The sample represented here consisted of White males in grades 7–12. Indexes and items in the table are described in Hirschi (1969). $N = 1,138–1,495$, except for English grade point average, where $N = 907$ because of missing grade point average information. *Not significant at .01. All other correlations significant at .001.

1985; Elliott, Huizinga, & Ageton, 1985; Hindelang, Hirschi, & Weis, 1981; Hirschi, 1969). For our purposes, we constructed a measure designed to match the common laboratory scenario wherein subjects are given the opportunity to punish deviance. In this analogous case, subjects were asked whether they would tell the police after witnessing four deviant or illegal acts: "a 14-year-old drinking in a bar," "a man beating his wife," "someone stealing a coat," and "a man peddling dope." Yes responses to these items were given a value of 1 and were summed to form a scale that might in Durkheimian terms be called a *measure of moral outrage* but in laboratory studies is used to measure aggression.[2] Evidence that the scale measures "moral outrage" is provided by its correlations with items measuring ambition (.18) and fatalism ($-.17$). The more aggressive the subjects' reactions to deviance, the more likely they are to be ambitious and future oriented.

In contrast, if, as in the psychological laboratory interpretation, punitive responses toward deviant behavior connote aggressiveness, such responses should also connote aggressiveness in natural settings. Therefore, punitive responses toward deviant behavior in natural settings should predict aggressive criminal acts. Other correlations in Table 1 address this question of construct validity.

Contrary to expectations derived from the psychological interpretation of laboratory studies, the more "aggressive" the subjects, the less likely they are to commit delinquent acts when such acts are measured by commonly used and widely validated self-report methods (for validity evidence, see Elliott et al., 1985; Hindelang et al., 1981). These results are not limited to self-report measures of delinquency; they generalize to delinquency as measured by police records ($r = -.15$). They also hold for general measures of delinquency and measures limited to acts of violence.

We recognize that the correlations in Table 1 are not large. They are, however, statistically significant and in the direction opposite to that expected were the laboratory measure of aggression tapping a more general tendency toward aggressive or violent behavior. In this case, convergent validity requires moderate to large negative correlations. The correlations observed, although small, are thus greatly different from those required by the psychological hypothesis.

---

[2] *In sociological theory, deviant behavior is often defined as a violations of others' expectations (Parsons, 1951). In this sense, our operational definition of laboratory aggression is identical to the definition in the original frustration–aggression formulation, wherein frustration is "an obstacle blocking the attainment of an expected gratification" and aggression is an attempt to inflict injury (Berkowitz, 1989, p. 61).*

Also contrary to clear expectations from laboratory research, Table 1 shows that moral outrage is negatively related to such forms of deviance as dropping out of school ($-.17$) and underage drug use (smoking and drinking; $r = -.18$). Consistent with the findings reported thus far, Table 1 also shows that this measure of moral outrage is positively related to verbal aptitude scores and to grade point average and that those with a punitive orientation toward deviation are more rather than less likely to perform well on these tests. Research has consistently shown that intelligence test scores and school grades are negatively correlated with crime, especially crimes of violence (Hirschi & Hindelang, 1977; Reichel & Magnusson, 1988). All correlations in Table 1 thus support the conclusion that the reaction of laboratory subjects to provocation represents the opposite of aggression as normally conceived. The greater the parental supervision, the higher the level of "aggression" as measured in the laboratory ($r = .18$). Also, the more the student likes school, the greater the "laboratory aggression" ($r = .20$). Again, these correlations are opposite in direction to the results required by the principles of construct validity.

Even the traditional demographic correlates of crime and violence behave incorrectly when "laboratory aggression" is the focus of attention. In Table 2, we extend the

TABLE 2

Laboratory Aggression by Race and Sex

Measure	Race and sex			
	White girls	White boys	Black girls	Black boys
Percent reporting three or more (of four) offenses to the police[a]	42 (n = 675)	33 (n = 1586)	20 (n = 813)	16 (n = 1001)
Percent refusing to tell the police or some other official what they know about a crime[b]	11 (n = 272)	22 (n = 846)	15 (n = 126)	31 (n = 368)

Note. These data represent original analyses from the Richmond (California) Youth Project described in Hirschi (1969) and the Seattle Youth Study described in Hindelang, Hirschi, and Weis (1981).
[a]From the Richmond, California, sample.
[b]From the Seattle, Washington, sample.

analysis to include a second large survey of adolescents conducted in Seattle. These data were originally collected to provide information on the reliability and validity of self-report measures of violence, crime, and drug use (Hindelang et al., 1981). Table 2 shows the connection between cooperativeness with authority and race and sex, two well-established correlates of violence. Research consistently shows that boys and members of ethnic minority groups are more likely than are girls and Whites to commit delinquent acts (see Wilson & Herrnstein, 1985). Table 2 shows that in two distinct data sets with rather different measures of "laboratory aggression," the groups typically lowest on delinquency are most likely to report offenses to the police. Thus, accepting the interpretation required by psychological research would force one to conclude that girls are more aggressive than boys and that Whites are more aggressive than Blacks. Once again, then, the correlates of "laboratory aggression" are opposite in sign from the well-established correlates of crime and delinquency.

To emphasize, aggression as measured in the laboratory by psychological researchers predicts conformity rather than deviance. The observed connection between moral outrage and conformity is, however, consistent with theories of social control.

Psychological researchers will, of course, argue that these survey responses do not measure aggression as they construe it. In the laboratory, subjects are asked to punish violations of norms they observe. In our surveys, respondents were asked if they would tell the police were they to observe certain delinquent acts. We would not contest the assertion that the laboratory measure may be a better measure of the underlying construct than is its survey equivalent. We would, however, question the relevance of this fact to a test of construct validity. If one could simulate the laboratory measure more precisely (e.g., by building into the description of the event an obligation to a higher authority), there is reason to believe that the results would be even more strongly contrary to a conception of the responses as reflecting aggression. For that matter, construct validation requires the use of different methods that do not share the same strengths or weaknesses.

As such, construct validation turns the meaning of laboratory experiments on aggression on its head. Rather than an aggressive person using unjustified or inappropriate force for personal advantage, laboratory experiments appear to show individuals defending their interests in the face of inappropriate or unjustified behavior on the part of the experimenter's confederate. In this interpretation, the aggressive subject in the experimental setting actually represents a citizen sensitive to social norms and willing to take steps to defend them (or perhaps an agreeable, compliant individual sensitive to social norms). The few efforts by laboratory researchers to establish the construct validity of laboratory measures are consistent with these results.[3]

If operational definitions of aggression in the laboratory do not meet ordinary standards of face validity and have not been subjected to tests of convergent validity, it is possible to understand these deficiencies as stemming from the inherent difficulties in assessing the validity of laboratory definitions. Difficulties of such magnitude should not be present in studies of aggression in natural settings, where behavioral measures of cognate concepts are readily available.

Aggression in Naturalistic or Field Studies

In a well-known study of the stability of aggression (see also Huesmann et al., 1984), Eron (1987) defined aggression as

> an act that injures or irritates another person. This definition excludes self-hurt . . . but makes no distinction between accidental and instrumental aggression or between socially acceptable and antisocial aggression. The assumption is that there is a response class, aggression, that can include a variety of behaviors, exhibited in numerous situations, all of which result in injury or irritation to another person. Thus, this category includes both hitting and hurting behaviors, whether or not these behaviors are reinforced by pain cues from the victim or target person. This category also includes *injury to or theft of property*. (p. 435, emphasis added)

This definition excludes nothing found in ordinary sociological definitions of crime and delinquency (Elliott et al., 1985; Hirschi, 1969; Wolfgang, Figlio, & Sellin, 1972). If the dependent or outcome variable in studies of aggression is some form of ordinary crime, as measured by self-reports of delinquent activities or by convictions for criminal offenses in a court of law, one cannot simultaneously use this variable as a measure of aggression. Put another way, if crime is used as a measure of aggression, aggression cannot be thought of as a cause of crime, contrary to the stated justification of much psychological research.

---

[3]*Milgram (1974) reported little success in his efforts to establish the convergent validity of obedience. In our view, such difficulties should not be taken to show the superiority of "behavioral measure" so much as an all-too-common lack of attention to the meaning or validity of these measures. For example, Milgram reported that obedient subjects are more authoritarian, but he appeared unwilling to put much faith in the measure of authoritarianism because it relies on "paper-and-pencil" responses rather than "actual submission." It seem plausible to assume that the shared variance in the two measures is due to the large acquiescence component in the measure of authoritarianism. If so, the operative meaning of obedience is something like "agreeableness stemming from diffidence," rather than the more sinister "willingness to punish the weak." Milgram's finding that obedience is correlated with low education (p. 205) is also consistent with our interpretation of his work as dealing with what survey researchers call acquiescence or "yea-saying" (Jackman, 1973).*

To illustrate this problem, consider the television-violence-causes-aggression-causes-crime issue. In this line of research, it is routinely assumed that aggression may be learned independently of other forms of deviant behavior. For example, Eron (1987) commented on a correlation between the frequency of viewing television at age 8 and criminal convictions 22 years later:

> What was probably important were the attitudes and behavioral norms inculcated by continued watching of those and similar programs. In this regard, we can consider continued television violence viewing as rehearsal of aggressive sequences. Thus, one who watches more aggressive sequences on television should respond more aggressively when presented with similar or relevant cues. From an information-processing perspective, sociocultural norms, reinforced by continual displays in the broadcast media, play an important role by providing standards and values against which the child can compare his or her own behavior and the behavior of others to judge whether they are appropriate. (p. 440)

This explanation appears in a different light when it is recalled that television viewing at age 8 would (given the operational definition of aggression used in this research) equally well predict theft, motor vehicle accidents, trivial nonviolent offending, drug consumption, and employment instability—behaviors hard to attribute to the number of shootings or fist fights watched on television 20 years previously. In fact, Eron (1987) wrote that "aggression at age 8 predicted social failure, psychopathology, aggression, and low educational and occupational success" 22 years later (p. 440). Huesmann et al. (1984) added as "measures of aggressiveness" (p. 1122) the number of moving traffic violations, the number of convictions for driving while intoxicated, and number of convictions for criminal acts. However, if psychologists treat aggression as a general concept that includes accidents, theft, withdrawal, lack of ambition, and drug use, they cannot at the same time treat it as a specific concept centered on physical assault. Because it behaves as a general tendency, it seems unlikely that television viewing at age 8 is independent of this general tendency at age 8. It therefore seems unlikely that the specific content of television programming viewed at age 8 could contribute independently to subsequent levels of "aggression."

Convergent and Discriminant Validity of Field Measures

To put our discussion of the validity of field measures of aggression in context, we use the following commonly accepted criteria of convergent and discriminant validity (Campbell & Fiske, 1959; see also Jackman, 1973, p. 332).

1. Valid measures of aggression should be correlated with other measures of aggression produced by the same and by different methods (convergent validity).
2. Measures of aggression can be invalidated by being too strongly correlated to measures of other concepts. Thus, valid measures of aggression will be more strongly correlated to other measures of aggression than to measures of concepts other than aggression produced by the same method (discriminant validity).
3. Valid measures of aggression should not be related to exogenous variables in precisely the same form or pattern as are measures of different concepts (i.e., predictors of aggression should not prove to be interchangeable with predictors of concepts distinct from aggression).

Convergent Validity

As we have reported, it has been established that aggression can be reliably measured, whether one is talking about stability or internal consistency. Table 3 shows intercorrelations among such measures of aggression as robbery, assault with weapons, physical assault, and fighting with authorities (teachers and police) as measured by standard self-reports of delinquency (Hindelang et al., 1981). The correlations among the measures are all positive, and nearly all are significant at the .001 level. The index of aggressive behavior produced by these 12 items has a split-half reliability of .76.

This measure of aggression correlates as expected with measures produced by other methods. Thus, Table 4 shows the relation between self-reported aggression and police record for delinquency. Among those reporting no violent acts, 39 percent had either police or court records. Among those reporting four or more violent acts, 79 percent had such records. These differences reflect a correlation of .27. (The Seattle study oversampled youth known to have police records. The base rate for delinquency, as shown, was 53%, considerably higher than would be found in a general population sample of White juveniles.)

If the validity of concepts is determined by empirical relations between their measures and measures of cognate concepts, the correlation between a reliable measure of aggression and independent measures of criminality would seem to establish at least provisionally the validity of the idea of aggression. The next criterion to consider is the ability to distinguish between measures of aggression and measures of crime.

TABLE 3

Correlations Among Measures of Aggression in White Males

Measure	1	2	3	4	5	6	7	8	9	10	11	12
1. Purse snatch	—	9*	16	07**	12	12	15	12	12	15	13	12
2. Armed robbery		—	33	20	34	25	15	19	22	18	31	8*
3. Threaten			—	33	21	16	20	17	16	21	26	10*
4. Strong arm				—	19	15	11	11	13	22	19	7**
5. Carry weapon					—	48	21	18	29	18	25	9*
6. Display weapon						—	24	18	31	20	24	7**
7. Resist arrest							—	19	28	21	14	19
8. Hit teacher								—	20	19	20	21
9. Aggravated Assault									—	24	31	10*
10. Picked fight										—	29	11
11. Jumped someone											—	14
12. Hit parent												—

Note. These data represent original analyses from the Seattle Youth Study described in Hindelang, Hirschi, and Weis (1981). $N = 833$.

*Significant at .01, one-tailed test.   **Not significant at .01. All other correlations significant at .001.

TABLE 4

Percentage of White Males With Police or Court Records, by Self-Reported Aggression

	Number of self-reported violent acts					
	0	**1**	**2**	**3**	**4+**	**Total**
Official record	39	58	60	69	79	53
	($n = 385$)	($n = 193$)	($n = 92$)	($n = 61$)	($n - 103$)	($n = 834$)

Note. These data represent original analyses from the Seattle Youth Study described in Hindelang, Hirschi, and Weis (1981).
$r = .27, gamma = .42, p < .001.$

Discriminant Validity

To examine the discriminant validity of aggression, we selected a large set of "nonaggressive" criminal and delinquent acts that connote stealth, passivity, or retreatism. One group of items within this set measures theft without the use of force or violence; the other measures drug use. Both sets of items are conceptually and empirically homogeneous, as was our measure of aggression. The split-half reliability coefficient for the 16 theft items is .80 and for the 10 drug items is .87 (for the content of the scales, see the Appendix). Recalling that the validity of a measure may be called into question if its correlation with measures of other concepts is too high, there is good reason to be concerned about the discriminant validity of aggression. The correlation between the theft and violence indexes was .43 in Richmond and .48 in Seattle; the correlation between drug use and aggression was .31 in Richmond and .44 in Seattle. (Theft was correlated with drug use .42 and .56 in Richmond and Seattle, respectively.) Given the generally moderate correlation among all measures of crime and delinquency, these correlations are high enough to question the assumption that aggression is independent of a more general construct encompassing violence, theft, and drug use.

The final test of discriminant validity involves comparison of the explanatory correlates of these potentially overlapping concepts. Can one discriminate between aggression and alternative measures of crime and delinquency on the basis of a set of standard explanatory variables? Table 5 presents correlations between violence, theft, and drugs and three indicators of concepts frequently used to explain delinquency: parental supervision, amorality, and ambition (Hindelang et al., 1981, p. 129). (The details of index construction are provided in the Appendix.) In all cases, in both data sets, the correlations of the three

TABLE 5
Correlations of Aggressive Behavior and Alternative Measures of Low Self-Control for White Males (Richmond/Seattle)

Variable	Theft	Violence	Drugs	General
Parental supervision	−.28/−.23	−.23/−.25	−.29/−.30	−.35/−.31
Amorality	.29/.30	.25/.30	.28/.28	.33/.35
Ambition	−.24/−.23	−.18/−.19	−.21/−.29	−.27/−.29
Theft	—	.43/.48	.42/.56	.89/.88
Violence	—	—	.31/.44	.76/.72

Note. These data represent original analyses from the Richmond (California) Youth Project described in Hirschi (1969) and the Seattle Youth Study described in Hindelang, Hirschi, and Weis (1981). $N = 1,034-1,052$ for Richmond sample; $N = 640$ for Seattle sample. For details of scale construction, see Appendix.

outside variables and the three dependent variables are indistinguishable. With respect to these independent variables, then, the three measures of "criminality" are interchangeable. Table 5 also shows that a composite scale constructed from the three separate measures of criminality produces results identical to those produced by the three taken one at a time. (Similar results are evident for a different set of independent variables in Table 1.) Thus, there is every reason within these sets of data to treat aggression as an idea indistinguishable from the more general idea of criminality. As would be expected from the results of much previous research in sociological criminology, the concept of aggression here fails an explicit test of discriminant validity.

Conclusions and Implications

The results of this study suggest that (a) measures of aggression used in laboratory studies lack convergent validity (i.e., are not correlated in the expected direction with other measures of aggression) and seem conceptually and empirically close to the concept of compliance and that (b) measures of aggression in field studies possess good convergent validity and stability but cannot be discriminated from measures of crime.

From a social control point of view, aggressive or violent acts are explicable as acts that produce immediate benefits and entail long-term social costs for the actor. Such acts are usually defined as criminal by the state and as deviant by society and are the very acts that social control theory is designed to explain (Gottfredson & Hirschi, 1990). There are also aggressive or violent acts that produce no immediate benefit to the actor but that are thought to produce long-term social benefits. Such acts are usually conceptualized as conformity and are therefore also easily explained within a control theory framework.

This chapter argues that psychological laboratory researchers confuse one of these forms of aggression with the other, that they treat conformity as deviance. As a consequence, the results of psychological laboratory research do not threaten the validity of sociological theories of deviance. This research provides no evidence of an individual personality trait or propensity that produces assaultive or violent behavior independent of its social consequences. An additional implication of our interpretation is that sociologists working on violence and aggression should not attempt to incorporate the findings of this laboratory research into their theories.

As noted, violent and assaultive acts that produce immediate benefit at the same time they produce long-term social costs are of interest to students of crime and deviance. Indeed, to the extent that aggressive acts share these defining characteristics of most forms of crime and deviance, they easily fall within the scope of a general control theory. Gottfredson and Hirschi (1990) argued that many violent acts can be understood in precisely this way. For example, on inspection, much homicide, child abuse, spouse abuse, and violent robbery is undertaken to gain some momentary advantage without regard for long-term social consequences. When a husband strikes his wife repeatedly as a way to end an argument, when a father physically assaults a child to end an annoyance of the moment, or when a robber shoots a clerk because he is nervous about his escape, the advantage of the moment has outweighed considerations of distant costs. Sociological control theorists focus on social forces that produce variability in the extent to which group members are influenced by the long-term costs of their behavior (Gottfredson & Hirschi, 1990; Heckathorn, 1990; Hirschi, 1969; Kornhauser, 1978).

This interpretation presupposes strong relations among forms of crime and deviance. Fortunately, a great deal of research in criminology and sociology is consistent with the assumption that offenders are versatile, that they do not specialize in violent or nonviolent behavior (Hindelang et al., 1981; Osgood, 1990; Osgood et al., 1988; Robins, 1966; Rojek & Erickson, 1982; Rowe et al., 1990; Sampson & Laub, 1990; Wolfgang et al., 1972). Such research indeed reveals a latent trait underlying the bulk of criminal, delinquent, and even imprudent behavior (Osgood et al., 1988; Rowe et al., 1990). The manifestations of this general trait (e.g., drug use, theft, and employment instability) are often inconsistent with the concept of aggression as used in psychological research (Gottfredson & Hirschi, 1990, pp. 65–72, 85–120).

Consistent with the finding of a general trait underlying many forms of criminal and deviant behavior, the concept of aggression does not survive an ordinary test of discriminant validity. Aggressive deviant acts share so much in common with nonaggressive deviant acts that individuals prone to commit aggressive criminal acts are prone to commit nonaggressive deviant acts as well. Thus, no individual-level trait of aggression is consistent with the results of behavioral research.

References

Anderson, C. A. (1989). Temperature and aggression: Ubiquitous effects of heat on occurrence of human violence. *Psychological Bulletin 106*, 74–96.

Bandura, A. (1973). *Aggression: A social learning analysis.* Englewood Cliffs, NJ: Prentice Hall.

Baron, R. (1976). The reduction of human aggression: A field study of the influence of incompatible reactions. *Journal of Applied Social Psychology, 6,* 260–274.

Berkowitz, L. (1989). Frustration–aggression hypothesis: Examination and reformulation. *Psychological Bulletin, 106,* 59–73.

Bernard, T. (1990). Angry aggression among the "truly disadvantaged." *Criminology, 28,* 73–96.

Blau, J., & Blau, P. (1982). The cost of inequality: Metropolitan structure and violent crime. *American Sociological Review, 47,* 114–129.

Blumstein, A., Cohen, J., Roth, J., & Visher, C. (1986). *Criminal careers and "career criminals."* Washington, DC: National Academy Press.

Buss, A. (1961). *The psychology of aggression.* New York: Wiley.

Campbell, D., & Fiske, D. (1959). Convergent and discriminant validation by the multitrait–multimethod matrix. *Psychological Bulletin, 56,* 81–105.

Cloward, R., & Ohlin, L. (1960). *Delinquency and opportunity.* New York: Free Press.

Cook, T., Kendzierski, D., & Thomas, S. (1983). The implicit assumptions of television research: An analysis of the 1982 NIMH report on television and behavior. *Public Opinion Quarterly, 47,* 161–201.

Dollard, J., Doob, L., Miller, N., Mowrer, O., & Sears, R. (1939). *Frustration and aggression.* New Haven, CT: Yale University Press.

Dornbusch, S., Merrill Carlsmith, J., Bushwall, S., Ritter, P., Leiderman, H., Hastorf, A., & Gross, R. (1985). Single parents, extended households, and the control of adolescents. *Child Development, 56,* 326–341.

Elliott, D., Huizinga, D., & Ageton, S. (1985). *Explaining delinquency and drug use.* Newbury Park, CA: Sage.

Eron, L. (1987). The development of aggressive behavior from the perspective of a developing behaviorism. *American Psychologist, 42,* 435–442.

Farrington, D. (1978). The family backgrounds of aggressive youth. In L. Hersov, M. Berger, & D. Shaffer (Eds.), *Aggression and antisocial behavior in childhood and adolescence* (pp. 73–93). Oxford, England: Pergamon Press.

Farrington, D., Ohlin, L., & Wilson, J. Q. (1986). *Understanding and controlling crime.* New York: Springer Verlag.

Gaebelein, J., & Taylor, S. (1971). The effects of competition and attack on physical aggression. *Psychonomic Science, 24,* 65–67.

Geen, R. (1968). Effects of frustration, attack, and prior training in aggressiveness upon aggressive behavior. *Journal of Personality and Social Psychology, 9,* 316–321.

Gelles, R. (1980). Violence in the family: A review of research in the seventies. *Journal of Marriage and the Family, 42,* 873–885.

Gentry, W. (1970). Effects of frustration, attack, and prior aggressive training on overt aggression and vascular processes. *Journal of Personality and Social Psychology, 16,* 718–725.

Gottfredson, M., & Hirschi, T. (1990). *A general theory of crime.* Stanford, CA: Stanford University Press.

Heckathorn, D. (1990). Collective sanctions and compliance norms—A formal theory of group-mediated social-control. *American Sociological Review, 55,* 366–384.

Hindelang, M., Hirschi, T., & Weis, J. (1981). *Measuring delinquency.* Newbury Park, CA: Sage.

Hirschi, T. (1969). *Causes of delinquency.* Berkeley: University of California Press.

Hirschi, T., & Gottfredson, M. (1990). Substantive positivism and the idea of crime. *Rationality and Society, 2,* 412–428.

Hirschi, T., & Hindelang, M. (1977). Intelligence and delinquency: A revisionist review. *American Sociological Review, 42,* 571–587.

Huesmann, L. R., Eron, L., Lefkowitz, M., & Walder, L. (1984). Stability of aggression over time and generations. *Developmental Psychology, 20,* 1120–1134.

Hynan, D. J., & Grush, J. E. (1986). Effects of impulsivity, depression, provocation, and time on aggressive behavior. *Journal of Research on Personality, 20,* 158–171.

Jackman, M. (1973). Education and prejudice or education and response-set? *American Sociological Review, 38,* 327–339.

Jensen, G., & Eve, R. (1976). Sex differences in delinquency: An examination of popular sociological explanations. *Criminology, 13,* 427–448.

Kornhauser, R. (1978). *Social sources of delinquency.* Chicago: University of Chicago Press.

Kulik, J., & Brown, R. (1979). Frustration, attribution of blame, and aggression. *Journal of Experimental Social Psychology, 15,* 183–194.

Matsueda, R. (1982). Testing control theory and differential association: A causal modeling approach. *American Sociological Review, 47,* 489–504.

Matsueda, R., & Heimer, K. (1987). Race, family structure, and delinquency: A test of differential association and social control theory. *American Sociological Review, 52,* 826–840.

Merton, R. (1938). Social structure and "anomie." *American Sociological Review, 3,* 672–682.

Milavsky, J., Kessler, R., Stipp, H., & Rubens, W. (1982). *Television and aggression: The results of a panel study.* New York: Academic Press.

Milgram, S. (1974). *Obedience to authority: An experimental view.* New York: Harper & Row.

Monahan, J. (1981). *Predicting violent behavior: An assessment of clinical techniques.* Newbury Park, CA: Sage.

National Institute of Mental Health. (1982). *Television and behavior: Ten years of scientific progress and implications for the eighties.* Rockville, MD: Author.

Olweus, D. (1979). Stability of aggressive reaction patterns in males: A review. *Psychological Bulletin, 86,* 852–875.

Olweus, D. (1980). Familial and temperamental determinants of aggressive behavior in adolescent boys: A causal analysis. *Developmental Psychology, 16,* 644–660.

Osgood, D. W. (1990). *Covariation among adolescent problem behaviors.* Paper presented at the meeting of the American Society of Criminology, Baltimore, MD.

Osgood, D. W., Johnston, L., O'Malley, P., & Bachman, J. (1988). The generality of deviance in late adolescence and early adulthood. *American Sociological Review, 53,* 81–93.

Parsons, T. (1951). *The social system.* New York: Free Press.

Reichel, H., & Magnusson, D. (1988). *The relationship of intelligence to registered criminality: An exploratory study* (Report No. 676). Stockholm, Sweden: University of Stockholm, Department of Psychology.

Robins, L. (1966). *Deviant children grown up.* Baltimore: Williams & Wilkins.

Rojek, D., & Erickson, M. (1982). Delinquent careers: A test of the career escalation model. *Criminology, 20,* 5–28.

Rowe, D., Osgood, D. W., Nicewander, W. A. (1990). A latent trait approach to unifying criminal careers. *Criminology, 28,* 237–270.

Sampson, R., & Laub, J. (1990). Crime and deviance over the life course: The salience of adult social bonds. *American Sociological Review, 55,* 609–627.

Sampson, R., & Laub, J. (in press). *Crime and deviance over the life course.* Cambridge, MA: Harvard University Press.

Straus, M., Gelles, R., & Steinmetz, S. (1980). *Behind closed doors: Violence in the American family.* Garden City, NY: Anchor Press.

Tedeschi, J. T., Gaes, G. G., & Rivera, A. N. (1977). Aggression and the use of coercive power. *Journal of Social Issues, 33,* 101–125.

Tedeschi, J. T., Smith, R. B., II, & Brown, R. C., Jr. (1974). A reinterpretation of research on aggression. *Psychological Bulletin, 81,* 540–563.

Widom, C. (1989a). The cycle of violence. *Science, 244,* 160–166.

Widom, C. (1989b). Does violence beget violence? A critical examination of the literature. *Psychological Bulletin, 106,* 3–28.

Wilson, J. Q., & Herrnstein, R. (1985). *Crime and human nature.* New York: Simon & Schuster.

Wolfgang, M., Figlio, R., & Sellin, T. (1972). *Delinquency in a birth cohort.* Chicago: University of Chicago Press.

Appendix

The Richmond violence and theft scales were constructed from six four-category items measuring frequency of involvement in delinquent acts. The two items "Not counting fights you may have had with a brother or sister, have you ever beaten up on anyone or hurt anyone on purpose?" and "Have you ever banged up something that did not belong to you on purpose?" were combined to form the violence measure. The theft scale was composed of three items measuring various amounts of theft and a single item measuring car theft. The drug scale summed responses to questions about smoking and drinking.

The Seattle delinquency indexes (Table 5) were constructed by dichotomizing all items between 0 and 1 or more and summing the results. (Such "ever variety" indexes have been shown to outperform indexes based on raw frequencies of offenses [see Hindelang et al., 1981].) Illustrative items include the following: Have you ever taken things worth between $10 and $50 from a store without paying for them? Have you ever used a club, knife, or gun to get something from someone? Have you ever drunk beer or wine? The items are reproduced in full in Hindelang et al. (1981).

In Seattle, the parental supervision index (Table 5) is based on the following five items: When you are away from home, does your mother (father) know where you are and who you are with? As far as my mother (father) is concerned, I am pretty much free to come and go as I please. I could stay away from home overnight, and no one would ask me where I had been. In Richmond, the supervision index (Tables 1 and 5) is based on four items assessing parental knowledge of the youth's whereabouts.

In Seattle, the amorality index (Table 5) is based on the following four items: It is alright to get around the law if you can get away with it. Suckers deserve what they get. To get ahead, you have to do some things that are not right. Everybody steals something once in a while. The Richmond index (Table 5) is based on the first three items listed above.

In Seattle, the measure of ambition (Table 5) is based on the following three items: How important is getting good grades to you, personally? I try hard in school. Whatever I do, I try hard. In Richmond (Tables 1 and 5), this index is based on the two "try hard" items and the item, A person should never stop trying to get ahead.

In Richmond, the measure of fatalism (Table 1) is based on the following three items: What is going to happen to me will happen, no matter what I do. A person should live for today and let tomorrow take care of itself. Planning is useless since one's plans hardly ever work out. The dropout measure (Table 1) combines self-reports of truancy and failure to complete homework.

CHAPTER 3

A Theory About Disputes and the Efficacy of Control

Mark C. Stafford and Jack P. Gibbs

O ne of sociology's many curses is its perennial pursuit of questions that for generations have defied a defensible answer. Such a question is, How is social order possible? The immediate problem is that the term *social order* refers to a quantitative
phenomenon even though there is no prospect of an empirically applicable measurement
procedure, not even with an enormous expansion of research resources.

Accordingly, the study of disputes is significant because it bears on social order
and yet offers the prospect of answerable questions. Few would deny that disputes
threaten social order; hence, a focus on disputes would facilitate pursuit of the social
order question. Specifically, implicit in the traditional question—How is social order possible?—should be the following question: Why does the dispute rate vary? The present
theory seeks to address the latter question, which has not been answered in the extensive
literature on disputes.

This chapter sets forth a theory in which the paramount generalization asserts a
negative causal relation among social units and over time between the average efficacy of
control attempts and the prevalence of disputes. The theory also encompasses generalizations about correlates of the perceived capacity for control (power), nonlethal interpersonal violence, and the homicide rate. Put briefly, the theory pertains to determinants of
variation in the prevalence of disputes and some consequences of that variation.

Postulate 1 and Two Related Conceptualizations

The theory commences with Postulate 1:

> Among social units (e.g., countries, tribes, cities, metropolitan areas) or for a social unit over time, the greater the average efficacy of control attempts in a unit, the less the prevalence of disputes within the unit.

The postulate and other premises should be judged in terms of the theory's predictive power rather than the preconceptions, background assumptions, or presuppositions of critics. Nonetheless, Postulate 1 cannot be understood fully without definitions of some key terms.

Definition of a Dispute

English-speaking people commonly treat the term *dispute* as though it is synonymous with *argument, claim, complaint, conflict, controversy, demand, problem,* or *quarrel.* Although these terms may be useful in describing particular disputes, it is not constructive to equate any of them with *dispute.*

A particular definition. Fortunately, Miller and Sarat (1980–1981) set forth a commendable definition: "A dispute exists when a claim based on a grievance is rejected either in whole or in part" (p. 527). That definition serves as the point of departure, and the first modification is the substitution of *complaint* for *claim,* the rationale being that *complaint* is more nearly relational and adversarial.

The modification is a minor one, and it does not resolve conceptual issues nor make the Miller–Sarat (1980–1981) definition compatible with all contenders. In particular, Silberman (1985, p. 3) rejected the definition, although his rationale is obscure and various objections can be made to his alternative: "A dispute is situationally defined as any disruption in daily or other routines produced through violations of normative expectations by some person, group, or organization" (p. 2). Because the definition does not call for anything like a complaint, let alone rejection of a complaint, evidently it would apply to the typical robbery or an ordinary citizen's vehement but purely private negative reaction to some legislative action. Although Silberman may object that the interpretation ignores "normative expectations" and "disruptions in daily routines," the meaning of those terms is so vague as to raise serious doubts about the definition's empirical applicability (i.e., *inter alia,* the extent to which independent observers agree when using a definition to identify particular events or things). Doubts grow when Silberman subsequently refers to a grievance as though it is an essential element of a dispute and even more when he persistently equates *dispute* with *problem* in conducting a survey and in analyzing the findings.

In stating their definition, Miller and Sarat (1980–1981, p. 528) expressed awareness of contending definitions, especially one favored by several anthropologists (Gulliver, 1979, in particular). According to that contender, a dispute comes into being only when a disagreement has become a public matter (perhaps meaning when a third party has intervened). Miller and Sarat (1980–1981, pp. 528–529) gave some compelling reasons for rejecting that contending definition, but there are several other contenders, and there is little prospect for an end to the conceptual debate. For that matter, the debate will not be constructive as long as critics (e.g., Cain & Kulcsar, 1981–1982; Kidder, 1980–1981) reject extant definitions without formulating an explicit alternative.

Beyond Miller and Sarat. Another modification of Miller and Sarat's (1980–1981) conceptualization is necessary because they define a grievance as the "belief that one is entitled to a resource controlled by another party" (p. 528). The reference to *resource* reduces the definition's intelligibility and, hence, its empirical applicability. For example, if the grievant demands an apology, is the meaning of *resource* to be stretched to the point of including the capacity for satisfying that demand? The problems suggested by such questions are reduced by this alternative definition: A grievance occurs when someone believes that he or she has been harmed, injured, demeaned, or unjustly deprived or has unfairly suffered some loss as a consequence of the wrongful action or inaction of someone else.

Still another problem is Miller and Sarat's (1980–1981) indication that a dispute comes into being when the grievance is voiced by the grievant to the alleged source of the grievance but the complaint is rejected. Given that a grievance can be communicated in various ways (e.g., whining, demands, recriminations, ultimata), it is better to characterize a complaint as a *grievance* expression, and Miller and Sarat notwithstanding, the grievance may be expressed directly or indirectly to the complaint target. However, the expression must indicate what action or inaction by the complaint target would placate the grievant. To be sure, the expression may be so vague that the complaint target has no real sense of what would placate the grievant, in which case the complaint will be rejected, although not explicitly. Alternatively, the complaint may be so abrasive as to generate an explicit complaint rejection rather than a placation attempt. Finally, contrary to Miller and Sarat's conceptualization, the complaint target is not merely anyone who happens to control a resource that the grievant believes he or she is entitled to possess; rather, the complaint target is identified by the grievant as responsible for the grievance.

Hence, we offer this definition: A dispute exists when (a) a grievance has been expressed directly or indirectly by the grievant to the party whom the grievant identifies as responsible for the grievance, meaning that a complaint has been made; (b) the complaint indicates what action or inaction by the responsible party would placate the grievant, meaning that a demand has been made; and (c) the responsible party has responded so as to indicate that the demand will be satisfied only partially, if at all, meaning that the complaint or the related demand has been totally rejected or responded to in a way deemed unacceptable by the complainant. Clearly, the definition is couched in terms that are thoroughly interactional.

A Definition of Control

If only to emphasize human behavior's purposive quality, *control* should be described in terms of successful or unsuccessful attempts, with the distinction determined by the attempter's perception. Accordingly, attempted control is overt behavior by an individual in the belief that (a) the behavior increases or decreases the probability of some subsequent condition and (b) the increase or decrease is desirable.

As demonstrated elsewhere (Gibbs, 1989, pp. 23–75), the definition encompasses three basic types of attempted control: (a) inanimate, meaning the control of lifeless objects or substances; (b) biotic, meaning the control of any feature of an organism, including behavior except in the case of humans; and (c) human control, meaning the control over the overt or internal behavior of one or more humans. The third basic type includes attempted self-control and three major types of attempts to control the behavior of others: (a) attempted proximate control, which is direct in the sense of not involving an intermediary; (b) attempted sequential control, meaning a chain of command or requests; and (c) attempted social control, meaning through a third party but by some means other than a chain of command or requests.

Brief treatments of a few other issues. The term *control* has been used extensively by sociologists since Ross's (1901) tome on social control. Unfortunately, Ross did not confront conceptual problems or issues, and their avoidance became a tradition.

The first issue is posed by the conventional preoccupation of sociologists with social control to the exclusion of other kinds of control over human behavior (i.e., self-control, proximate, or sequential) as well as to the exclusion of inanimate control and biotic control. One counterargument is that inanimate and biotic control lack sociological relevance. To the contrary, technology is an unmanageably broad notion unless defined in material terms, which makes each technological item the product of inanimate control. Indeed, for all practical purposes, inanimate control is the creation, use, or maintenance of technological items, the connection being significant if only because sociologists readily grant technology's importance. The same will be true of *biotic control* once it is recognized that the term refers to, *inter alia*, plant domestication, animal domestication, and genetic engineering. Then there are numerous occupations that cannot be described adequately without reference to inanimate or biotic control. Indeed, humans commonly interact with and become dependent on other humans through inanimate and biotic control.

Even if sociologists should grant the need to go beyond social control, they are likely to balk at the present definition of control. Commencing with Ross's (1901) use of the term *social control* and perpetuated by Parsons's (1951) conceptualization, sociologists have tended to deny that intention, perception, beliefs, or affective behavior is necessarily involved in control. There are at least four objections to any such denial. First, it ignores the purposive quality of human behavior. Second, the denial obliterates the distinction between control and other kinds of human causation, such as influence. Third, the denial negates the very notion of attempted control; hence, the distinction between control success and control failure is lost. Fourth, absurdities ensue if control is defined strictly in terms of "consequences," making internal behavior irrelevant. Illustrating the last objection, suppose that someone emerges from a bank building with pistol in hand and is shot by a police officer. Although the bank robber was shot as a consequence of his or her behavior, it would be bizarre to conclude that he or she controlled the police officer's behavior. Anticipating an objection, it does not tax credulity to argue that "suicide through robbing a bank" is so rare that it can be ignored in this illustration.

One major counterargument is that making internal behavior conceptually relevant results in a too narrow definition of control. Yet, the phrase "behavior in the belief that" (see the definition of control given earlier) refers to more than intentional behavior in the conscious and deliberate sense. To illustrate, an automobile driver commonly does not hold the steering wheel consciously and deliberately, but surely he or she holds the wheel in the belief that it reduces the probability of a collision and that such reduction is desirable.

Perhaps most important, the present definition of control applies to diverse everyday human behavior thought to be habitual or uncritical, such as saying hello, and many social or behavioral scientists appear reluctant to recognize such behavior as a control attempt, perhaps because it is not clearly "intentional." But if saying hello is not attempted control, why are we surprised and miffed if there is no response? Then there is another reason for the reluctance to recognize that the bulk of human interaction involves attempted control. Although they rarely express it, sociologists appear prone to think of control over human behavior as an evil; hence, contrary to the present definition, they would balk at recognizing that inviting someone for dinner is an attempt to control human behavior.

A Particular Property of Control

Just as various types of control should be recognized, such is the case for properties of control. In the present theory, *efficacy* pertains to all control attempts by social unit members over some stipulated period, but the term actually refers to two things: (a) the effectiveness of control attempts, meaning the proportion of attempts perceived by the would-be controllers as having been successful, and (b) control efficiency, meaning the amount of time and human energy invested in the attempts. Although the implied definition excludes the extent of control (the frequency and intensity of attempts), it is assumed that extent is positively associated with effectiveness and efficiency. Finally, some connection between social position (e.g., class, race, ethnicity, gender, age) and control efficacy is not denied, although such a connection is not directly relevant in the context of the theory.

Even if a clear and complete definition of *control efficacy* could be realized, there would be no prospect of an intelligible measurement formula and a related procedure for gathering the requisite data in even a few social units, let alone a procedure that could be applied given the practical limits of research. Hence, the term must be identified as a construct rather than a concept, and for that reason Postulate 1 by itself is not testable. Evidence can be brought to bear on it only indirectly.

The Rationale for Postulate 1

Postulate 1 should be interpreted this way: From one social unit to the next or for a particular social unit over time, an increase in control efficacy is followed by a decrease in the prevalence of disputes, but the reverse temporal sequence is not claimed. The appropriate time lag is unknown; nonetheless, the asserted relation qualifies as a causal claim by conventional conceptions of causation.

Although the postulate's validity can be judged only through indirect tests, numerous supporting observations can be made. Unless humans are innately belligerent creatures, why would two individuals ever become involved in a dispute with each other if one has absolute and total effective control over the other? In such a condition, even a grievance is unlikely. Should it be objected that grievances are inevitable if only because of accidents, the reply is simple. For all practical purposes, any accident results from a failure in attempted control, be it inanimate, biotic, or human (e.g., automobile collisions involve failures in attempted inanimate control).

Of course, a grievance does not necessarily result in a complaint, much less become a dispute that generates violence. Rather, the grievant may sublimate or displace aggressive inclinations or may simply suffer in silence, but those possibilities require effective self-control.

Prevalence of Disputes and a Proposition

The term *prevalence of disputes* refers to the proportion of social unit members who at some stipulated time are involved in a dispute. The term is identified as a concept not just because the previous definition of a dispute is empirically applicable; in fact, the literature clearly suggests that data on disputes can be gathered through surveys (see, especially, issue No. 3–4 of Vol. 15, *Law and Society Review*, Kennedy, 1990, pp. 38–42).

Some components of the theory pertain to the consequences of disputes, one such component of which is Proposition 1:

> Among social units or for a social unit over time, the greater the prevalence of disputes, the greater the nonlethal interpersonal violence rate.

As in all propositions, both constituent variables are concepts; hence, the generalization is testable. Tests are not reported here, but anyone who doubts Proposition 1 should read police reports of assaults and battery. Those reports clearly support this metaphorical claim: Disputes are the very soil for the growth of interpersonal violence.

There would be grave doubts about the validity of Proposition 1 if the independent variable pertained not to dispute prevalence but, rather, to the incidence of disputes—the number that commenced in a given social unit during some stipulated period. The doubts would stem from recognition that most disputes do not end in violence, the principal reason being that there are several ways to avoid violence.[1] One major possibility is the solicitation by a disputant of a third party's intervention for a peaceful settlement, a possibility that, in addition to others, illustrates how the association between disputes and interpersonal violence is contingent on various features of human interaction. The solicitation of the third party may fail; if so, the dispute simmers until the disputant solicits the intervention of another third party, or the complainant repeats the grievance expression, or the complainant chooses to become a sufferant at least temporarily. Similarly, even if the third party does intervene, the intervention itself may fail; if so, there are the same alternative outcomes as when an intervention solicitation fails.

The crucial consideration is that solicitation and intervention failures tend to perpetuate disputes; hence, even if two social units have the same incidence of disputes, they may have quite different prevalence rates. Viewed that way, dispute prevalence is much more indicative of third-party solicitation failures and third-party intervention failures. Because such failures reduce alternatives to violence, dispute prevalence is asserted to be more strongly associated with the nonlethal interpersonal violence rate than is dispute incidence.

More Premises

Efficacious control reduces dispute prevalence not just through the prevention of grievances but also through successful complaints (i.e., the complaint target complies with the complainant's demands). After all, a complaint is in itself an attempt at control. A complaint may aggrieve the complaint target, and a dispute could result from the "new" grievance; but if so, the complaint would be a failure in attempted control.[2] Should the complaint target attempt to negotiate, his or her behavior also constitutes attempted control; if the attempt is successful, it prevents a dispute. Hence, assuming a fairly strong positive association between the efficacy of complaints as control attempts in particular

---

[1] Although police reports are strategic in showing that the bulk of interpersonal violence involves disputes, those reports exaggerate the extent to which disputes result in violence. The reason is that "nonescalating" cases (disputes that do not end in violence) rarely come to the attention of the police. It is even more true that most grievances do not result in violence, and that is the primary rationale for focusing the theory on disputes rather than grievances.

[2] Sometimes the success of a complaint as a control attempt is facilitated by the "weight of custom." Howard (1990, pp. 272–274) reported that on the island of Rotuma in the Republic of Fiji, the most effective mechanism for dispute management is *faksoro*, a ritual of formal apology. Among Rotumans, a complaint target is expected to offer *faksoro*, and the complainant is obliged to accept it under most circumstances. As for the consequences of the ritual, Howard indicated that Rotumans are "remarkable for their gentleness—physical violence is a great rarity" (p. 263).

situations and the efficacy of control in general within each social unit, there should be a negative association among social units between general control efficacy and dispute prevalence.

Postulate 2

A dispute is more likely to result in violence if the unplacated grievant solicits the intervention of a third party for a peaceful settlement but the solicitation or the intervention fails.[3] However, such failures are unsuccessful control attempts. Consequently, control efficacy is negatively associated with the nonlethal interpersonal violence rate through a positive association between control efficacy and two other rates, the solicitation success rate and the intervention success rate. Each of the two associations could be asserted as a separate postulate, but for the sake of simplicity, the two are combined in Postulate 2:

> Among social units or for a social unit over time, the greater the average efficacy of control attempts, the less the nonlethal interpersonal violence rate.[4]

Some complexities. Several complexities should be recognized even though none of them jeopardizes Postulate 2's validity. The very processes that generally reduce the probability of violence occasionally result in a dispute and thereby increase that probability. To illustrate, the solicitation of a third-party intervention may anger the complaint target and thereby create another grievance and possibly another dispute. Nevertheless, the argument is that, in general, such solicitations reduce the probability of violence. Even so, an angry response to a solicitation by the complaint target represents a failure in attempted control. The unplacated grievant does not solicit the intervention of a third party as an end in itself; rather, the solicitation constitutes attempted control, with the perceived source of the grievance as the ultimate target. Hence, it is unlikely that the solicitor—the unplacated grievant—hopes to anger the complaint target.

Whether angered by the third party's intervention, the complaint target may attempt to negotiate the terms of a settlement. Although negotiation is an alternative to

---

[3] *There is currently no truly systematic evidence that solicitations of a third party's intervention for a peaceful settlement of a dispute reduce the probability of interpersonal violence, but numerous general observations can be made in support of the assertion. As a case in point, Hallpike (1977, p. 120) reported numbers indicating an average annual homicide rate of 211.1 per 100,000 population (533.3 including intertribal cases) for New Guinea's Goilala tribe. That rate is at least 20 times the U.S. rate. Hallpike made this comment on the "basic mode of social control" in the tribe: "There is no idea of a meeting between disputants and of their case being mediated by some respected arbitrator or council of elders" (pp. 188–189).*

[4] *Postulate 2 asserts that control efficacy has a direct effect on the nonlethal interpersonal violence rate, while Postulate 1 and Proposition 1 (taken together) identify an indirect effect through dispute prevalence. Hence, Postulate 2 expresses the idea that control efficacy has an effect on interpersonal violence above and beyond any indirect effect it has.*

violence, it is also an attempt at control, and a failure may result in an angry third party (i.e., still another grievance).

Postulate 2 should not be construed as an implicit denial that interpersonal violence can be an attempt to control human behavior (Black, 1983). However, particularly at the interpersonal level, violence is likely not only to fail as a means of control but also to eventually result in retaliatory violence (see, e.g., Feld & Straus, 1989).

Postulate 3 and Axiom 1

The theory would be incomplete without recognizing an indirect relation between control efficacy and dispute prevalence. A grievant is unlikely to complain unless he or she perceives some prospect that the complaint target will comply with the demand (Felstiner, 1974, p. 81). Such perception pertains to the grievant's power in that particular situation because *power* is defined here as the "perceived capacity for control" (for elaboration, see Gibbs, 1989, pp. 64–68). But even the complaint target's perceptions are relevant because in complying with the grievant's demands, or even in negotiating, the complaint target is attempting control. Hence, presuming a substantial positive association between average perceived capacity for control and perceptions of particular social unit members in particular situations, we have Postulate 3:

> Among social units or for a social unit over time, the greater the average perceived capacity for effective control, the less the prevalence of disputes.

Figure 1 shows how the average efficacy of control attempts is related to the prevalence of disputes through two paths, direct and indirect. Postulate 1 is the direct path, and Postulate 3 is one of two links in the indirect path. The other link in the indirect path is Axiom 1:

> Among social units or for a social unit over time, the greater the average efficacy of control attempts, the greater the average perceived capacity for effective control.

Despite the terminology, Figure 1 should not be interpreted as being akin to a conventional path model or causal model, which would depict all constituent variables as though they were measurable (far from the case in Figure 1). For that matter, mastery of Figure 1 is not imperative for understanding the theory.

Perceptions of control capacity may be shaped largely by actual experience, being enhanced by successful control attempts and diminished by failures. However, the variables are at the aggregate level because the theory pertains to differences among social

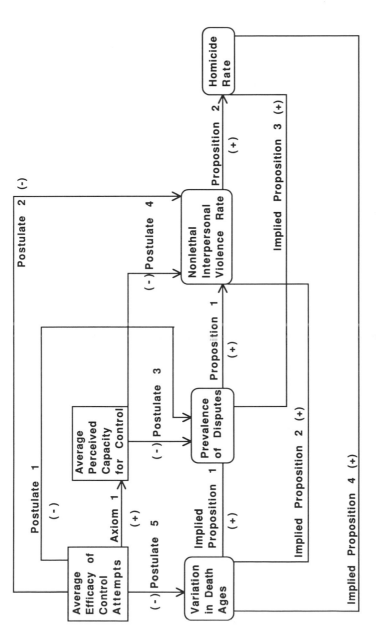

FIGURE 1 Diagram of a theory pertaining to properties of social units. (An axiom connects concepts [in square boxes], a postulate connects a construct and a concept [in rounded boxes], and a proposition connects concepts. A plus sign [+] signifies a positive relation, and a negative sign [−] signifies a negative realtion. Arrows indicate causal direction.)

units rather than among individuals. More specifically, *average efficacy of control attempts* refers to all attempts in a given social unit over some stipulated period, and *average perceived capacity* refers to what all social unit members ostensibly believe about effective control by humans in general. Those beliefs may be shaped in part by vicarious experiences that transcend the social unit. For example, Captain Cook's sojourn may have changed substantially the beliefs of many Hawaiians about what humans can control, but the change had nothing to do with the efficacy of control attempts in Hawaii before Cook's landing. Hence, both Postulate 3 and Axiom 1 are likely to hold much better for totally isolated social units, the nearest contemporary approximations of which are countries.

Another Determinant of Interpersonal Violence

Contemplate two distinct possibilities: first, that the unplacated grievant does not solicit the intervention of a third party for a peaceful settlement and, second, that even if there is a solicitation, the third party declines to intervene. Both possibilities are conducive to violence, but they are much less likely if the unplacated grievant and the third party perceive a real prospect of success, meaning that both solicitation and intervention are largely functions of perceived control capacity. Accordingly, assuming a substantial positive association between average perceived control capacity and perceptions by particular social unit members in particular situations, we have Postulate 4:

> Among social units or for a social unit over time, the greater the average perceived control capacity, the less the nonlethal interpersonal violence rate.[5]

Perceived control capacity reduces the probability of violence through promoting one or more of the following inclinations: (a) that of a grievant to express a complaint, (b) that of the complaint target to comply and thereby terminate the complaint, (c) that of the unplacated grievant to solicit a third party's intervention, and (d) that of the third party to intervene. Therefore, were there no need to simplify, Postulate 4 could be restated in the way of four more detailed postulates and four propositions, with each postulate–proposition pair linking perceived control capacity and nonlethal interpersonal violence.

---

[5]*Postulate 4 is based on the assumption that perceived capacity for control has an effect on interpersonal violence above and beyond its indirect effect through dispute prevalence (the indirect effect being by way of Postulate 3 and Proposition 1, as shown in Figure 1).*

Homicide Rates

An examination of police or other official reports of homicide cases is needed to appreciate the frequency with which a killing terminates a sequence of escalating violent interactions (see, e.g., Felson & Steadman, 1983; Luckenbill, 1977; Savitz, Kumar, & Zahn, 1991).[6] Such a sequence is essential because it is the proximate determinant of variation in the homicide rate. That generalization is expressed as Proposition 2:

> Among social units or for a social unit over time, the greater the nonlethal interpersonal violence rate, the greater the homicide rate.

The proposition should not be construed as implying that even most nonlethal interpersonal violence results in homicide. Rather, the proposition expresses the claim that the nonlethal interpersonal violence rate is the major link between dispute phenomena and the homicide rate.[7] Even if it should be argued that the two rates are manifestations of the same condition and are not causally connected, the proposition would still hold.

Serial killings, mass murders, and infanticide are largely alien to Proposition 2 because they are not preceded by a sequence of escalating violent interactions, but those behaviors are so rare (as a proportion of all homicides) that their contribution to variation in the homicide rate is negligible. Felony homicides (killings that are incidental to other felonies) also may not be preceded by a sequence of escalating violent interactions, although they present a more difficult problem because they are more frequent, at least in the United States (19 percent of all U.S. homicides according to Maxfield, 1989). Consequently, variation among social units in the incidence of felony homicides may reduce the association between the nonlethal interpersonal violence rate and the homicide rate. Variation in the quality of medical care of violence victims may also reduce the association (see, e.g., Doerner & Speir, 1986), but none of these contingencies should invalidate the proposition.

---

[6]*Gottfredson and Hirschi (1990) described a typical case: "People who are known to one another argue over some trivial matter, as they have argued frequently in the past. In fact, in the past their argument has on occasion led to physical violence, sometimes on the part of the offender, sometimes on the part of the victim. In the present instance, one of them decides that he has had enough, and he hits a little harder or with what turns out to be a lethal instrument. Often, of course, the offender simply ends the dispute with a gun" (p. 33).*

[7]*The theory pertains to two particular consequences of variation in the prevalence of disputes—the direct consequence being variation in the nonlethal interpersonal violence rate and the indirect consequence being variation in the homicide rate. The theory should not be construed as identifying all determinants of variation in the homicide rate, and it is not actually an alternative to theories about those determinants. There is, however, a "control" theory about those determinants. That theory is much more extensive than the present theory, and it is an alternative to the "culture of violence" theory and the "economic deprivation" theory. For a statement of the control theory and a critique of the other two theories, see Stafford and Gibbs (1991).*

A Very Special Correlate of Control Efficacy

In virtually all social units, some members regularly or occasionally undertake, organize, or facilitate certain kinds of activities in the belief that they reduce the probability of human morbidity and mortality. When highly organized, such activities result in sewer lines, hospitals, public water works, public information campaigns, and mass inoculations, to mention only five of numerous public health measures. Those measures are all attempts at control; in regard to the reduction of human mortality, the attempts are more extensive and efficacious in some social units than in others. Consequently, various arguments could be made to support the following generalization: The greater the average efficacy of control attempts, the lower the human mortality rate.

If the generalization were testable, the findings would indicate that the degree of association depends on the extent to which the kind of mortality rate takes age composition into account. To illustrate, two social units may have identical levels of control efficacy but substantially different crude death rates, with the mortality differential reflecting variation in age composition. Age is relevant primarily because, regardless of control efficacy, deaths of the very elderly are inevitable. However, ineffective control attempts are clearly indicated when the death rate is more or less uniform among age groups, one manifestation being substantial variation in the ages of population members at death. Hence, the theory's final premise, Postulate 5:

> Among social units or for a social unit over time, the greater the average efficacy of control attempts in a unit, the less the variation in death ages within the unit.[8]

The second (dependent) variable refers not to differences in the mortality rates of social units but to differences among deceased members of the same social unit as to age at death.

If only because social unit members may make extensive use of medical or health facilities located outside the social unit, Postulate 5 applies best to social units that are totally isolated.[9] Hence, international comparisons should provide the most support when

[8] *It is assumed for Postulate 5 (and all of the other premises involving control efficacy) that there is a substantial positive association between the three basic types of control—inanimate, biotic, and human. However, the assumption is not crucial because the independent variable has to do with the efficacy of control attempts in general. Hence, a social unit with high levels of all three types of control efficacy would have a greater general control efficacy than would a social unit with high levels of only two types of control efficacy. A more crucial assumption for Postulate 5 is that the various types of control are more or less equally important in preventing deaths.*

[9] *There is still another qualification and one that applies to all generalizations in which "variation in death ages" is a constituent variable. Specifically, the generalization is limited to social units and periods in which there were no deaths of members as consequences of warfare, revolutions, rebellions, or genocide. The point is not that such historical events or*

testing generalizations derived in part from Postulate 5 (i.e., indirect tests of the postulate).

Some critics may regard variation in death ages as more a measure or an indicator than a consequence of control efficacy. That preference reflects a common belief among social and behavioral scientists that all constructs can be "operationalized" and, hence, that all premises in a theory are directly testable. Space limitations permit only a very brief rejoinder. After nearly a century of attempts, there is no real prospect of a defensible measure of anomie, class conflict, social cohesion, normative consensus, or social integration, to mention only five major sociological terms. As for use of the term *indicator* rather than *measure*, the practice is conducive to ambiguity and prematurely terminates theory construction. Hence, if someone identifies "frequency of deaths from political violence" as an indicator of the "amount of class conflict" in a country, one must wonder why the identification is not translated into the following generalization as a component of the theory in question: Among countries, the greater the amount of class conflict, the greater the frequency of deaths from political violence. Without something like this translation, the connection between the two variables is ambiguous. Yet, there is really no mystery as to why the "indicator language" is so favored. If the identification of an indicator is translated into an explicit generalization as part of the theory itself, the matter is more likely to become an issue.

Four Implied Propositions

Because propositions are more nearly directly testable than are axioms and postulates, the theory has been stated so as to facilitate their deduction. They are identified in Figure 1 as *implied propositions* to distinguish them from Propositions 1 and 2, which are stated as premises. Figure 1 provides an overview of the theory, but it does not reveal the deduction rule. It is the "sign rule" that requires that each premise be characterized by a plus sign (+) if its relational term is "greater . . . greater" and a negative sign (−) if its relational term is "greater . . . less." Given such characterizations, the rule is this: A deduced statement's sign is positive unless it has been deduced from a series of premises in which there is an odd number of negative signs.

---

episodes have nothing to do with control (on the contrary, they are studies in attempted coercive control); rather, they contribute to diversity in death ages but are not necessarily indicative of inefficacious control attempts (especially noncoercive attempts) within the social unit.

Implied Proposition 1

As deduced from Postulates 1 and 5, Implied Proposition 1 reads:

> Among social units or for a social unit over time, the greater the variation in death ages, the greater the prevalence of disputes.

The relation is not causal, and should the generalization appear puzzling, it is because the theory does what a theory is supposed to do—among other things, anticipate empirical relations that otherwise would be unexpected or puzzling.

If comparisons of social units do not reveal a substantial positive association between values that represent death age variation and values that represent dispute prevalence, the validity of Postulates 1 and 5 will be jeopardized. However, whether both would be invalidated should depend on tests of certain other implied propositions; for reasons indicated earlier, tests of Implied Proposition 1 should provide more support for the theory when based on international comparisons.

Implied Proposition 2

As deduced from any one of four combinations of premises (see Figure 1), Implied Proposition 2 reads:

> Among social units or for a social unit over time, the greater the variation in death ages, the greater the nonlethal interpersonal violence rate.

The generalization is another instance of an anticipated relation that would be puzzling apart from the theory, and it is also another instance wherein more support is expected when tests are based on international comparisons.

A formal mode of theory construction permits a more informative interpretation of test outcomes than does the conventional discursive mode. The present theory provides several illustrations, but only one can be considered, and all too briefly. Should tests indicate that of all of the propositions only Implied Propositions 2 and 4 are false, that outcome would indicate that Postulate 2 is the only false premise. The interpretation would be justified because of all of the premises (including Propositions 1 and 2) only Postulate 2 enters exclusively into the derivation of false implied propositions.

Implied Proposition 3

As deduced from Propositions 1 and 2 or from Postulate 3, Postulate 4, and Proposition 2, Implied Proposition 3 reads:

> Among social units or for a social unit over time, the greater the prevalence of disputes, the greater the homicide rate.

The alternative deduction paths introduce a complexity but not an insurmountable problem when interpreting test outcomes.

Another complexity is that the interpretation of tests of Implied Proposition 3 will depend largely on tests of Propositions 1 and 2. There are eight possible outcomes if tests of each of the three propositions are either predominantly positive or predominantly negative.[10] Space limitations permit a commentary on only two outcomes, the first of which is predominantly positive tests of both Proposition 1 and Implied Proposition 3 but predominantly negative tests of Proposition 2. That outcome would indicate that nonlethal violence is not a factor in homicide; additionally, the findings would suggest that control phenomena do have an impact (somehow) on the homicide rate but not through nonlethal violence.

The other outcome consists of predominantly positive tests of Proposition 2 but predominantly negative tests of Proposition 1 and Implied Proposition 3. That outcome would indicate that disputes play no discernible role in nonlethal interpersonal violence and that control phenomena do play a role but not through reducing the prevalence of disputes.

Implied Proposition 4

As deduced from any one of four combinations of premises, Implied Proposition 4 reads:

> Among social units or for a social unit over time, the greater the variation in death ages, the greater the homicide rate.

In this case, it is not just a matter of a covariational relation that would be puzzling outside the theory. Given the length of the chain connecting the two variables, a substantial statistical association between them is not expected.[11] In any case, the interpretation of

---

[10] A test outcome would be considered positive if and only if the statistical association between the two sets of values is in the direction predicted and of such magnitude as to be considered statistically significant by some conventional standard. By contrast, an outcome is considered negative if an association is not in the predicted direction (regardless of magnitude) or an association is in the predicted direction but is not statistically significant. A set of tests is predominantly positive if and only if the proportion of positive tests is significant by some conventional standard; otherwise, the set is judged as predominantly negative.

[11] Nor should there be a strong association between the homicide rate and any other concept that might be considered a correlate or manifestation of the average efficacy of control attempts. For example, there should be a positive association among countries between the average efficacy of control attempts and the level of development, but Messner (1989, pp. 603–604) reported that development is only moderately negatively associated with the homicide rate.

tests of Implied Proposition 4 is likely to be the most complex and conjectural. One illustrative interpretation of predominantly positive tests and one of predominantly negative tests must suffice.

Predominantly positive tests would provide the most general support for the theory, the reason being that all of the premises can be construed as somehow influencing the relation asserted by Implied Proposition 4. However, if the tests are predominantly positive but tests of all other propositions (implied or not) are predominantly negative, that outcome would indicate that the theory is completely false.

A complex interpretation would be inevitable if tests of Implied Proposition 4 are predominantly negative, especially if the tests are based on international comparisons, the condition that is expected to maximize support for the proposition. Should tests of Proposition 2 also be predominantly negative, the predominantly negative tests of Implied Proposition 4 would not necessarily be evidence that the other premises are invalid. However, there would be serious doubts about the other premises if tests of Proposition 2 but not Implied Proposition 4 are predominantly positive.

Interpretation of Tests of Propositions 1 and 2

Only occasional comments have been made about Propositions 1 and 2 because both are premises rather than derivations. However, the interpretation of tests of the two propositions cannot be equally simple if only because Proposition 1 but not Proposition 2 is both a causal assertion and a relation implied by other premises. Specifically, the prevalence of disputes is asserted to be related to the nonlethal interpersonal violence rate in two ways—directly (as indicated by Proposition 1) and by virtue of both variables being effects of the two control variables.

Tests of Proposition 1

If tests of Proposition 1 are predominantly positive, the findings would suggest that disputes play a major role in the etiology of nonlethal violence, although the following question would not be answered: Do disputes enter directly into the etiology of homicide, or is the relation totally indirect, as indicated by Figure 1? At least a partially indirect relation would be suggested if taking the nonlethal interpersonal violence rate into account reduces the association between dispute prevalence and the homicide rate (i.e., Implied

Proposition 3).[12] However, should the association be reduced to insignificance, there would be doubts about Postulates 1–4.

As indicated by Figure 1, the control variables (control efficacy and perceived control capacity) are asserted to be related to the homicide rate only indirectly and by two paths. One path is through the prevalence of disputes (Postulates 1 and 3) and the nonlethal interpersonal violence rate (Propositions 1 and 2), and the other path is through the nonlethal interpersonal violence rate independently of dispute prevalence (i.e., Postulate 2, Postulate 4, and Proposition 2). Hence, if tests of Proposition 1 and also those of Implied Proposition 3 are predominantly negative but those of Proposition 2 and Implied Proposition 4 are predominantly positive, the inference would be that the two control variables and the homicide rate are connected only through the nonlethal interpersonal violence rate.

Tests of Proposition 2

Should tests of Proposition 2 prove to be predominantly negative but those of Implied Proposition 3 predominantly positive, the suggestion would be that the control variables cause variation in the homicide rate through dispute prevalence but not through nonlethal interpersonal violence. However, even that suggestion would not require rejection of Postulates 2 and 4, especially if the tests of Proposition 1 are predominantly positive.

A much more disturbing possibility would be predominantly negative tests for both Proposition 2 and Implied Proposition 3 but predominantly positive tests for Implied Proposition 4. In that case, the conclusion would be that the theory fails to identify the causal path between the control variables and the homicide rate.

Further Observations on Testability

Six of the theory's twelve constituent generalizations can be tested because they are propositions, meaning that they link concepts. A concept is a term defined such that the theorist regards the definition as clear and complete, and when a concept pertains to

---

[12] *The following is another question that would not be answered by predominantly positive tests of Proposition 1: Is there a causal relation between dispute prevalence and interpersonal violence? Both variables are direct effects of the control variables (control efficacy and perceived control capacity); hence, predominantly positive tests of Proposition 1 cannot be taken as incontrovertible evidence of causation. If the proposition is not causal, then it will need to be identified as an implied proposition in the theory. However, because the control variables are constructs, confident inferences about causation cannot be made on any simple basis.*

quantitative phenomena, it is linked in the theory with a formula and the stipulation of a procedure for acquiring the requisite data. The formula is empirically applicable to the extent that (a) it is intelligible, (b) research resources and observational methods permit acquisition of the data along the lines specified by the procedure, and (c) the values reported by independent investigators for the same units (particular individuals or populations) do not differ substantially.

Each concept in the theory (variation in death ages, prevalence of disputes, the nonlethal interpersonal violence rate, and the homicide rate) pertains to quantitative phenomena. Hence, only three things are needed to make the propositions subject to systematic tests: (a) define each concept, (b) designate the appropriate formula (or alternatives), and (c) stipulate the requisite data and the acquisitional procedure.

Variation in Death Ages

A brief definition of the concept will suffice: overall differences in the age at death of the population's members who died during some stipulated time period. The term *population* is used in a generic sense; as such, it applies to all types of social units, such as households, organizations, tribes, cities, or countries.

Research procedure. An ideal variation measure would require access to all death records (possibly "mortality tapes") and their use to compute the standard deviation and coefficient of variation in death ages or some special measure of variation. Because access may be difficult, there is a need for an alternative procedure that can be applied to published data. The data are virtually always tabulated by age groups (e.g., 0–4, 5–9, . . . 85+ years), and the lack of uniformity (especially internationally) in the age groups is only one problem in attempting to apply a conventional variation measure (e.g., the standard deviation). The residual character of the upper age group (e.g., over 74, over 84) is a problem in itself. For that matter, the meaning of *amount of variation* is more debatable than conventional measures suggest (contemplate 1, 1, 1, 7 vs. 1, 2, 3, 4).

The simplest and most feasible measure for published data is $1\text{-}[(\Sigma\ Dp - 1)/(Na - 1)]$, where Dp is the proportion of all age-known deaths during some designated period in a particular age group and all older age groups and Na is the number of age groups. The measure has an absolute minimum of 0 and an absolute maximum of 1, but it is not applicable unless the oldest age group exceeds 50 and the age groups are the same for all of the social units being compared. Each value of the measure reflects the extent of concentration of deaths among the elderly, and although concentration in any age group reduces variation in death ages, deaths of elderly population members are the least indicative of inefficacious control. So the formula might be more appropriately described as a measure of geriatric mortality, but it does reflect the amount of variation in death ages. Bear in mind, however, that the limitation of mortality to infants borders on the impossible for some types of social units, and a high infant mortality rate contributes to variation in death ages because it is the deaths of the elderly and not the young that are inevitable, at least until there are revolutionary changes in the efficacy of human control, especially in connection with genetic engineering.

Data acquisition. Despite the increasing availability of mortality tapes, few researchers have access to many of them. Hence, the primary data sources will be official vital statistics reports in published form.

The most accessible sources will be publications of the World Health Organization and the United Nations' Statistical Office. The publications of national statistical agencies are also relevant because they permit experimentation with the number and limits of the age groups.

Units of comparison for tests. Although the various formulas (i.e., standard deviation, coefficient of variation, and the designated alternative for published data) can be applied both to countries and to various types of intranational territorial units (e.g., cities, provinces), for reasons previously stated any test of Implied Propositions 1, 2, and 4 should be based on international comparisons. The suggestion is not that the relations asserted by the generalizations cannot hold for intranational units; rather, the expectation is a less strong association at that level than for international comparisons. Should special tests not reveal the expected contrast, a reexamination of the theory (Postulate 5 especially) would be in order.

Unfortunately, for reasons indicated subsequently, research resources are not likely to permit international tests of Implied Propositions 1 and 2. Consequently, tests of Implied Proposition 4 will be especially strategic in assessing the theory's predictive power, and it is fortunate that virtually all of the premises can be construed as possibly entering into the derivation of that generalization (see Figure 1).

Prevalence of Disputes

The concept *prevalence of disputes* refers to the proportion of social unit members who at some designated time are involved in a dispute. As for the meaning of *involved,* an individual is involved in a dispute if he or she has made a complaint or is a target of a complaint and at present the complainant does not perceive the dispute as resolved.

The computational formula is simple: Rd/Nr, where Rd is the number of respondents in a survey of a sample of social unit members who report being the complainant in at least one on-going dispute and Nr is the number of respondents who are actually questioned and respond in a "codeable" way. Lest the suggested procedure for gathering the requisite data appears impractical, there is now an extensive literature on surveys pertaining to disputes (e.g., Kennedy, 1990; Kritzer, 1980–1981; Silberman. 1985).

The essential survey questions. After posing questions pertaining to the demographic characteristics of the respondent, the interviewer would make this statement: "I want you to think about the last time that someone did something wrong to you or that you were treated unfairly and as a result felt insulted, or thought that you had been cheated, or suffered some loss. Now keep thinking about it and answer two questions for me. First question: Did you ask or demand that the person responsible for what happened to you do something about it? Second question: Has the person done enough for you to consider the matter as settled?"

Rd for a social unit would be the number of respondents who answered the first question affirmatively but the second question negatively.[13] Each negative response to the second question would indicate an on-going dispute in one sense or another, including cases wherein the complainant anticipates no prospect of ever obtaining "satisfaction" (Yngvesson, 1976).

The "last time" qualification in the statement preceding the two questions makes it much easier for respondents to answer the questions, but the qualification precludes the possibility of the respondent reporting more than one on-going dispute. Hence, the data would not be suited for comparing dispute frequency among individuals, but it can be assumed that among populations there is a substantial positive association between the Rd/Nr ratio and the true prevalence of disputes.

Units of comparison for tests. Because the cost of gathering data for even a few countries would be prohibitive, the surveys must be limited to localities (e.g., metropolitan

---

[13] *The proportion of respondents who answered the first question negatively would be indicative of the frequency of "unexpressed grievances" (i.e., no ensuing complaint). Exploratory analysis could be undertaken to ascertain if that grievance variable should be a component of the theory in addition to or instead of the dispute variable (i.e., with a view to explaining variation in the interpersonal violence rate). Note also that Nr would include the unlikely cases in which respondents ostensibly were unable to recall having suffered a grievance. The proportion of all respondents who could be so described also should be considered in an exploratory analysis because that proportion could be construed as indicative of the rarity of grievances in a social unit. Yet, the survey would not be designed to estimate the frequency of grievances, not just because of the cost and difficulty entailed but also because the focus of the theory is on disputes rather than grievances (for the reason suggested in footnote 1).*

areas). Accordingly, there is no prospect for basing tests of Implied Proposition 1, Proposition 1, or Implied Proposition 3 on international comparisons. However, there can be tests of Proposition 1 and Implied Proposition 3 even if research resources permit only a survey for one locality. In that case, the units of comparison in each test would be age–sex divisions of the population (possibly race or ethnicity in some cases), but Implied Proposition 3 would be testable only if homicide rates could be computed for those divisions.

Limiting tests along the lines indicated will be unfortunate but necessary for practical reasons. Specifically, it would be desirable to maximize variation in the prevalence of disputes, a condition that may be realized best through international comparisons.

The Nonlethal Interpersonal Violence Rate

The nonlethal interpersonal violence rate (NIVR) can be defined by three statements. First, violence is nonlethal if it does not result in the death of any of the participants. Second, violence is interpersonal if none of the participants acted in an official capacity as an agent of the government or as a representative of such a social unit as a tribe or clan. Third, violence is the physical injury (not just a threat to injure) of one human by the action of another human, with the action undertaken in the belief that it increased the probability of such injury and that the increase was desirable.

The formula for computing NIVR is conventional. Specifically, NIVR $= (Nv/P)100,000$, where Nv is the number of instances of nonlethal interpersonal violence in some designated social unit during some designated period and P is the estimated number of social unit members who could have been involved in at least one instance. *Data acquisition.* Official data on assaults or battery should not be used to test any of the propositions. Such data are excluded because of doubts about their reliability.

One alternative way to acquire the requisite data is through a "victimization" survey. Again, the feasibility problem is lessened by the existence of an extensive literature on victimization surveys (see, especially, Karmen, 1990). The prescribed data acquisition procedure is all the more feasible because the survey questions can be added to the schedule pertaining to disputes.

Only two victimization questions need be asked in the survey. First, "During the past 12 months, have you ever been physically injured by someone who intended to harm or hurt you?" If the respondent answers affirmatively, the second and final question would be, "How many times did that happen during the past 12 months?" The computational formula would be $\Sigma\ X/Nr$, where X is the value given by a respondent in answering the second question and Nr is the total number of people who gave a codeable response to the question or questions, including those who did not answer the first question affirmatively. Although the formula does not correspond to the definition of NIVR, the discrepancy is not crippling because it is reasonable to assume a substantial positive association between $\Sigma\ X/Nr$ (an average) and NIVR.

Units of comparison for tests. Like Proposition 1, there is no theoretical reason for limiting tests of Proposition 2 to any particular type of social unit. The only exceptions are social units that have a small population because both rates (nonlethal interpersonal violence and homicide) are likely to be very unstable.

The truly difficult problem is again one of limited research resources. It is feasible to gather data on the incidence of nonlethal interpersonal violence and the prevalence of disputes in the same survey; but, as pointed out earlier, research resources do not permit such a survey in even a few countries. Nonetheless, as victimization surveys become more common throughout the world, international tests of Proposition 2 will become more feasible.

Homicide Rates

A homicide occurs when violence results in the death of an individual who has been physically injured. Although a distinction between legal homicides (e.g., executions) and illegal or extralegal (justifiable) homicides should be drawn because legal homicides are scarcely the product of disputes or nonlethal interpersonal violence, the distinction is not essential because legal homicides do not contribute appreciably to the homicide rate (HR). Given the foregoing definition, HR can be defined by this conventional formula: HR $= (Nh/P)100,000$, where Nh is the number of population members who became homicide victims during some designated period and P is the total number of population members at some time point during that period or the average number at two or more time points during the period.

Data acquisition. In testing Implied Proposition 4 through international comparisons, data on the annual incidence of homicide are to be obtained from publications by international statistical agencies, such as the World Health Organization, the Statistical Office of the United Nations, or INTERPOL. If the data are reported as absolute incidence figures, those data can be converted into rates by using population figures for the corresponding year as reported in publications of international statistical agencies. In any case, the data can be supplemented with or replaced by data from the publications of national statisti-cal agencies.

Official homicide data are prescribed because there is no alternative, such as vic-timization surveys. However, questions concerning reliability are less serious in the case of homicide than in the case of crime in general (see, e.g., Krahn, Hartnagel, & Gartrell, 1986, p. 271).

Demands for Direct Evidence

Regardless of the number of tests of the six propositions or test outcomes, there may be a demand for direct evidence of a negative relation among social units or for a particular social unit over time between the average efficacy of control and the prevalence of dis-putes. The relation is the core of the theory, especially given that both a direct and an indirect connection between the variables are asserted, with the indirect connection being through the perceived capacity for control. Nonetheless, a demand for direct evidence of the relation will reflect a refusal to recognize that many of the major notions in the social and behavioral sciences are constructs, not concepts, meaning that they are theoretical notions.

Distant Prospects for Direct Evidence

A construct may become a concept, and that possibility takes on added importance in the case of any term that denotes a property or dimension of control. Unlike such terms as *anomie, social integration,* and *class conflict,* the term *control* can be conceptualized such that it is empirically applicable when it comes to specific acts by particular individuals. To illustrate, if a particular conceptualization already in the literature (Gibbs, 1989) is ac-cepted, independent investigators are likely to agree that the following statement by a customer to a store manager constitutes attempted control: "Give me back what I paid for this piece of junk or I'm going to see a lawyer!"

Unfortunately, application of a control terminology at the micro level is one thing, but its application at the macro level is quite another. No matter how small the social unit, not even enormous research resources would permit computation of the average ef-ficacy of control attempts during a given day, let alone a year. The reason is that a feasi-ble observational procedure is lacking.

Surveys as the most realistic possibility. Granted that there is no prospect of truly systematic observations on actual control behavior outside of experimental situations, a representative sample of social unit members can be questioned about their control attempts during some stipulated period. Consider two illustrative survey questions: "During the past year, how many times have you applied or asked for a job or position that would pay you a salary or wage? How many of those times did you get the job or position?"

No illustrations are needed in the case of survey questions pertaining to the perceived capacity for control. Indeed, there are conventional ways of asking a respondent to assess or estimate his or her power, influence, or ability, all of which can be linked conceptually with the perceived capacity for control. The general point is that the study of control behavior can make use of a large body of conventional survey methods.

Some Caveats

Despite what has been said, there remains a very difficult problem, although one not peculiar to gathering data on control behavior. Throughout each day, virtually any social unit member engages in thousands of diverse kinds of control attempts, and currently there is no feasible procedure for framing survey questions such that they are demonstrably representative of all questions that could be asked. The same problem is confronted in the case of questions pertaining to perceived control capacity because for each kind of control attempt there is a possible corresponding perceptual question.

It would be illusory to suppose that some conventional measurement procedure offers a solution. In particular, the locus-of-control instrument (see Lefcourt's, 1984, literature survey) does not even pertain to effectiveness of actual control attempts. For that matter, the instrument is not based on a defensible conceptualization of control, and it constitutes an amalgamation of distinct notions, such as the belief in fate, perceptions of capacity to control others, perceptions of vulnerability to control by others, and perceptions of capacity for self-control.

The Possible Benefits of a Challenge

It may well be that not even a majority of sociologists think of tests of a theory as a truly essential or valued activity. Perhaps tests are not viewed as creative work. In any case, sociologists appear much more inclined to interpret, debate, or restate theories rather than test them.

The present theory offers something to those who are not interested in testing theories. Methodologically inclined investigators can work on procedures for the measurement of control efficacy and perceived capacity for control, especially procedures that are applicable at the macro level. Fortunately, however, tests of the theory can be conducted even if such procedures are never developed. Indeed, the theory can be expanded by adding postulates that link the constructs to additional concepts, but tests of the six constituent propositions should have priority over such expansion.

References

Black, D. (1983). Crime as social control. *American Sociological Review, 48*, 34–45.

Cain, M., & Kulcsar, K. (1981–1982). Thinking disputes: An essay on the origins of the dispute industry. *Law and Society Review, 16*, 375–402.

Doerner, W. G., & Speir, J. C. (1986). Stitch and sew: The impact of medical resources upon criminally induced lethality. *Criminology, 24*, 319–330.

Feld, S. L., & Straus, M. A. (1989). Escalation and desistance of wife assault in marriage. *Criminology, 27*, 141–161.

Felson, R. B., & Steadman, H. J. (1983). Situational factors in disputes leading to criminal violence. *Criminology, 21*, 59–74.

Felstiner, W. L. F. (1974). Influences of social organization on dispute processing. *Law and Society Review, 9*, 63–94.

Gibbs, J. P. (1989). *Control: Sociology's central notion.* Urbana: University of Illinois Press.

Gottfredson, M. R., & Hirschi, T. (1990). *A general theory of crime.* Stanford, CA: Stanford University Press.

Gulliver, P. H. (1979). *Disputes and negotiations: A cross-cultural perspective.* San Diego, CA: Academic Press.

Hallpike, C. R. (1977). *Bloodshed and vengeance in the Papuan mountains: The generation of conflict in Tauade society.* Oxford, England: Clarendon Press.

Howard, A. (1990). Dispute management in Rotuma. *Journal of Anthropological Research, 46*, 263–292.

Karmen, A. (1990). *Crime victims: An introduction to victimology* (2nd ed.). Pacific Grove, CA: Brooks/Cole.

Kennedy, L. W. (1990). *On the borders of crime: Conflict management and criminology.* New York: Longman.

Kidder, R. L. (1980–1981). The end of the road?: Problems in the analysis of disputes. *Law and Society Review, 15*, 717–725.

Krahn, H., Hartnagel, T. F., & Gartrell, J. W. (1986). Income inequality and homicide rates: Cross-national data and criminological theories. *Criminology, 24*, 269–295.

Kritzer, H. M. (1980–1981). Studying disputes: Learning from the CLPP experience. *Law and Society Review, 15*, 503–524.

Lefcourt, H. M. (1984). New directions in research with the locus of control construct. *Psychological Studies, 29*, 107–111.

Luckenbill, D. F. (1977). Criminal homicide as a situated transaction. *Social Problems, 25*, 176–186.

Maxfield, M. G. (1989). Circumstances in supplementary homicide reports: Variety and validity. *Criminology, 27*, 671–695.

Messner, S. F. (1989). Economic discrimination and societal homicide rates: Further evidence on the cost of inequality. *American Sociological Review, 54*, 597–611.

Miller, R. E., & Sarat, A. (1980–1981). Grievances, claims, and disputes: Assessing the adversary culture. *Law and Society Review, 15*, 525–566.

Parsons, T. (1951). *The social system.* New York: Free Press.

Ross, E. A. (1901). *Social control: A survey of the foundations of order.* New York: Macmillan.

Savitz, L. D., Kumar, K. S., & Zahn, M. A. (1991). Quantifying Luckenbill. *Deviant Behavior, 12*, 19–29.

Silberman, M. (1985). *The civil justice process.* San Diego, CA: Academic Press.

Stafford, M. C., & Gibbs, J. P. (1991). *Control, disputes, interpersonal violence, and homicide.* Unpublished manuscript.

Yngvesson, B. (1976). Responses to grievance behavior: Extended cases in a fishing community. *American Ethnologist, 3*, 353–373.

PART TWO

Aggression and Social Conflict

CHAPTER 4

Aggression as a Struggle Tactic in Social Conflict

Dean G. Pruitt, Joseph M. Mikolic, Robert S. Peirce, and Mark Keating

S ome aggressive actions have instrumental goals; their aim is to achieve victory or avoid defeat in social conflict. We call such actions *struggle tactics*. Struggle tactics are used both inside and outside negotiation. Those used inside negotiation are designed to persuade the opponent to make concessions on the road to an agreement. They tend to be relatively mild forms of aggression. Examples are threatening to break off negotiation, committing oneself to stick to one's current position, imposing time pressure on the opponent, or belittling the opponent's arguments (Pruitt, 1981; Pruitt & Carnevale, in press). Struggle tactics used outside negotiation often involve much heavier forms of aggression that are designed to impose one's will on the other party. Examples are seizing common resources, denouncing the opponent, laying in weapons, building political strength, or threatening to do all of these things. Because struggle tactics are usually milder inside than outside negotiation, negotiation provides benefits to the disputants and the broader community quite apart from any agreement that can be reached as part of it.

Other procedures in addition to struggle tactics are available in conflict, including problem solving (trying to find a mutually acceptable solution), yielding (moving in the direction of the other party's desires), inaction (doing nothing), and withdrawal (severing contact with the other party; Pruitt & Rubin, 1986). Like struggle tactics, these procedures can be used both inside and outside negotiation. Still other procedures that are sometimes available include seeking arbitration (binding third-party intervention) and seeking mediation (nonbinding third-party intervention).

The choices that disputants make among the procedures just mentioned and among the various forms of struggle tactics are sometimes influenced by affect (e.g., anger), but they are more often a matter of rational calculation, aimed at achieving benefits and avoiding losses. The latter implies that aggression is more probable when a disputant concludes that struggle tactics are likely to be inexpensive and effective. It also implies that the likelihood of aggression depends on a rational evaluation of alternatives to struggle tactics.

The latter point deserves special attention. It means that the likelihood of struggle, and hence of aggression, decreases when alternative procedures seem feasible and increases when alternative procedures do not seem feasible. An example of the former can be seen in an experiment by Moser and Levi-Leboyer (1985), in which observers watched people trying to use a broken public telephone. Aggression, in the form of hitting the telephone, was common in this situation. But the incidence of aggression decreased markedly when a sign was placed in the phone booth giving information about nearby phones and procedures for recovering lost money. An example of the latter can be seen in a number of studies to be reviewed later showing that the likelihood of struggle tactics increases under conditions that make it hard to adopt the alternative procedure of yielding.

Our aim in this chapter is to examine conditions that affect procedural choice in social conflict, thus increasing or diminishing the attractiveness of struggle and alternative procedures as ways of dealing with social conflict. We present material from several lines of inquiry, including laboratory research on negotiation, case studies of mediation in nonindustrial society, and theory about the design of dispute resolution systems. In addition, we present the results of several laboratory and interview studies we have done on procedural choice in everyday interpersonal conflict.

Evidence From Studies of Negotiation

A good deal of the evidence about procedural choice comes from research on negotiation. In negotiation, two or more parties try to reach a verbal agreement that resolves a divergence of interest between them. Negotiation can be thought of as a mild form of social conflict. The approaches that are commonly available in negotiation include mild struggle tactics (also called *contending* and *competitive tactics*), problem solving, yielding (concession making), inaction, and withdrawal. These procedures have their parallels outside negotiation. Hence, evidence about conditions that encourage these procedures has implications for conflict as a whole.

The Nature of Struggle Tactics

Several different kinds of struggle tactics can be used in negotiation. A *threat* is a tactic wherein one makes a commitment to punish another if the other does not accept one's demands. Threats are often low-cost tactics because if they work, one does not have to deliver the punishment. However, costs can become large if the other does not concede and one has to deliver the punishment. Delivery may be costly in that the punishment may be elaborate or expensive. It may be costly because of the risk of retaliation from the other party and the danger of alienating third parties who sympathize with the other party.

A second kind of struggle tactic involves making positional commitments. A positional commitment is a statement that one will not concede a particular point. The hope is that the other will concede to avoid disagreement. Positional commitments are only effective if failure to reach agreement is costly to the other (e.g., if the alternative to agreement is a strike).

Struggle may also be pursued by imposing time pressure on the other. The most common method is to impose a deadline (e.g., if the other does not meet one's demands or if an agreement is not worked out by a certain time, then one will take a certain course of action). In industrial negotiation, this course of action could be going on strike; in commercial settings, it could be starting negotiation with another party. One can also impose time pressure by making time more costly to the other (e.g., by dragging out negotiations or engaging in a work slowdown).

A fourth kind of struggle tactic involves harassment. Harassment is like threat in that it uses punishment but is unlike threat in that the punishment comes first. For example, people may engage in verbal abuse, annoying or menacing actions, or physical assault in the hope that the other party will comply with their demands as a way to stop the harassment. Harassment has a downside in comparison with threat in that it always involves the costs associated with delivering punishment. On the other hand, harassment is more credible than threat because the opponent actually gets a taste of the punishment. Harassment is sometimes used in negotiation, but it is more often used in nonnegotiatory conflict wherein one or both parties try to impose their will on the other party.

Reciprocation of Struggle Tactics

There is considerable evidence that negotiators tend to reciprocate their opponent's use of struggle tactics. Druckman (1986) observed reciprocation of contentious rhetoric in a study of international negotiation. Another study, which was done in the laboratory, showed that threats tended to evoke counterthreats (Michener, Vaske, Schleiffer, Plazewski, & Chapman, 1975). Two other laboratory experiments showed a high level of reciprocation between negotiators in the use of threats and positional commitments (Kimmel, Pruitt, Magenau, Konar-Goldband, & Carnevale, 1980; Pruitt & Lewis, 1975).

Trust moderates the likelihood of reciprocating an opponent's struggle tactics. When a "trusted" other uses a struggle tactic, the tactic will likely be attributed to the situation and hence not seen as indicative of the other's true character or beliefs. As a result, there should be less retaliation. Similar allowances are not likely to be made when a "distrusted" other engages in struggle tactics; in this case, the struggle tactics are likely to be reciprocated. Evidence favoring this generalization can be seen in Gottman's (1979) finding that retaliation for negative remarks was higher in distressed marriages than in nondistressed marriages. Trust is presumably weaker in the former.

Credibility of Struggle Tactics

Threats and positional commitments, two of the struggle tactics used in negotiation, work only if credibility is established—if the opponent comes to believe the commitment that the tactics embody. The opponent must believe that one will actually do what one has committed oneself to do—carry through with the threat or hold firm regardless of consequences.

Sources of credibility in general. There are a number of conditions that make both threats and positional commitments more credible. First, credibility is affected by one's history of fulfilling past commitments. Research has shown that consistent enforcement of past commitments has a positive impact on the credibility of current commitments (Horai & Tedeschi, 1969; Schlenker, Helm, & Tedeschi, 1973). Second, credibility is positively affected by one's relative status. Faley and Tedeschi (1971) found that high-status individuals were more effective in threatening low-status individuals than were low-status individuals in threatening high-status individuals. Third, credibility can be affected by the cost of carrying through with the commitment; the higher the cost, the less credible the commitment (Mogy & Pruitt, 1974).

Commitments are also seen as more credible if they are made in public so that they reflect on one's reputation (Schelling, 1960). The possible image loss that is associated with nonfulfillment of a commitment will motivate one to follow through. Logically, this motivation will be stronger the more concerned one is about one's reputation and the larger the sector of the public that knows of this commitment. Credibility is also likely to be enhanced when one expects to have a continuing relationship with the other (Pruitt, 1981). Another way to enhance credibility is to get a third party to guarantee one's commitment (e.g., to sign a legal contract or obtain an injunction).

Sources of the credibility of threats. The credibility of threats is affected by the aforementioned general sources of credibility and also by other factors. A threat's credibility is dependent on whether one can monitor the other's behavior to see whether the other is acting as requested. If the other's noncompliance cannot be verified through surveillance, the threat loses some credibility. For example, a parent tells a child "Don't eat any of the cookies I've made for tomorrow's party. If you do, you'll get a paddling." If the child can keep his or her cookie eating from the adult, the adult's threat of punishment loses credibility.

Threats are also seen as more credible if they come from people who are viewed negatively or are known to view themselves negatively (Schlenker, Bonoma, Tedeschi, & Pivnick, 1970). This is because it is easier to believe that the source of the threat does not have the other's best interests in mind and hence may actually carry out the threat.

The credibility of one's threats is also enhanced to the degree that one is free from the social control of neutral third parties, who might punish or censure one for carrying out the threat. This can result from a lack of interaction with such third parties (as in a frontier or wartime situation) or from having high status in the eyes of third parties (being known as above the law). Threats will be seen as more credible if the other has no avenues of redress. One need not worry about the other's reactions if the other does not have anybody to complain to or does not have any way to punish or reward one in the future.

Sources of the credibility of positional commitments. There are some specific sources of the credibility of positional commitments in addition to the aforementioned general sources. A positional commitment is seen as more credible if one can demonstrate that an agreement with another is not imperative. For example, one may be able to demonstrate that one can absorb the cost of no agreement, as when one has a reasonable outside alternative. This is why negotiators are often urged to seek their best alternative to negotiated agreement (Fisher & Ury, 1981). The key here is to demonstrate that one can absorb the cost of no agreement. Related to this is demonstrating that one is not under any time pressure to reach an agreement. This makes it more credible that one will not move away from one's stated position and, hence, that the other must concede if agreement is to be reached in a reasonable period of time.

People can also enhance the credibility of their positional commitments by demonstrating that they cannot easily make concessions or that their bargaining limits are high. This can be done in many different ways. To demonstrate that they cannot easily make concessions, they can claim that the limit contained in their commitment is set by a third party, such as a supervisor. They can justify high bargaining limits by demonstrating that their costs or needs are high.

Positional commitments also gain credibility if people can demonstrate that they are acting on principles that they hold dear. For example, payment for work done is a widely held principle in our society. Hence, it will be hard for the other to doubt a positional commitment that is justified in this way.

Antecedents of the Use of Struggle Tactics

Credibility. We know of no research on the relation between the credibility that people believe they have and the strategies that they choose, but it is possible to speculate about this issue. One possibility is that people are more likely to use threats and positional commitments the more credible that they think they can make these tactics (e.g., the higher their status, the smaller the cost that is anticipated in carrying the tactic through). Another possibility is that this is true only up to a point. With extremely high levels of credibility, it may sometimes be unnecessary to actually use these tactics because the other side can see that it will have to make concessions and hence does so without being prodded. This suggests that instrumental aggression is an inverted U-shaped function of credibility, first rising and then falling. Research is needed to sort out these two possibilities.

Punitive power and threat use. For a threat to succeed, it is usually necessary for threateners to have punitive power (i.e., the capacity to punish others for failing to comply). Threats are sometimes shams (e.g., the gun is actually a toy), and shams often do not work.

An experiment by Hornstein (1965) examined the impact of punitive power possession on threat use. Subjects in an experiment on negotiation had the capacity to fine (take points from each other). Power was manipulated by varying the size of the possible fines. In some conditions, the negotiators were unequal in power. The larger the power discrepancy was, the more threats were made by the party with greater power and the fewer threats were made by the party with lesser power. This suggests, unsurprisingly, that aggression is a function of the size of the power discrepancy in a negotiator's favor.

However, there was a strange anomaly in the condition in which there was a small discrepancy in power. In this condition, the less powerful negotiators were found to make more threats than were the more powerful negotiators. A possible interpretation of this anomaly is that when there was a small power discrepancy, the less powerful negotiators refused to accept their inferior status and tried to compensate for it with a display of unusual aggressiveness. In contrast, when there was a large power discrepancy, the less powerful negotiators accepted their diminished status as inevitable. It is interesting to note that more points were made by both sides in the large power discrepancy condition than in the small power discrepancy condition (the party with greater power made more points than did the one with less power in both conditions). This suggests that the status rivalry produced by a small power discrepancy produced an escalation that hurt both parties.

More research is clearly needed on these issues. Nevertheless, the results of this study may have a parallel in relations between the United States and the former Soviet Union. There was considerable escalation in the relation between these two powers so long as Soviet Union saw itself as nearly equal in power to the United States. This was probably a result of status rivalry (see Organski, 1958). However, the tension diminished when it became clear that the Soviet economy was in a shambles and that the United States was far ahead. At this point, the Russians all but stopped competing on the world scene. The result of this large power discrepancy was negotiation, which produced greater benefit to both sides than had previously been possible.

In the international case just cited, threats from the higher power party (the United States) actually declined as the power discrepancy increased. This suggests that there may be an inverted U-shaped relation between the possession of punitive power and its actual use, as was speculated earlier for credibility. More powerful parties are more likely to use their power up to a point, but beyond that point, power use diminishes. A party with overwhelming power usually does not need to flaunt its power to achieve its ends (although occasionally very weak parties, such as Saddam Hussein's Iraq, are willing to challenge strong parties to test the latter's readiness to use their power).

Barriers. Barriers that block negotiators from seeing each other tend to dampen their competitive tendencies. Lewis and Fry (1977) found that negotiators with individualistic (competitive) orientations made significantly higher joint profits when they were negotiating with a barrier between them. Pruitt (1981) explained this by postulating that the barriers interfere with dominance behaviors. In negotiation, dominance behaviors are often nonverbal (e.g., icy stares, moving into the other's territory or personal space, or positioning one's body in an aggressive stance). Barriers make it difficult to enact such tactics. An alternative explanation is that the visual image of the other party heightens a negotiator's competitive impulses. These impulses are not heightened when a barrier blocks this image.

Antecedents of Resistance to Concession

A major alternative to struggle is yielding to the opponent. This suggests that conditions affecting the likelihood of yielding will have an opposite effect on the likelihood of using struggle tactics. The greater the resistance to yielding, the more likely are struggle tactics to be used. In negotiation, yielding implies concession making—lowering one's demands. Many of the conditions that produce resistance to concession have been found to encourage aggressive tactics such as threats and positional commitments (Pruitt, 1991).

Goals and limits. We know a great deal about the conditions that produce resistance to concession in negotiation. One source of this resistance is high goals and limits. Goals are what parties hope to achieve in a situation, and goals change as the negotiation between the parties progresses. Limits are outcomes that parties find minimally acceptable—parties will take them, but they would prefer more. When goals or limits are high, there is greater resistance to concession making (Holmes, Throop, & Strickland, 1971; Kelley, Beckman, & Fischer, 1967; Schoeninger & Wood, 1969; Smith, Pruitt, & Carnevale, 1982; Yukl, 1974a, 1974b), and struggle tactics are common (Fischer, 1969; Kelley et al., 1967). Principles of fairness exert a major influence on the goals and limits that parties set and accept. People commonly refuse to make concessions when they believe that principles of fairness are at issue because they feel that their demands are justified. Hence, one can expect them to be prone to resort to struggle tactics.

Representation. People who negotiate on behalf of others are called *representatives.* Those whom they represent are called *constituents.* In general, representatives are eager to please their constituents. This has a great effect on the resistance to concession making. If representatives believe that their constituents want them to be competitive and win in the negotiation, they will resist concession making; conversely, if they believe that their constituents want them to accommodate the other side, they will make more concessions (Benton & Druckman, 1974; Tjosvold, 1977). In the event that representatives have no information about their constituents' preferences, they tend to believe that the constituents want victory, which enhances resistance to concession making. Constituents are usually quite competitive in their outlook. Hence, having a representative ordinarily discourages concession making and encourages the use of struggle tactics (Benton, 1972; Benton & Druckman, 1973; Druckman, Solomon, & Zechmeister, 1972).

The effects just described are heightened when representatives are accountable to their constituents. If they have to answer to the group about their actions, they will make especially strong efforts to determine these preferences and to carry them out. The same is true if they are unsure about their standing in the group or are under surveillance by their constituents (Organ, 1971; Pruitt, Carnevale, Forcey, & Van Slyck, 1986). Because constituents are usually quite competitive, these conditions ordinarily produce slower concession making (Bartunek, Benton, & Keys, 1975; Carnevale, Pruitt, & Britton, 1979; Klimoski, 1972; Wall, 1975) and more use of struggle tactics (Ben-Yoav & Pruitt, 1984a).

Positive and negative framing. *Framing* refers to a perspective on the issues being negotiated. A positive frame means that people see the issues as involving various degrees of gain; a negative frame means that people see them as involving various degrees of loss. Because losses are harder to accept than gains, negative frames encourage slow concession making (Bazerman, Magliozzi, & Neale, 1985; Bottom & Studt, in press; Carnovalo & Keenan, 1990) and probably encourage the use of struggle tactics.

Concern about the other party's interests. In all of the negotiation research mentioned so far, the subjects were primarily concerned with their own interests or those of their constituents. But this is by no means universally the case in social conflict. There is often a concern about the opponent's interests as well. This concern may be genuine owing to the fact that people may like their opponent, may see their opponent as a fellow group member, may be in a good mood, or so on. The concern also may be instrumental owing to dependence on the opponent for future cooperation (Pruitt & Rubin, 1986).

Friendly, cooperative relations between parties have been shown to produce concession making (Fry, Firestone, & Williams, 1983), to increase problem solving (Ben-Yoav & Pruitt 1984a, 1984b; Carnevale & Keenan, 1990), and to inhibit the use of struggle tactics (Sillars, 1981; Syna, 1984). These are signs of concern about the other party's interests. In addition, positive mood, which is known to enhance concern for others (Isen, 1970), has been shown to reduce the use of struggle tactics (Carnevale & Isen, 1986; Pruitt, Carnevale, Ben-Yoav, Nochajski, & Van Slyck, 1983).

More important, these studies show that the antecedents of resistance to concession, the topic of the previous section, have a different impact on behavior when there is also a concern about the other party's interests as well as one's own. As we have shown, resistance to concession encourages the use of struggle tactics when people are concerned only about their own interests. But these tactics are replaced by problem solving when there is concern about the other party's interests as well as one's own. In other words, the parties seek options that will satisfy one another's interests. This effect has been shown for high limits (Schoeninger & Wood, 1969), accountability to constituents (Ben-Yoav & Pruitt, 1984b), and negative framing (Carnevale & Keenan, 1990)—all sources of resistance to concession.

Time pressure. Time pressure has a different effect from the variables just mentioned in that it encourages both concession making (Hamner, 1974; Hamner & Baird, 1978; Komorita & Barnes, 1969; Pruitt & Johnson, 1970; Pruitt & Lewis, 1975; Smith et al., 1982; Yukl, 1974b) and increased use of struggle tactics (Carnevale & Lawler, 1986). This is probably because the basic effect of time pressure is to heighten the urgency of moving toward agreement (i.e., to diminish the attractiveness of inaction). Both concession making and struggle tactics have the potential for facilitating movement toward agreement; hence, both are encouraged by time pressure.

Evidence From Nonnegotiation Studies

We have recently begun a series of studies that examine procedural choice in everyday interpersonal conflict. This series was inspired by a tradition of research started by Thibaut and Walker (1975). These scholars and their students looked at preferences among the following procedures: autocratic decision making, arbitration, advisory arbitration, negotiation, and several variants of these procedures. In our studies, we dropped autocratic decision making and added mediation, inaction, and struggle because we believe that they are more common in everyday life. Thus, we examined choices involving an aggressive procedure (struggle) and five alternatives to this procedure.

Experiments on Procedural Choice

Two of our studies (Peirce, Pruitt, & Czaja, 1991) involved laboratory experiments using undergraduates as subjects. We used an anticipated role-playing methodology wherein subjects were led to believe that they would actually be resolving a conflict. In Study 1, the subjects played the roles of a tenant and a landlord who were in conflict about a badly dyed rug. In Study 2, they played the roles of a student and a professor who were in conflict about whether a final examination should be cumulative. After learning about the dispute and their roles, subjects ranked and rated the attractiveness of the six conflict resolution procedures in the belief that they would actually have to enact their first-choice procedure. As mentioned, these procedures were inaction (doing nothing about the conflict), negotiation (talking directly to the other party), mediation (having a third party assist in the resolution of the conflict), advisory arbitration (having the third party make a nonbinding decision regarding the resolution of the conflict), arbitration (having a third party make a legally binding decision), and struggle (denouncing the other party publicly or threatening to harm that party's interests).

One of our main interests in these studies involved complainant–respondent difference. A complainant is a party who seeks redress; a respondent is a party from whom redress is sought. In the Peirce et al. (1991) studies, the student and the tenant were the complainants; the student wanted the final to be noncumulative, and the tenant wanted a new rug. The teacher and landlord were the respondents; the teacher wanted to keep the final cumulative, and the landlord wanted the tenant to make do with the old dyed rug. A crucial difference between the two roles is that complainants are usually trying to change the status quo, whereas respondents are usually trying to maintain it. Most disputes involve both roles (Felstiner, Abel, & Sarat, 1980).

In both studies, complainants saw arbitration as more attractive and inaction as less attractive than did respondents. These results follow from an analysis of self-interest: Arbitration has the potential to change the status quo, whereas inaction favors it.

Our most interesting findings concerned preferences among the six procedures. We learned from answers to an open-ended question in Study 1 that many people think of procedural choice in terms of sequences of procedures, with each procedure in the sequence used if the prior procedure proves unworkable.

In Study 2, we asked the subjects to rank the procedures in their preferred order of use. Half (50%) chose negotiation as their most preferred form of action, whereas less than a fifth (19%) chose mediation. Half (50%) of those starting with negotiation were willing to move to mediation and then to advisory arbitration if negotiation failed. Struggle tactics were ordinarily ranked last or next to last. However, 62% of our subjects indicated a readiness ultimately to use struggle tactics if other approaches were ineffective. In other words, most subjects were willing to take aggressive action if all else failed, but aggression was a last resort.

In Study 2, we also measured perceptions of each procedure on the dimensions of self-interest (whether favoring one's own or the other's position) and normativeness (what subjects believed other people would view as the proper approach). Multivariate analyses suggested that both kinds of perceptions affect procedural choice, with perceived normativeness having the stronger impact. Perceived normativeness predicted a subject's order of preference among the procedures better than did perceived self-interest.

Unexpectedly, however, both complainants and respondents rated struggle as highest among the procedures in perceived self-interest. In other words, both sides thought they could win by using aggressive tactics. Yet, struggle was a nonpreferred procedure, used only as a last resort. A possible explanation for this paradox is implied by the finding that struggle was also perceived as very low in normativeness. The sense that struggle was an improper approach appears to have vastly overshadowed the belief that struggle would be effective in achieving one's ends. This shows how powerful social norms are in inhibiting instrumental aggression.

An Interview Study[1]

In an effort to assess whether some of our experimental results would generalize to real-life settings, we interviewed 17 complainants who had called the Dispute Settlement Center in Buffalo, New York. All had complaints about the behavior of other individuals (e.g., a neighbor not letting the complainant park on the street in front of her house, a boy repeatedly hitting the complainant's daughter, vermin living in a neighbor's yard). We asked them to describe the steps they had gone through in dealing with their dispute before they called the center.

We divided the tactics that they described into three classes: inaction (with hope that the problem would go away), negotiation (talking with the other party), and contacting a third party (usually in an effort to bring pressure on the other party). Struggle tactics were seldom mentioned, perhaps because of embarrassment about reporting the use of nonnormative approaches. Most of the subjects used a sequence of tactics, involving two or all three of these classes of procedures. The initial tactic chosen was as follows: negotiation (42%), inaction (29%), and third party (29%). Of the 5 who chose inaction first, 3 chose negotiation second; hence, 59% chose to talk to the other party as their first form of action. This matches one of the findings in our experimental studies: Discussion with the other party is the most popular starting point for action in everyday disputes. This

[1] We wish to thank the following officers of the Dispute Settlement Center at the Better Business Foundation of Western New York for their help in making this study possible: Charles Underhill, Judith Peter, and Mary Beth Goris.

conclusion is also supported by Valley's (1990) finding that 64% of a sample of company executives said that they would "sit down with the other party and discuss the possibilities for resolving the conflict" when dealing with an organizational controversy.

Developing Workable Alternatives to Aggression

Several of the results reviewed so far imply that aggressive tactics are unlikely to be used if other procedures work or seem promising. This implies that aggression can be prevented by effective conflict management. The challenge is to develop workable alternatives to aggression.

Designing Dispute Resolution Systems

A similar point was made by Ury, Brett, and Goldberg (1988). These authors distinguished three general approaches that disputants can take to conflict: determining each other's interests and reconciling these interests (problem solving and mediation), determining who is right (arbitration), and determining who is more powerful (struggle). They proposed ways to design systems for dealing with conflict that will make consensual procedures (problem solving and mediation) so attractive that people will not be tempted to turn to arbitration or struggle. Their area of application is conflict within organizations, such as between management and labor.

Some of their principles are designed to make problem solving and mediation readily available when grievances arise. They suggest designing systems that provide disputants with the following:

1. Immediate and fully legitimate access to the other side, so as to avoid the build-up of resentment and rash struggle activity. The best approach is to have regular meetings between potential antagonists so as to detect problems in their incipient stages.
2. Several points of contact between disputants in case the first does not work.
3. Representatives of both sides who have authority to make decisions, so that problems will be dealt with effectively.
4. Access to accomplished mediators.

Ury et al. (1988) also recommended training potential adversaries in problem-solving skills. Among the skills that could be included in such training are attacking the problem and not the people, active listening, being firm about ends but flexible about means, and enhancing the positive mood of all people involved (Fisher & Ury, 1981; Pruitt & Rubin, 1986).

Alternatives to Aggression in Nonindustrial Societies

The development of workable alternatives to aggression has been carried to a high art in some nonindustrial societies. These are societies in which, unlike most parts of Western society, it is normative to use violence in response to major crimes such as murder, rape, and theft. Such norms pose a danger to the social fabric if the alleged perpetrator and the victim of a crime are from the same village or family. Hence, these societies provide mediation services to forestall the outbreak of violence in such relationships (Gulliver, 1979).

Merry (1989) listed the typical characteristics of these mediation services:

1. Mediation begins immediately at the first sign of conflict. Although mediators in some circumstances have the luxury of waiting to intervene until the situation is "ripe" (Touval & Zartman, 1985), this is not a practical approach when violence is pending.
2. Mediators have high status and are often quite powerful, with access to both sides and the capacity to impose a solution if agreement is not reached. Thus, the procedure is one of mediation followed by arbitration if mediation fails, which has been shown to be more effective at producing problem solving than simple mediation (McGillicuddy, Welton, & Pruitt, 1987).
3. Community members join with the mediator to impose a solution if agreement is not reached and to enforce this solution after the mediation is finished.
4. The solutions reached often require the respondent to compensate the complainant (e.g., in money, cattle, or sheep).
5. The solutions reflect community norms, including status norms. Hence, mediated settlements between unequals are "unequal," providing a larger reward to the party with higher status.

Such mediation services are conflict management systems. But they differ from the systems envisioned by Ury et al. (1988) in that mediation is often mandatory, imposed by a community that watches carefully to be sure a solution is reached and followed. Furthermore, mediators have the power to impose a solution if agreement is not reached.

Although some critics might question whether such systems should actually be called *mediation* in light of their coercive features, the systems do constitute mediation in the sense that the third parties make an effort to achieve a consensual agreement.

It can be argued that mandatory mediation would also be useful in our own society for resolving festering disputes that are too small for the courts to spend time on or too complicated for the courts to solve. Requiring people to engage in mediation seems improper to many proponents of mediation, but it is becoming an increasingly popular part of our legal system (Roehl & Cook, 1989).

Struggle Followed by Negotiation

Ury et al. (1988) pointed out that struggle may be a necessary prelude to effective problem solving in some controversies. This is true when (a) one or both parties are unwilling to come to the negotiation table, or (b) both parties are so sure of their own strength that their goals are too ambitious to permit agreement. An example of the latter is the Vietnam War, in which both sides seemed confident of victory at first. The war had to be fought to convince the losing side (the United States) to reduce its goals to a point at which they were compatible with those of the other side.

The challenge to conflict management in such cases is to keep the struggle within bounds and to begin problem solving as soon as possible. Ury et al. (1988) alluded to four procedures for meeting this challenge:

1. Substitute posturing for actual struggle; for example, line troops up on opposite sides of the border or have gangs of boys yell at each other rather than fight. Such procedures will sometimes clarify which side is stronger, making actual struggle unnecessary.
2. Fight only in a limited realm wherein relative strength can nevertheless be assessed. In the authors' words, "a strike in which workers refuse only overtime work is less costly than a full strike" (p. 18).
3. Observe a cooling-off period whenever a controversy threatens to move into the struggle phase. A related norm would require a pause in hostilities once they get going. Friends who separate two fighters are enforcing the latter sort of norm.
4. Require negotiation during the cooling-off periods and provide crisis mediation services to encourage problem solving.

Another approach is for one or both parties to change leadership at the point of transition from struggle to negotiation. Such a change can facilitate settlement, since the ill feelings resulting from struggle are often directed at the other side's leader. An example is the easy transition into effective negotiation with the West that occurred when Gorbachev took over the leadership of the Soviet Union. The transition to peace making would have been more difficult if Gorbachev had begun his term with a round of threats and menacing moves against the West.

Conclusion

Viewing aggression as a struggle tactic in social conflict is not a new perspective. However, it needs to be taken more seriously because it links aggression theory to other bodies of knowledge in the realms of negotiation, mediation, procedural choice, and dispute management systems. This perspective implies, for example, that the likelihood of aggression is a function of one's level of punitive power and one's assessment of the credibility of struggle tactics in the eyes of the opponent.

Another important implication of this perspective is that the likelihood of aggression is a function of the assessment of alternative procedures, including yielding, problem solving, mediation, arbitration, and inaction. This implies, for example, that conditions that make it hard to yield tend to encourage aggressive behavior. Examples of such conditions are ambitious goals, being an accountable representative, and framing the options negatively.

In most parts of our society, it appears that consensual procedures, such as problem solving and mediation, are more popular than is aggression for dealing with everyday controversies. Our evidence suggests that aggression, although often effective, tends to be rejected because it is not viewed as normative. Aggression is, nevertheless, usually available as a residual procedure if others seem unworkable. Hence, strengthening the consensual procedures (e.g., encouraging easy access between the disputants or providing mediation services) should reduce the probability of aggression. This is probably why mandatory mediation is so common in nonindustrial societies in which the disputes between people who are parts of larger social units might otherwise tear these units apart. Ury et al. (1988) developed guidelines for building systems in which consensual procedures are readily available and workable.

It may be impossible to prevent aggression when both disputants feel they are so powerful that they need not make substantial concessions. In such cases, the challenge for conflict management is to keep the resulting struggle within bounds and to shift to problem solving as soon as it is clear which side will prevail.

References

Bartunek, J., Benton, A., & Keys, C. (1975). Third party intervention and the behavior of group representatives. *Journal of Conflict Resolution, 19,* 532–557.

Bazerman, M. H., Magliozzi, T., & Neale, M. A. (1985). Integrative bargaining in a competitive market. *Organizational Behavior and Human Decision Processes, 35,* 294–313.

Benton, A. A. (1972). Accountability and negotiations between group representatives [Summary]. *Proceedings of the 80th Annual Conference of the American Psychological Association,* 227–228.

Benton, A. A., & Druckman, D. (1973). Salient solutions and the bargaining behavior of representatives and nonrepresentatives. *International Journal of Group Tensions, 3,* 28–39.

Benton, A. A., & Druckman, D. (1974). Constituent's bargaining orientation and intergroup negotiations. *Journal of Applied Social Psychology, 4,* 141–150.

Ben-Yoav, O., & Pruitt, D. G. (1984a). Accountability to constituents: A two-edged sword. *Organizational Behavior and Human Performance, 34,* 283–295.

Ben-Yoav, O., & Pruitt, D. G. (1984b). Resistance to yielding and the expectation of cooperative future interaction in negotiation. *Journal of Experimental Social Psychology, 34,* 323–335.

Bottom, W. P., & Studt, A. (in press). The nature of risk and risk preference in bargaining. *Organizational Behavior and Human Decision Processes.*

Carnevale, P. J., & Isen, A. M. (1986). The influence of positive affect and visual access on the discovery of integrative solutions in bilateral negotiation. *Organizational Behavior and Human Decision Processes, 37,* 1–13.

Carnevale, P. J., & Keenan, P. A. (1990). *Decision frame and social goals in integrative bargaining: The likelihood of agreement versus the quality.* Paper presented at the meeting of the International Association Conflict Management, Vancouver, British Columbia.

Carnevale, P. J., & Lawler, E. J. (1986). Time pressure and the development of integrative agreements in bilateral negotiation. *Journal of Conflict Resolution, 30,* 636–659.

Carnevale, P. J., Pruitt, D. G., & Britton, S. D. (1979). Looking tough: The negotiator under constituent surveillance. *Personality and Social Psychology Bulletin, 5,* 118–121.

Druckman, D. (1986). Stages, turning points, and crisis: Negotiating military base rights, Spain and the United States. *Journal of Conflict Resolution, 30,* 327–360.

Druckman, D., Solomon, D., & Zechmeister, K. (1972). Effects of representative role obligations on the process of children's distributions of resources. *Sociometry, 35,* 387–410.

Faley, T. E., & Tedeschi, J. T. (1971). Status and reactions to threats. *Journal of Personality and Social Psychology, 17,* 192–199.

Felstiner, W. L. F., Abel, R. L., & Sarat, A. (1980). The emergence and transformation of disputes: Naming, blaming, claiming. *Law and Society Review, 15*, 629–654.

Fischer, C. S. (1969). The effects of threats in an incomplete information game. *Sociometry, 32*, 301–314.

Fisher, R., & Ury, W. (1981). *Getting to YES: Negotiating agreement without giving in.* Boston: Houghton Mifflin.

Fry, W. R., Firestone, I. J., & Williams, D. L. (1983). Negotiation process and outcome of stranger dyads and dating couples: Do lovers lose? *Basic and Applied Social Psychology, 4*, 1–16.

Gottman, J. M. (1979). *Marital interaction: Experimental investigations.* San Diego, CA: Academic Press.

Gulliver, P. H. (1979). *Disputes and negotiations: A cross-cultural perspective.* San Diego, CA: Academic Press.

Hamner, W. C. (1974). Effects of bargaining strategy and pressure to reach agreement in a stalemated negotiation. *Journal of Personality and Social Psychology, 30*, 458–467.

Hamner, W. C., & Baird, L. S. (1978). The effect of strategy, pressure to reach agreement and relative power on bargaining behavior. In H. Sauermann (Ed.), *Contributions to experimental economics* (Vol. 7). Tubingen, Germany: Mohr.

Holmes, J. G., Throop, W. F., & Strickland, L. H. (1971). The effects of prenegotiation expectations on the distributive bargaining process. *Journal of Experimental Social Psychology, 7*, 582–599.

Horai, J., & Tedeschi, J. (1969). Effects of credibility and magnitude of punishment on compliance to threats. *Journal of Personality and Social Psychology, 12*, 164–169.

Hornstein, H. A. (1965). Effects of different magnitudes of threat upon interpersonal bargaining. *Journal of Experimental Social Psychology, 1*, 282–293.

Isen, A. M. (1970). Success, failure, attention, and reaction to others. The warm glow of success. *Journal of Personality and Social Psychology, 15*, 294–301.

Kelley, H. H., Beckman, L. L., & Fischer, C. S. (1967). Negotiating the division of reward under incomplete information. *Journal of Experimental Social Psychology, 3*, 361–398.

Kimmel, M., Pruitt, D. G., Magenau, J., Konar-Goldband, E., & Carnevale, P. J. (1980). The effects of trust, aspiration, and gender on negotiation tactics. *Journal of Personality and Social Psychology, 38*, 9–23.

Klimoski, R. J. (1972). The effect of intragroup forces on intergroup conflict resolution. *Organizational Behavior and Human Performance, 8*, 363–383.

Komorita, S. S., & Barnes, M. (1969). Effects of pressures to reach agreement in bargaining. *Journal of Personality and Social Psychology, 13*, 245–252.

Lewis, S. A., & Fry, W. R. (1977). Effects of visual access and orientation on the discovery of integrative bargaining alternatives. *Organizational Behavior and Human Performance, 20*, 75–92.

McGillicuddy, N. B., Welton, G. L., & Pruitt, D. G. (1987). Third party intervention: A field experiment comparing three different models. *Journal of Personality and Social Psychology, 53*, 104–112.

Merry, S. E. (1989). Mediation in nonindustrial societies. In K. Kressel & D. G. Pruitt (Eds.), *Mediation research* (pp. 68–90). San Francisco: Jossey-Bass.

Michener, H. A., Vaske, J. J., Schleiffer, S. L., Plazewski, J. G., & Chapman, L. J. (1975). Factors affecting concession rate and threat usage in bilateral conflict. *Sociometry, 38*, 62–80.

Mogy, R. B., & Pruitt, D. G. (1974). Effects of a threatener's enforcement costs on threat credibility and compliance. *Journal of Personality and Social Psychology, 29,* 173–180.

Moser, G., & Levy-Leboyer, C. (1985). Inadequate environment and situation control: Is a malfunctioning phone always an occasion for aggression? *Environment and Behavior, 17,* 520–533.

Organ, D. W. (1971). Some variables affecting boundary role behavior. *Sociometry, 34,* 524–537.

Organski, A. F. K. (1958). *World politics.* New York: Knopf.

Peirce, R. S., Pruitt, D. G., & Czaja, S. J. (1991). *Complainant–respondent differences in procedural choice.* Unpublished manuscript.

Pruitt, D. G. (1981). *Negotiation behavior.* San Diego, CA: Academic Press.

Pruitt, D. G. (1991). Strategy in negotiation. In V. Kremenyuk (Ed.), *International negotiation: Analysis, approaches, issues* (pp. 78–89). San Francisco: Jossey-Bass.

Pruitt, D. G., & Carnevale, P. J. (in press). *Negotiation in social conflict.* Pacific Grove, CA: Brooks/Cole.

Pruitt, D. G., Carnevale, P. J., Ben-Yoav, O., Nochajski, T. H., & Van Slyck, M. (1983). Incentives for cooperation in integrative bargaining. In R. Tietz (Ed.), *Aspiration levels in bargaining and economic decision making* (pp. 22–33). New York: Springer.

Pruitt, D. G., Carnevale, P. J., Forcey, B., & Van Slyck, M. (1986). Gender effects in negotiation: Constituent surveillance and contentious behavior. *Journal of Experimental Social Psychology, 22,* 264–275.

Pruitt, D. G., & Johnson, D. F. (1970). Mediation as an aid to face-saving in negotiation. *Journal of Personality and Social Psychology, 14,* 239–246.

Pruitt, D. G., & Lewis, S. A. (1975). Development of integrative solutions in bilateral negotiation. *Journal of Personality and Social Psychology, 31,* 621–633.

Pruitt, D. G., & Rubin, J. Z. (1986). *Social conflict: Escalation, stalemate, and settlement.* New York: Random House.

Roehl, J. A., & Cook, R. F. (1989). Mediation in interpersonal disputes: Effectiveness and limitations. In K. Kressel & D. G. Pruitt (Eds.), *Mediation research* (pp. 31–52). San Francisco: Jossey-Bass.

Schelling, T. (1960). *The strategy of conflict.* Cambridge, MA: Harvard University Press.

Schlenker, B. R., Bonoma, T. V., Tedeschi, J. T., & Pivnick, W. P. (1970). Compliance to threats as a function of the wording of the threat and the exploitativeness of the threatener. *Sociometry, 33,* 394–408.

Schlenker, B. R., Helm, B., & Tedeschi, J. T. (1973). The effects of personality and situational variables on behavioral trust. *Journal of Personality and Social Psychology, 25,* 419–427.

Schoeninger, D. W., & Wood, W. D. (1969). Comparison of married and ad hoc mixed-sex dyads negotiating the division of a reward. *Journal of Experimental Social Psychology, 5,* 483–499.

Sillars, A. L. (1981). Attributions and interpersonal conflict resolution. In J. H. Harvey, W. Ickes, & R. F. Kidd (Eds.), *New directions in attribution research* (Vol. 3, pp. 279–305). Hillsdale, NJ: Erlbaum.

Smith, D. L., Pruitt, D. G., & Carnevale, P. J. (1982). Matching and mismatching: The effect of own limit, other's toughness, and time pressure on concession rate in negotiation. *Journal of Personality and Social Psychology, 42,* 876–883.

Syna, H. (1984). *Couples in conflict: Conflict resolution strategies, perceptions about sources of conflict and relationship adjustment.* Unpublished doctoral dissertation, State University of New York at Buffalo.

Thibaut, J., & Walker, L. (1975). *Procedural justice: A psychological analysis.* Hillsdale, NJ: Erlbaum.

Tjosvold, D. (1977). Commitment to justice in conflict between unequal persons. *Journal of Applied Social Psychology, 7,* 149–162.

Touval, S., & Zartman, I. W. (1985). *International mediation in theory and practice.* Boulder, CO: Westview Press.

Ury, W., Brett, J. M., & Goldberg, S. (1988). *Getting disputes resolved.* San Francisco: Jossey-Bass.

Valley, K. L. (1990). *Rank and relationship effects on formality in conflict management.* Paper presented at the meeting of the International Association of Conflict Management, Vancouver, British Columbia.

Wall, J. A., Jr. (1975). Effects of constituent trust and representative bargaining orientation on intergroup bargaining. *Journal of Personality and Social Psychology, 31,* 1004–1012.

Yukl, G. A. (1974a). Effects of opponents initial offer, concession magnitude, and concession frequency on bargaining behavior. *Journal of Personality and Social Psychology, 30,* 332–335.

Yukl, G. A. (1974b). The effects of situational variables and opponent concessions on a bargainer's perception, aspirations, and concessions. *Journal of Personality and Social Psychology, 29,* 227–236.

CHAPTER 5

Reciprocity of Coercion and Cooperation Between Individuals and Nations

Martin Patchen

T he actions of one person toward another often follow and may be primarily a reaction to the other's prior actions. If A threatens or punishes B, B may respond with his or her own threats or punishments. Alternatively, B may submit to A's coercion without reciprocating, perhaps complying with some demand of A in order to avoid further punishment. Similarly, if A promises or gives rewards to B, B may or may not reciprocate.

Do people generally reciprocate coercive or cooperative actions by their interaction partners? Under what conditions is reciprocation more or less likely to occur? What is the nature of reciprocation when it does occur? Is it usually a simple "tit-for-tat," or is the nature of reciprocation more complex?

This chapter will review evidence and theoretical explanations concerning reciprocity. It will give special attention to research on interaction between national leaders. Although there has been considerable development of research on this topic, studies of reciprocity between national leaders have been done largely in isolation from research on reciprocity of coercive and cooperative behaviors in other settings.

There are, of course, differences between actions at the national level and those between people in other types of settings (e.g., between parents and children, wives and husbands, bosses and workers). For example, national actions sometimes may be more the product of a group or organizational process than are, say, the actions of family members.

However, the interactions between national leaders and people in other settings are not completely different. People at many institutional "levels" often make decisions in groups. For example, two parents often decide together how to deal coercively with a misbehaving child, and a group of executives may decide together how to react co-ercively to what they see as problematic behavior by one or more workers. Second, just as final decisions on important matters are often made by a single person (e.g., the president of a business, the principal of a school), there is considerable evidence that most important actions by nations are decided ultimately by a single top decisionmaker (Hoagland & Walker, 1979).

Thus, although the analyst should be alert to differences among settings, it seems useful to consider work on internation reciprocity in the context of more general work on this topic. What does research on the actions of national leaders have to contribute to the study of reciprocity as a general social process? And how can studies of reciprocity at the national level benefit from a broader range of social psychological research and theory?

This chapter begins by considering research, based on international studies, concerning the extent to which the behaviors of one actor are reactions to those of another actor, rather than to internal forces. Second, research from several substantive areas concerning general tendencies toward reciprocity will be reviewed. Third, studies of internation interaction that attempt to specify the nature of reciprocity will be summarized. Fourth, the central issue of the conditions under which reciprocity occurs will be discussed, drawing on research in a variety of settings. Fifth, theoretical explanations of the occurrence of reciprocity will be reviewed, and an explanatory framework based on decision theory will be presented. The final section presents a summary and overall conclusions.

Importance of the Other's Actions

Before studying the process of interaction, a prior question must be addressed. To what extent are the actions of each actor taken in response to those of another, as opposed to being a result of internal forces such as personal motives or habits?

This question has received attention and some systematic investigation with respect to the actions of national leaders. Some scholars (e.g., Nincic, 1989) have argued that national leaders act primarily because of factors internal to their own nation, such as their own foreign policy goals, domestic political and economic pressures, habits, and bureaucratic momentum. From this perspective, each nation's leaders tend to continue the same type of actions they have taken recently toward a rival nation, which reflect these internal forces.

A number of studies have investigated the relative impact of a nation's own recent behavior and its rival's recent behavior on each nation's cooperative and conflictive actions toward the other. A review of research on U.S.–Soviet interactions indicated that neither the rival's recent actions nor the actor's own recent actions were consistently found to be a more important influence on each actor's behavior (Patchen, 1991). Cooperative behavior seemed to be affected as much or more by the actions of a rival as by a nation's own prior behavior. Conflict behavior appeared generally to be influenced more by each nation's own prior behavior than by the actions of its rival. However, the rival's behavior appeared to increase in importance as a predictor of the most extreme conflict behavior.

Some scholars have investigated the hypothesis that in crisis situations, a nation's reactivity to the actions of a rival depends on the phase of the crisis. The evidence suggests that national leaders react most to each other's behavior when conflict is intensifying but that this is less true of the initiator of a crisis than of the other side (Corson, 1970; Tanter, 1974).

Scholars concerned with interaction in other settings (e.g., between parent and child or husband and wife) also have recognized that the actions of each person may be affected by both internal forces (e.g., motives, traits) and the actions of the other person. However, there appears to be little systematic evidence about the relative impact of these two general types of influence or about the conditions under which reactivity to another is greatest.

General Tendencies Toward Reciprocity

When people do respond to the actions of others, what is the nature of this reaction? Do they generally follow a modified "golden rule" to "Do unto others what they have recently done unto you"?

There is, in fact, evidence from studies of interaction in a wide variety of settings that indicates that people do tend to reciprocate both the negative and the positive actions of others. Studies of aggression indicate that people generally retaliate against punishing responses directed at themselves. This has been found, for example, in laboratory settings (e.g., O'Leary & Dengerink, 1973; Taylor, 1967), in the relations between police and residents of innercity neighborhoods (Toch, 1969), in interactions leading to criminal violence (Felson & Steadman, 1983), and in relations between husbands and wives (Patterson, 1982; Wills, Weiss, & Patterson, 1974). Violence or punishing action usually follows a provocation and often leads to further reciprocation.

The use of coercion (threat and actual punishment) also has been studied in bargaining situations. Coercion often is effective in gaining compliance with bargainers' demands, at least in the short run. However, the use of coercion usually leads to countercoercion, often resulting in an escalating spiral of coercion and countercoercion (Hornstein, 1965; Pruitt & Rubin, 1986; Tedeschi & Bonoma, 1977). As the escalation of coercion progresses, the stakes of the dispute may seem higher to both sides (Brockner & Rubin, 1985; Deutsch, 1973), and their inhibitions about hurting the other side may be reduced (J. H. Goldstein, Davids, & Herman, 1975).

In relations between nations there also is a general tendency for the target of coercive actions to reciprocate in kind (Patchen, 1988). Thus, for example, several studies have found a moderate tendency for both the United States and the former Soviet Union to reciprocate conflictive actions toward each other during the Cold War period (e.g., Dixon, 1988; J. S. Goldstein & Freeman, 1990). Terrorist raids by Arab groups against Israel have met consistently with Israeli reprisals, and these reprisals have in turn been followed by further Arab violence (Blechman, 1972).

Actions that reward another actor also are likely to be reciprocated. Anthropologists have described patterns of reciprocation in helping and gift giving among primitive peoples (Malinowski, 1961; Mauss, 1954). Many studies of helping behavior in modern society, involving both children and adults, show that people are inclined to help those who have helped them earlier (Bar-Tal, 1976). Studies of interaction in bargaining situations indicate a tendency for each side to match concessions with concessions (Druckman, 1983; Pruitt, 1981; Putnam & Jones, 1982). A strategy of unilateral conciliatory initiatives has been found to be generally effective in eliciting cooperation from a bargaining partner (Lindskold, 1978). And husbands and wives—both those involved in marital therapy and those in nonclinical situations—have been found generally to reciprocate positive behaviors of their spouses while interacting in a variety of tasks (Gottman, 1979).

Consistent with findings in these disparate areas, studies of interaction between nations have shown that national leaders also tend to reciprocate cooperative actions, including those from adversaries (Patchen, 1991). Thus, for example, conciliatory initiatives from U.S. leaders toward Soviet leaders and from Soviet toward Chinese leaders generally have been reciprocated to some extent (J. S. Goldstein & Freeman, 1990).

In addition to the consistency with which a general tendency toward reciprocity has been found in different types of interaction, another consistency emerges across substantive areas. A number of studies have shown a tendency toward greater reciprocity of cooperative actions than of coercive actions. Bargainers in simulated labor–management situations (Putnam & Jones, 1982), husbands and wives in standardized task situations (Gottman, 1979), and U.S. and Soviet leaders (Patchen, 1991) all were more likely generally to reciprocate cooperative than conflictive actions.

In both the labor–management bargaining and the husband–wife interactions, reciprocation of conflictive actions by a partner was characteristic of a pair who were relatively unsuccessful in handling their problems. Similarly, in U.S.–Soviet relations, high reciprocity of conflictive actions was found only in situations of intensifying conflict or crisis (e.g., Holsti, Brody, & North, 1969) wherein the relation had gotten somewhat "out of control." Thus, although reciprocity of both positive and negative behaviors generally occurred in relationships of various kinds, the participants generally seemed to be aware of the need to control the possibly damaging escalation of punitive responses. A high level of coercive interaction indicates that such controls have failed and that the relationship is in difficulty.

Specifying the Nature of Reciprocity

Probably the most distinctive contribution of internation studies to an understanding of reciprocity has come from detailed investigations of the nature of reciprocity. Specifically, attention has been given to (a) the issue areas in which reciprocity may occur, (b) undermatching and overmatching of responses, (c) the shape of the response function, (d) trends in the rival's behavior, (e) differences between the rival's and one's own behavior, and (f) short-term versus long-term reciprocity.

Issue Area

Reciprocity, when it occurs, does not necessarily occur in the same issue area. Dixon (1986) found that there was a "mixed reciprocity process" operating in U.S.–Soviet relations. Both the United States and the former Soviet Union tended to reciprocate the friendliness or hostility of political actions by its rival with political actions of its own. However, military actions by one side tended to come more often in response to nonmilitary (political, cultural, scientific) actions by the other side. Similarly, actions by each side on cultural or scientific issues were related most strongly to actions by the rival in different areas (e.g., political). Thus, reciprocity may involve choice among a wide range of possible actions that reflect friendliness or hostility rather than matching the specific actions or even the type of action taken by the rival.

Undermatching and Overmatching

A simple reciprocity model predicts that each side will respond to the other's action with equal strength. James and Harvey (1989) investigated whether the United States and the former Soviet Union actually responded in such a proportional way in 27 crisis situations. They found that the simple reciprocity model was not as accurate as was a model that predicts a more than proportional response in cases of minor provocation and a less than proportional response in cases of major provocation. Similar tendencies were found by Berkowitz and Geen (1966) in a laboratory study of aggression, but little attention has been given to this phenomenon by writers on aggression.

Shape of the Response Function

A simple reciprocity model would predict a linear response function (i.e., for a given increase in the magnitude of cooperative or conflictive action by Side A, Side B would increase the magnitude of its own response in a constant manner). Greffenius (1989), drawing on earlier theoretical work by Pruitt (1969), used the Behavioral Correlates of War data set to plot the joint behavior of many pairs of rival nations in 36 internation crises. He found that, although some nations exhibited linear response functions to their rival's actions, in most cases the response function was nonlinear.

The most common nonlinear functions included the following reactions by Nation B to increases in hostile actions by Nation A:

1. B increased its own hostile actions but with a decreasing slope.
2. B increased its hostile actions with an increasing slope at first and then with a decreasing slope (an S-shaped function).
3. B increased its hostile actions with an increasing slope.

Greffenius (1989) noted that these results indicate a wide range of potential patterns once a dispute has begun. Some patterns of response are likely to lead to escalation of the conflict to violence, whereas other response patterns (even though involving some reciprocation) lead to deescalation and resolution short of violence.

Absolute Level Versus Deviations in Behaviors

Whereas a simple reciprocity model predicts that Side A will respond to the magnitude of Side B's cooperative or conflictive behavior, some researchers have explored models that postulate that nations react primarily to unexpected foreign policy "innovations" (or changes from previous behavior patterns) in ways that indicate reciprocity. Freeman and Goldstein (1989; see also J. S. Goldstein & Freeman, 1990) analyzed events data on U.S.–Soviet interactions and found not only evidence of "simple" reciprocity but evidence that each nation reacted to "innovations" in the other's behavior. Stoll and McAndrew (1986) found some support for a model that predicted that the United States and the former Soviet Union would respond to trends in the level of cooperativeness exhibited by the rival in arms negotiations.

Differences Between Other's and One's Own Behavior

An actor may respond not to a rival's actions in isolation but to the differences between the rival's recent behavior and his or her own recent behavior. According to this model, if the other's concessions have been greater than the actor's own recently, the actor increases his or her concessions; if the other's concessions have been less than the actor's own, the actor decreases his or her concessions. Druckman and Harris (1990) and Stoll and McAndrew (1986) found strong support for this model of reciprocation in their studies of arms negotiations.

Short-Term and Long-Term Reciprocity

Rajmaira and Ward (1990) suggested that empirical studies that examine the shortest time periods do not find robust evidence of reciprocity. They reported evidence of long-term trends in which the behaviors of the United States, the former Soviet Union, and China "drift[ed] together in a loosely coupled way over the past four decades" (p. 468). They concluded that reciprocity does occur but "on a much expanded time scale" (p. 473).

So far, only a limited amount of work has been done to test alternative models of the reciprocity process. Two studies that tested several models of arms negotiations between nations give greatest overall support to the "comparative reciprocity" model (i.e., the one that predicts A's behavior on the basis of the difference between its own recent behavior and that of B; Druckman & Harris, 1990; Stoll & McAndrews, 1986; see also Freeman & Golstein, 1989).

Conditions Under Which Reciprocity Occurs

Although people tend to reciprocate the actions of others, sometimes reciprocity does not occur. The target of coercive actions may endure threat or punishment without responding, or he or she may reward the coercer by complying with his or her wishes. Similarly, the target of cooperative actions may give nothing in return or may even inflict threats or punishments on the actor who has just rewarded him or her. Under what conditions is reciprocation of another's action likely to occur?

Responses of one actor to the actions of another may be affected by (a) the actor's perceptions of the other and the other's actions, (b) the actor's own motives, (c) conflicting and common interests between the two parties, (d) the power of the two parties to affect each other's outcomes, (e) third-party pressures, and (f) prior responses of the other to the actor's behavior. The following sections will discuss the effects of these factors, plus some additional ones, on reciprocity.

Perceptions of the Other and the Other's Actions

Whether the action of another is reciprocated depends in part on the actor's perception of the other and the nature of the other's actions.

First, the identity of the other in relation to the actor may be important (Tedeschi & Felson, 1993). If, for example, the other is an authority figure (parent, teacher, etc.) who has a socially sanctioned right to use coercion against the actor, then the actor is not likely to retaliate against coercion. However, if the other is an equal-status competitor for status (e.g., a fellow gang member), then coercion by the other is more likely to be reciprocated. (See Milburn & Watman, 1981, on the actor's tendency to reciprocate coercion when his or her status is threatened.)

The perceived legitimacy of the other's action may affect the actor's response. The greater the perceived wrong inflicted on the actor and the more resentful he or she feels, the more probable is retaliation (Milburn & Watman, 1981; Tedeschi & Bonoma, 1977). If, however, the target of the original action believes that he or she was deserving of punishment, retaliation is less likely (Fishman, 1965).

The perceived intentions of the other also may be important. Thus, retaliation against aggressive actions is increased when the potential retaliator believes that the harm done was intentional (Ferguson & Rule, 1983). Similarly, people are more likely to help those who helped them earlier when they believe that the benefactor's intentions were good (e.g., when the original help was given voluntarily; Greenberg & Frisch, 1972) and motives not selfish (Greenberg, 1980).

The perceived future intentions and goals of the other also may be important. The actor may interpret coercive actions by the other as an indication that the other has aggressive intentions and will continue to make further demands and use more coercion if his or her present tactics are successful (Bacharach & Lawler, 1981; Pruitt, 1981).

The importance of the actor's perceptions of the other's future goals has been emphasized especially in research on reciprocation of threats and coercion by national leaders. Reactions by national leaders to threats by other nations are influenced greatly by the leaders' interpretation of what the threats indicate about the more general intentions of the other nation (i.e., whether its long-term aims might be "sinister and unpredictable"; Cohen, 1979, p. 165). (Illegitimate actions by the other are especially apt to signal such malign future intention; Cohen, 1979).

Gamson and Modigliani (1971) maintained that whether national leaders will reciprocate belligerent behavior by a rival depends in part on their perceptions of the rival's goals. If the rival is seen as acting for defensive reasons, they will tend to chose a conciliatory response to the rival's bellicose actions (to calm fears). If, on the other hand, leaders perceive that the rival's bellicose behavior reflects expansionist goals, they will tend to respond with bellicose actions of their own to show that they cannot be intimidated. Consistent with the latter prediction, the actions of national leaders have been found to be influenced greatly by concern for their "reputation for resolve" and how their responses to coercive actions will affect the future intentions and actions of rivals (Snyder & Diesing, 1977).

Reciprocation of cooperative actions by other nations also may be affected by leaders' perceptions of the long-term aims of rivals. Thus, for example, data from Gamson and Modigliani's (1971) study of U.S.–Soviet interaction patterns suggest that the United States did not reciprocate cooperative moves by the former Soviet Union at a time when it distrusted Soviet aims (Patchen, 1991).

Perceptions of the intentions of another may derive in part from more general attitudes toward the other. Such general attitudes may influence an actor's response to the other's behavior (Pruitt, 1969). In addition to influencing expectations about the other's behaviors, they may affect the actor's motives to help or to hurt the other. If the actor dislikes the other, he or she is apt to be more willing to inflict harm on the other.

Actor's Own Motives

The nature of an actor's responses to another's behavior may be affected by the actor's own motives or goals. For example, if the actor is anxious to avoid a fight with the other, he or she may be slow to reciprocate coercion; if he or she is most concerned with not losing in a dispute with the other, then he or she is more likely to reciprocate coercion.

The vigor of reciprocity also may depend on the actor's motives. Tedeschi and Felson (1993) suggested that when the actor is motivated primarily by a desire to restore justice, reciprocation of coercion will be proportional to the provocation; when the actor is motivated primarily to enhance his or her social identity, he or she will give more than proportional responses to coercion.

Scholars who have studied interactions between nations have paid particular attention to the aims of national leaders with respect to winning advantage over a rival. Studies of escalation of coercion between nations have emphasized that each side in a dispute may raise the level of coercion—especially overmatching the other's actions—in an attempt to pressure the other side to concede (Patchen, 1987).

The long-term goals of national leaders also are important. Gamson and Modigliani (1971) suggested that if national leaders aim primarily to defend and consolidate what they already have, they will interpret a rival's conciliatory moves as receptive to cooperation and reciprocate. If their own goals involve expansion or even destroying the rival, they generally will interpret a rival's conciliatory behavior as indicating weakness and will respond with belligerence. In the same vein, Kaplowitz (1984) asserted that cooperative actions by national leaders will be reciprocated only by a rival who is seeking accommodation rather than victory.

Conflicting and Common Interests

The actions of people toward each other are affected in a fundamental way by the extent to which they can achieve good outcomes at the same time (Kelley & Thibaut, 1978). This general principle should also affect the occurrence of reciprocity. Thus, reciprocity of cooperation is more likely and the payoffs to each side greater when they both cooperate than when they both compete (Patchen, 1988, p. 284).

Pruitt (1969) hypothesized that one party is more likely to underreact to provocations from the other party if it feels more dependent on the other. Some evidence relevant to the effects of economic dependence on reciprocity comes from a study by Smith (1987) of hostile and cooperative interactions between nations.

As trade with the former Soviet Union became more important to the United States, U.S. reciprocation of cooperative actions by the Soviet Union increased. However, as U.S.–Soviet trade became more asymmetric, whichever side was disadvantaged at the time (i.e., had a trade deficit) increased its reciprocation of hostile actions by the other.

Increased interdependence increased the cooperative reactivity of the United States and West Germany toward each other. As their dyadic trade relative to the other nation's total trade increased, each side reacted more positively to cooperative behavior by the other.

Overall, these results suggest that although greater dependence on exchange with another makes reciprocation of cooperative acts more likely, being disadvantaged in the exchange makes reciprocation of conflictive acts more likely.

Power

Another fundamental factor affecting social interaction is the power of each side to affect the outcomes of the other (Kelley & Thibaut, 1978). The power of each depends on its resources, the needs of the other, and the other's alternative sources of reward.

Experimental studies have found that people with greater power tend to use coercion, whereas those with less power tend to submit when a more powerful adversary uses coercion against them. When the parties are more equal in power, coercion is likely to be resisted, and a spiral of conflict often ensues (Rubin & Brown, 1975, pp. 214–221; Tedeschi, Schlenker, & Lindskold, 1972).

Experimental studies also indicate that the absolute, as well as relative, power of actors may affect the reciprocation of coercion. The greater the magnitude of harm threatened by another, the more likely is compliance (Horai & Tedeschi, 1969). Also, the ability of actors to inflict great harm on each other tends to inhibit retaliation against coercion, even when the actors have equal power (Hornstein, 1965).

In international relations, Leng (1980) found that when one nation threatens another, the target of threat is more likely to respond defiantly when the rivals are equal in power than when the threatener is stronger. Several studies of interaction between the United States and the former Soviet Union also indicate that reciprocation of conflictive actions is most likely when the potential reciprocator is relatively strong (Patchen, 1991).

Some writers have pointed out that a more powerful party is not necessarily more likely than a weaker party to use coercion (Tedeschi & Felson, 1993). A weaker party may use coercion to indicate its resolve to resist intimidation, whereas a powerful party may not feel the need to respond to provocation. Evidence indicating such a "reverse" effect of relative power with respect to reciprocation of hostile behavior comes from a study of interaction between nations (Smith, 1987). Both the United States and the former Soviet Union reciprocated less strongly the hostile behavior of 49 other nations than those other nations reciprocated hostile actions of the superpowers.

It may be that the effect of a party's relative power on whether it retaliates against hostile actions will vary with its perception of how likely the other is to use its power fully. Thus, a small nation may reciprocate vigorously hostile behavior of the United States in the expectation that the United States will choose not to use its full power against that small nation. One reason for the greater "slowness to anger" of a superpower as compared with a weaker nation may be that the former usually is affected less by hostile actions than is the latter, both in pragmatic terms and in symbolic damage to its national sensitivities.

Relative power also affects reactions to cooperative behavior. Experimental studies indicate that a person is more likely to cooperate in response to a strategy of conciliation when the initiator of conciliation is equal in power to, or stronger than, itself (Chertkoff & Esser, 1976; Lindskold & Aronoff, 1980). In internation interaction, however, reciprocity by other nations to cooperative actions by the United States from 1952 to 1977 was less than was U.S. reciprocity to other nations' cooperative behavior, whereas other nations reciprocated Soviet cooperative actions more fully than the Soviets reciprocated others' cooperation (Smith, 1987). Again, the effect of relative power on reciprocity may depend on expectations about the use of power. It may be that many nations expected U.S. cooperation to continue despite their own limited reciprocity but believed that full reciprocity was needed to encourage continued Soviet cooperation.

Third-Party Pressures and Norms

Reciprocity may be encouraged or discouraged by pressures from third parties, sometimes stemming from norms or law. People have reported that reciprocity norms influence their behavior (Muir & Weinstein, 1962). Pruitt (1969) pointed out that both laws within nations and international law require aggrieved parties to take others to court rather than to respond themselves when their interests are hurt. He noted too that there are "proportionality" norms that may provide outside pressures against overreacting to another's harmful actions.

Third parties, acting as either active parties (e.g., mediators) or an audience, also may affect reactions to another's behavior. Evidence from both experimental and natural settings indicates that people are more likely to retaliate against coercion from a person of the same gender if an audience is present (Felson, 1982). On the other hand, the presence of an audience that the actor believes opposes the use of coercion will inhibit retaliation (Borden, 1975). Thus, retaliation against coercion appears to be affected by the actor's beliefs about the effects of such actions on social approval and on his or her social identity. Presumably, audiences with differing norms about proper behavior also would differentially affect the likelihood that people will reciprocate reward or cooperation.

Prior Responses of Others

Whether an actor responds to the actions of another with conflictive or cooperative actions may be influenced by how the other has reacted to the actor's behavior in the past. In experimental studies, the probability of a person responding with a cooperative or with a conflictive action is related to the previous sequence of behaviors (e.g., if he or she cooperated previously, whether the other responded with cooperation; Rapoport, 1963). Similarly, the actor's reciprocation of cooperative or conflictive actions by another may be affected by the other's past responses to his or her behavior. Consistent with this proposition, a number of experimental studies (e.g., Reychler, 1979) have found that cooperative actions of Person A are not likely to be reciprocated by Person B when A's cooperation has been unconditional (i.e., he or she has cooperated regardless of what B has done). Given a situation wherein unilateral competitiveness has a higher payoff than does mutual cooperation, B has learned that it pays better not to reciprocate A's cooperative actions. There appears to be little systematic evidence from natural settings, including the international arena, about the effects on reciprocity of the past responses by the other to one's own behavior.

Other Circumstances Affecting Reciprocity

This review of conditions affecting reciprocity is not intended to be exhaustive; other circumstances also may have some effect. I will give attention here to a few other interesting findings from research on interaction between nations (see Smith, 1987).

High levels of reciprocity, both of hostile and cooperative behavior, have been found to be associated with small constants in the equations describing these relations, whereas low levels of reciprocity have been found to be associated with large constants. For example, if leaders of Nation A generally display little hostility toward Nation B, the former tend to react vigorously to any hostile behavior they receive from the latter. On the other hand, if leaders of Nation A generally show much hostility toward Nation B, the former tend to react only slightly to hostile behavior from the latter. It appears, then, that hostility from a friend evokes a stronger reaction than does hostility from a rival, whereas friendly actions from a rival evoke a stronger reaction than does friendly action from a friend.

Contrary to what many would expect, reciprocity of both hostile behavior and cooperative behavior from another nation tend to be positively correlated (i.e., the more a given nation reciprocates hostile behavior from another nation, the more it also reciprocates cooperative behavior). For example, Soviet reciprocity of hostile and of cooperative behavior from the United States from 1952 to 1977 was highly and positively correlated (Smith, 1987).

The average time for national leaders to respond (usually in a reciprocal way) to the actions of another nation is generally shorter when they receive cooperative actions, rather than conflictive actions, from the other. However, in some dyads (e.g., the U.S.–Soviet dyad), the mean time lags for responses to hostile actions were shorter than were those for responses to cooperative actions (Smith, 1987). Smith interpreted these results as a result of variations among dyads in the dominant form of behavior. When one type of behavior toward another nation is usual, officials can respond quickly by following customary patterns. When response involves nontypical behavior (e.g., cooperation during the Cold War), inertia leads to slower speed of response.

Relating Reciprocity to General Theories

Much of the research concerning reciprocity has not been done within the framework of a general theory of interaction. However, there are several types of theoretical explanations that have been explicitly or implicitly applied to this phenomenon.

Social Processes

Some explanations of reciprocity have focused on the social context in which reciprocity occurs. Reciprocity has been seen as occurring in the course of social exchange processes, as being determined by social norms, and as reflecting a competition for favorable social identities.

Exchange processes. Reciprocation of rewards has been seen as part of an ongoing process of social exchange (Blau, 1964; Cook, 1987). If individuals value what they receive from each other, each is likely to give more to his or her partner to provide incentives for the other to increase his or her own contributions as well as to avoid becoming indebted to the other.

Within this theoretical framework, A is more likely to reciprocate B's rewarding actions (i.e., continue the exchange process) when A has a high need for B's rewards, when A lacks alternative sources of such rewards, and when A lacks the ability to seize these rewards by force. Exchange theory has focused on exchanges of rewards and has dealt little with exchanges of punishments.

Norms. Related to, but distinct from, a perspective that views reciprocity as a continuing exchange of rewards, reciprocity has been seen as stemming from acceptance of a norm of appropriate behavior.[1] Gouldner (1960) proposed the widespread existence of a reciprocity norm that stipulates that people should help those who help them and should not hurt those who help them. Individuals act in accordance with this norm both because they seek social approval for desirable behavior and because they have internalized the norm. Although Gouldner's statement of the reciprocity norm does not call for reciprocating punishment, Tedeschi, Smith, and Brown (1974) suggested that norms of equity also extend to the distribution of punishment. They suggested that a person may punish another to redress an unfair distribution of punishments and thus restore equity.

Competition for identities. Reciprocity also has been seen as occurring when individuals compete for the most favorable social identities. From this perspective, the actions of each are intended to manage the impression that the individual has on some audience of significant others and thus to enhance his or her power and status compared with others. A number of researchers have discussed retaliation against aggressive behavior from this perspective (e.g., Felson, 1981; Toch, 1969). Actions by another that inflict insult or harm on a person tend to place him or her in a position of weakness and inferiority. By retaliating, the target of aggression may attempt to show that he or she is strong, courageous, and superior (or at least equal) relative to competitors.

Similarly, reciprocation of cooperative behavior sometimes has been seen as a social process in which actors attempt to manage impressions of wealth, generosity, fairness, and the like in a competition for status (Goffman, 1959; Mauss, 1954; Reis, 1981).[2]

---

[1] *A norm of reciprocity may grow out of exchange processes, but those who emphasize norms do not always discuss their origin.*

[2] *Although the impression management approach focuses on the attempt of people to manipulate their public images, symbolic interaction theory directs attention also to peoples' efforts to maintain and enhance their self-concepts. Thus, the individual may reciprocate against coercive actions to maintain his or her self-image as strong and courageous and may reciprocate*

Psychological Processes

In addition to explanations that focus on the social context of reciprocity, some theoretical approaches focus on the individual psychological processes that may be involved. These include emotional arousal, learning, and decision making.

Emotional arousal. Reciprocation may be seen as occurring because the initial action arouses the emotions of the other. This explanation has been used especially with respect to retaliation against aggressive actions by another (Zillman, Bryant, Cantor, & Day, 1975). Aggressive action by A causes B to become angry, which increases the likelihood of aggressive actions occurring.

Several links between anger and aggressive behavior have been found. A person who is angry usually experiences physiological arousal, which increases the probability that aggressive behavior will occur (Bandura, 1973). Arousal also may increase imitation of aggressive models (O'Neal, McDonald, Hori, McClinton, 1977). In addition, arousal may increase responsiveness to aggressive cues (Caprara, Passerini, Pastorelli, Renzi, & Zelli, 1986). Aggression is most likely to occur when physiological arousal is labeled by the actor as anger, perhaps because such a label helps justify aggressive behavior (Geen, Rakosky, & Pigg, 1972).

Learning. Reciprocation or nonreciprocation of another person's actions may be seen as depending on whether such reciprocation has positive consequences (Rapoport, 1963). Bandura (1973, p. 163) commented that retaliation against verbal or physical assaults may be frequent because retaliation tends to reduce later mistreatment. Conversely, he noted, when a person's retaliatory responses are punished, he or she will tend to submit to, rather than retaliate against, further aggressive actions by the other.

Tendencies to reciprocate cooperative responses also have been seen as being strengthened by a learning process. Thus, Axelrod's (1984) description of the process by which mutual cooperation evolves emphasized peoples' tendencies to repeat actions that have been rewarded.

Decision processes. Reciprocation or nonreciprocation of the conflictive or cooperative actions of another may be seen as resulting from a decision process. Most theories of decision making (Abelson & Levi, 1985) see a person's choice among actions as being the result of (a) the values he or she gives to various possible outcomes of his or her actions, combined with (b) his or her expectancies that particular actions will lead to particular

---

cooperation to maintain a self-image as a person who is kind, generous, Christian, and so on—regardless of the effect on his or her public image.

outcomes. Each action has an expected value based on a combination of (a) and (b). Thus, a person will reciprocate a coercive action by another if he or she expects that action to have an expected value higher than the expected value of nonreciprocation. A number of scholars have used decision models to predict when conflictive and cooperative behaviors will be chosen and reciprocated in both interpersonal and internation interactions (e.g., Bueno de Mesquita, 1981; Tedeschi et al., 1972).

Elaboration of a Decision Theory Framework

A decision theory model provides a theoretical framework within which the various factors discussed earlier as affecting the occurrence of reciprocity may be organized. A decision model also can encompass the variables and processes dealt with by other explanations of reciprocity (i.e., emotional arousal, learning, social norms, social exchange, and competition over identities). A conceptual framework for explaining reciprocity from a decision perspective is shown in Figure 1.

Figure 1 shows in the right-hand side a number of values and expectancies that are relevant to an actor's choice to reciprocate a recent action (conflictive or cooperative) of

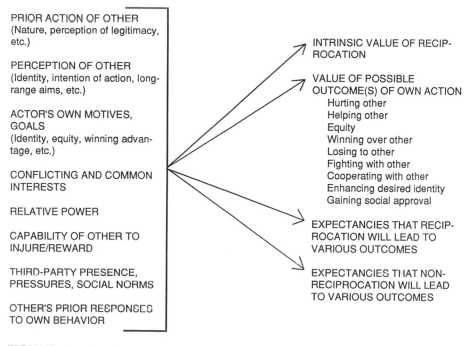

FIGURE 1   A decision theory framework for explaining reciprocity.

another or to take some alternative nonreciprocal action. The values are those that the actor gives to various possible outcomes of his or her action. They include such outcomes as hurting the other, helping the other, securing justice or equity, winning over the other with respect to a dispute in which they are engaged (with whatever material and nonmaterial benefits winning brings), losing to the other, fighting (physical, verbal, legal, etc.) with the other, cooperating with or recieving help from the other, enhancing one's own desired identity (e.g., as tough, courageous, fair, benevolent), and getting social approval. The value of each of these possible outcomes to the actor will be determined by the rewards and costs (physical and psychological) perceived to be associated with the outcome and the importance of such rewards or costs to the actor.

The right-hand side of Figure 1 also includes the actor's expectancies that either reciprocation or nonreciprocation (e.g., of coercive actions) by the other will lead to any or all of the outcomes just discussed.

The factors listed in the left-hand side of Figure 1 may affect the occurrence of reciprocity by affecting the valuation that the actor gives to various outcomes or the actor's expectancies about the outcomes of his or her actions. Without attempting to be exhaustive in indicating all such possible connections, I suggest some of the possible linkages.

If the prior action of the other is seen by the actor as provocative and illegitimate, the actor may give greater value to hurting ("getting even with") the other and also may give high value to winning over the other.

If the other is a competitor for status or is seen as having dangerous long-range aims, then the value to the actor of winning over the other may be enhanced, and his or her expectancy that reciprocating cooperative moves by the other will lead to lasting cooperation will be decreased.

The actor's own motives will, of course, affect the value to him or her of particular outcomes. If, for example, the actor generally is motivated to defend and enhance his identity as a tough macho man, this will increase the value of that outcome in this interaction. However, the impact of general motives will vary in different circumstances. For example, if the actor is a young man and the other is an elderly women (i.e., not a competitor with respect to toughness), the actor will not be likely to place high value on enhancing his macho image in this interaction.

If the actor and the other have conflicting interests (e.g., over who will possess some valuable object), then the value to the actor of winning over the other will be increased and the value of losing decreased. The greater the common interests of the parties, relative to conflicting interests, the more valued will be cooperation with the other.

The absolute and relative power of the other will affect the value to the actor of a fight. The greater the ability of the other to impose damage (or to withhold rewards), the greater the cost of a fight. The greater the relative power of the other, the less likely is the actor to be the winner of any fight. Relative power also is likely to affect the actor's expectancies about the likely responses of the other to his or her own action. For example, if the other is relatively strong, the actor probably will expect that if he or she reciprocates coercion, the other will continue (and even intensify) coercive actions.

Social norms and third-party pressures may affect the actor's valuation of some outcomes. If there are clear social norms that apply to the interaction and if third parties pressure the actor to do "what is right," then the value to the actor of restoring equity may be increased. Active involvement by third parties also may affect the actor's expectancies. For example, a third party may serve as a "guarantor" of pacific actions by both sides and thus lead the actor to expect that his or her reciprocation of some cooperative move by the other will lead to long-range cooperation.

Finally, the other's prior history of responses to the actor's behavior may affect the actor's values and especially his or her expectancies. If, for example, the other has often responded to cooperative moves with conflictive actions, the actor may be angry and may wish to hurt the other. More important probably, the actor will not expect that his or her reciprocation of a cooperative action by the other will lead to long-range cooperation.

The relations shown in Figure 1 encompass a number of processes that have been highlighted in the various explanations of reciprocity discussed thus far. Some of the effects shown in Figure 1 involve emotional arousal; for example, provocative, "illegitimate" actions may make the actor angry and lead him or her to value highly hurting the other person. Learning processes are involved in that the actor's expectancies about the outcomes of his or her actions are shaped to a considerable extent by past experience. This is shown most clearly by the connection between the other's past responses to the actor's behavior and the actor's current values and expectancies. But other connections also are affected by the actor's more general prior experiences. For example, he or she may have learned that when a person with a certain identity (e.g., a motorcycle gang member) makes a threat, reciprocation of this threat is highly likely to lead to a physical fight.

The role of social norms in reciprocity is shown in the connection between the presence of particular norms of reciprocity and (a) valuing equity and especially (b) the actor's expectations that reciprocation of coercion or cooperation will lead to social approval.

Several of the factors in the left-hand side of Figure 1 are especially relevant to possible attempts by a person to enhance his or her public identity relative to that of others. If the actor's own motives include the desire to enhance his or her public image with respect to a given characteristic and the other person is a competitor or plausible comparison person with respect to this characteristic and also there is an audience, then the actor is apt to be concerned with enhancing his or her public identity in this situation and to expect that reciprocation will have this result.

Finally, several of the determinants of values and expectancies listed in the left-hand side of Figure 1 are relevant to exchange processes. The extent of common and conflicting interests between the actor and the other and their capability to reward and injure each other determine the extent to which the actor is dependent on the other. When dependence on the other is high, each actor will tend to give high value to cooperation and low value to a fight (and thus tend to reciprocate cooperation but not coercion). The social exchange perspective, which emphasizes actors' concerns with establishing equity in exchange, also is consistent with attention to the valuation given by the actor to justice or equity in his or her relationship with the other.

The decision theory framework shown in Figure 1 is intended to take into account a wide range of variables, suggested by diverse theoretical perspectives. Within this framework, a large number of specific variables may be understood in terms of the same basic factors—values and expectancies—that determine choice. Although this theoretical approach focuses on the choices of individuals, it incorporates in the decision process variables that derive from the social relationships in which the individual is involved, as well as individual variables.

Summary and Conclusions

This chapter has reviewed evidence and theory concerning reciprocity, with special attention to research on interaction between nations.

A preliminary but important question is the extent to which each actor reacts to the actions of another rather than being impelled by internal forces. Research on internation interaction indicates that reactivity by national leaders to another nation's behavior varies with the type of behavior and with the intensity of conflict between the two nations. It would be interesting to know more about whether these results at the internation level are found also in various interpersonal settings.

The most distinctive contribution from research on interaction between nations concerns the nature of the reciprocity process. Reciprocity between nations has been found to be more complex than a simple tit-for-tat process. Among other things, national leaders may overmatch or undermatch the other's actions, depending on the magnitude of the provocation; they may respond to changes in, rather than the absolute nature of, the other's behavior; and they may respond to differences between the other's prior behavior and their own prior behavior. More research is needed to test the relative predictive power of alternative models of the reciprocity process and also to construct models that incorporate variables from several models. For example, the responses of an actor may depend on the absolute nature of the other's actions, plus the direction of change in the other's recent actions, plus the difference between the other's and the actor's own recent behaviors. Testing of such specific models of reciprocity is needed with respect to interaction between nations. Parallel research is needed also concerning reciprocity in other settings.

People tend to reciprocate both conflictive and cooperative behaviors in many types of relationships, including those between leaders of different nations. Reciprocation of cooperative acts has been found to be greater in general than has reciprocation of conflictful acts. Evidence from a number of settings, including the international, is consistent in indicating that vigorous reciprocation of conflictful behavior often is a sign of an unhealthy relationship.

Whether reciprocity occurs depends on a variety of conditions: The nature of the other's prior actions, the actor's perception of the other, the actor's own motives, the extent of conflicting and common interests between the parties, their relative power, social norms, and the other's prior responses to the actor's own behavior are among the conditioning factors that may determine the occurrence of reciprocity. Research bearing on conditions of interaction between national leaders is generally consistent with research on other types of interactions, although studies in different areas have focused on somewhat different sets of conditions. Future research concerning the occurrence of reciprocity in any specific type of relationship (husband–wife, parent–child, employer–worker, national leaders) should take fuller account of the entire range of conditioning factors that have been studied in a broad range of settings.

Most research on reciprocity, and especially that on interaction between nations, has not been guided explicitly by general theories of social interaction. However, there have been some efforts to explain reciprocity in terms of social exchange, social norms, competition for favorable identities, emotional arousal, learning, and decision making. There is a great need to anchor studies of reciprocity more firmly in general theory.

I have outlined a possible conceptual framework for understanding reciprocity in terms of the actor's decision making. I have attempted to show how the various factors found to be related to reciprocity may have their effects by linking them to the valuations given by the actor to possible outcomes of his or her actions and to his or her expectancies that the actions will result in these outcomes. Such an analysis may help us understand the circumstances under which reciprocity occurs.

Research on reciprocity to date generally has been done with respect to specific types of behavior and interaction—aggression, altruism, bargaining, marital relations, internation interaction, and so on—with researchers in each specific area paying little attention to work on reciprocity in other areas. This review suggests that work on reciprocity between nations and in other relationships may have mutual benefits. More generally, researchers interested in particular types of relationships may benefit from theory and research about reciprocity as a general social process.

References

Abelson, R. P., & Levi, A. (1985). Decision-making and decision theory. In G. Lindzey & E. Aronson (Eds.), *Handbook of social psychology* (3rd ed., Vol. 1, pp. 231–310). New York: Random House.

Axelrod, R. (1984). *The evolution of cooperation.* New York: Basic Books.

Bacharach, S. B., & Lawler, E. J. (1981). *Bargaining.* San Francisco: Jossey-Bass.

Bandura, A. (1973). *Aggression: A social learning analysis.* Englewood Cliffs, NJ: Prentice-Hall.

Bar-Tal, D. (1976). *Prosocial behavior: Theory and research.* New York: Halsted.

Berkowitz, L., & Geen, R. G. (1966). Film violence and the cue properties of available targets. *Journal of Personality and Social Psychology, 3,* 525–530.

Blau, P. (1964). *Exchange and power in social life.* New York: Wiley.

Blechman, B. M. (1972). Impact of Israel's reprisals on Arab behavior. *Journal of Conflict Resolution, 16,* 155–181.

Borden, R. J. (1975). Witnessed aggression: Influence of an observer's sex and values on aggressive responding. *Journal of Personality and Social Psychology, 31,* 567–573.

Brockner, J., & Rubin, J. Z. (1985). *Entrapment in escalating conflicts: A social psychological analysis.* New York: Springer-Verlag.

Bueno de Mesquita, B. (1981). *The war trap.* New Haven, CT: Yale University Press.

Caprara, G. V., Passerini, S., Pastorelli, S., Renzi, P., & Zelli, A. (1986). Instigating and measuring interpersonal aggression and hostility: A methodological contribution. *Aggressive Behavior, 12,* 237–247.

Chertkoff, J. M., & Esser, J. K. (1976). A review of experiments in explicit bargaining. *Journal of Experimental Social Psychology, 12,* 464–487.

Cohen, R. (1979). *Threat perception in international crisis.* Madison: University of Wisconsin Press.

Cook, K. (Ed.). (1987). *Social exchange theory.* Newbury Park, CA: Sage.

Corson, W. H., II. (1970). *Conflict and cooperation in East–West crises: Dynamics of crisis interaction.* Unpublished doctorial dissertation, Department of Social Relations, Harvard University, Cambridge, MA.

Deutsch, M. (1973). *The resolution of conflict.* New Haven, CT: Yale University Press.

Dixon, W. J. (1986). Reciprocity in United States–Soviet relations: Multiple symmetry or issue linkage? *American Journal of Political Science, 30,* 421–445.

Dixon, W. J. (1988). The discrete sequential analysis of dynamic international behavior. *Quality and Quantity, 22,* 238–254.

Druckman, D. (1983). Social psychology and international negotiations: Processes and influences. In R. F. Kidd & J. M. Saks (Eds.), *Advances in applied social psychology* (Vol. 2, pp. 51–81). Hillsdale, NJ: Erlbaum.

Druckman, D., & Harris, R. (1990). Alternative models of responsiveness in international negotiations. *Journal of Conflict Resolution, 34,* 234–251.

Felson, R. B. (1981). An interactionist approach to aggression. In J. T. Tedeschi (Ed.), *Impression management theory and social psychological research* (pp. 181–200). San Diego, CA: Academic Press.

Felson, R. B. (1982). Impression management and the escalation of aggression and violence. *Social Psychology Quarterly, 45,* 245–254.

Felson, R. B., & Steadman, H. J. (1983). Situations and processes leading to criminal violence. *Criminology, 31,* 59–74.

Ferguson, T. J., & Rule, B. G. (1983). An attributional perspective on anger and aggression. In E. Donnerstein & R. G. Geen (Eds.), *Aggression: Theoretical and empirical reviews* (Vol. 1, pp. 41–74). San Diego, CA: Academic Press.

Fishman, C. G. (1965). Need for approval and the expression of aggression under varying conditions of frustration. *Journal of Personality and Social Psychology, 2,* 809–816.

Freeman, J. R., & Goldstein, J. S. (1989). *U.S.–Soviet–Chinese relations: Routine, reciprocity, or rational expectations.* Minneapolis: Department of Political Science, University of Minnesota.

Gamson, W., & Modigliani, A. (1971). *Untangling the Cold War.* Boston: Little-Brown.

Geen, R. G., Rakosky, J., & Pigg, R. (1972). Awareness of arousal and its relation to aggression. *British Journal of Social and Clinical Psychology, 11,* 1115–1121.

Goffman, E. (1959). *The presentation of self in everyday life.* New York: Doubleday.

Goldstein, J. H., Davids, R. W., & Herman, D. (1975). Escalating of aggression: Experimental studies. *Journal of Personality and Social Psychology, 31,* 162–170.

Goldstein, J. S., & Freeman, J. R. (1990). *Three-way street: Strategic reciprocity in world politics.* Chicago: University of Chicago Press.

Gottman, J. M. (1979). *Marital interaction: Experimental investigations.* San Diego, CA: Academic Press.

Gouldner, A. (1960). The norm of reciprocity: A preliminary statement. *American Sociological Review, 25,* 161–178.

Greenberg, M. (1980). A theory of indebtedness. In K. J. Gergen, M. Greenberg, & R. H. Willis (Eds.), *Social exchange: Advances in theory and research* (pp. 3–26). New York: Plenum Press.

Greenberg, M., & Frisch, D. (1972). Effect of intentionality on willingness to reciprocate a favor. *Journal of Experimental Social Psychology, 8,* 99–111.

Greffenius, S. (1989, March). *Measure for measure: Patterns of reciprocity in militarized disputes, 1816–1975.* Paper presented at the meeting of the International Studies Association, London.

Hoagland, S. W., & Walker, S. G. (1979). Operational codes and crises outcomes. In L. S. Falkowski (Ed.), *Psychological models in international politics* (pp. 125–168). Boulder, CO: Westview.

Holsti, O. R., Brody, R., & North, R. C. (1969). The management of international crises: Affect and interaction in American–Soviet relations. In D. G. Pruitt & R. C. Snyder (Eds.), *Theory and research on the causes of war* (pp. 62–79). Englewood Cliffs, NJ: Prentice-Hall.

Horai, J., & Tedeschi, J. T. (1969). The effects of credibility, magnitude of punishment and compliance to threats. *Journal of Personality and Social Psychology, 12,* 164–169.

Hornstein, H. A. (1965). The effects of different magnitudes of threat upon interpersonal bargaining. *Journal of Experimental Social Psychology, 1,* 282–293.

James, P., & Harvey, F. (1989, November). *The most dangerous game: Superpower rivalry in international crises, 1948–1985.* Paper presented at the meeting of the Peace Science Society, Columbus, OH.

Kaplowitz, N. (1984). Psychopolitical dimensions of international relations: The reciprocal effects of conflict strategies. *International Studies Quarterly, 28,* 373–406.

Kelley, H., & Thibaut, J. (1978). *Interpersonal relations.* New York: Wiley.

Leng, R. J. (1980). Influence strategies and interstate conflict. In J. D. Singer (Ed.), *The correlates of war* (Vol. 2, pp. 124–160). New York: Free Press.

Lindskold, S. (1978). Trust development, the GRIT proposal, and effects of conciliatory acts on conflict and cooperation. *Psychological Bulletin, 85,* 772–779.

Lindskold, S., & Aronoff, J. R. (1980). Conciliatory strategies and relative power. *Journal of Experimental Social Psychology, 16,* 187–198.

Malinowski, B. (1961). *Argonauts of the Western Pacific.* New York: Dutton.

Mauss, M. (1954). *The gift.* Glencoe, IL: Free Press.

Milburn, T. W., & Watman, K. H. (1981). *On the nature of threat: A social-psychological analysis.* London: Praeger.

Muir, D., & Weinstein, E. (1962). The social debt: An investigation of lower-class and middle-class norms of social obligation. *American Sociological Review, 27,* 532–539.

Nincic, M. (1989). *Anatomy of hostility: The U.S.–Soviet rivalry in perspective.* San Diego, CA: Harcourt Brace Jovanovich.

O'Leary, M. R., & Dengerink, H. A. (1973). Aggression as a function of the intensity and pattern of attack. *Journal of Experimental Research in Personality, 7,* 61–70.

O'Neal, E. C., McDonald, P., Hori, R., & McClinton, B. (1977). Arousal and imitation of aggression. *Motivation and Emotion, 1,* 93–100.

Patchen, M. (1987). The escalation of inter-nation conflicts. *Sociological Focus, 20,* 95–110.

Patchen, M. (1988). *Resolving disputes between nations: Coercion or conciliation?* Durham, NC: Duke University Press.

Patchen, M. (1991). Conflict and cooperation in U.S.–Soviet relations: What have we learned from quantitative research? *International Interactions, 17,* 127–143.

Patterson, G. R. (1982). *Coercive family process.* Eugene, OR: Castalia.

Pruitt, D. G. (1969). Stability and sudden change in interpersonal and international affairs. *Journal of Conflict Resolution, 13,* 18–38.

Pruitt, D. G. (1981). *Negotiation behavior.* San Diego, CA: Academic Press.

Pruitt, G., & Rubin, J. Z. (1986). *Social conflict: Escalation, stalemate, and settlement.* New York: Random House.

Putnam, L. L., & Jones, T. S. (1982). Reciprocity in negotiations: An analysis of bargaining interactions. *Communication Monographs, 49,* 171–191.

Rajmaira, S., & Ward, M. D. (1990). Evolving foreign policy norms: Reciprocity in the superpower triad. *International Studies Quarterly, 34,* 457–476.

Rapoport, A. (1963). *A stochastic model for prisoner's dilemma.* Ann Arbor, MI: Mental Health Research Institute.

Reis, H. T. (1981). Self-presentation and distributive justice. In J. T. Tedeschi (Ed.), *Impression management theory and social psychological research* (pp. 269–291). San Diego, CA: Academic Press.

Reychler, L. (1979). The effectiveness of a pacifist strategy in conflict resolution: An experimental study. *Journal of Conflict Resolution, 23,* 228–260.

Rubin, J. Z., & Brown, B. R. (1975). *The social psychology of bargaining and negotiation.* San Diego, CA: Academic Press.

Smith, D. L. (1987). *Linking the foreign policy process to international action.* Unpublished doctoral dissertation, Department of Political Science, Massachusetts Institute of Technology, Cambridge, MA.

Snyder, G., & Diesing, P. (1977). *Conflict among nations.* Princeton, NJ: Princeton University Press.

Stoll, R. J., & McAndrew, W. (1986). Negotiating strategic arms control, 1969–1979: Modelling the bargaining process. *Journal of Conflict Resolution, 30,* 315–326.

Tanter, R. (1974). *Modelling and managing international conflicts: The Berlin crises.* Newbury Park, CA: Sage.

Taylor, S. P. (1967). Aggressive behavior and physiological arousal as a function of provocation and the tendency to inhibit aggression. *Journal of Personality, 35,* 297–310.

Tedeschi, J. T., & Bonoma, T. V. (1977). Measures of last resort: Coercion and aggression in bargaining. In D. Druckman (Ed.), *Negotiations: Social psychological perspectives* (pp. 213–242). Newbury Park, CA: Sage.

Tedeschi, J. T., & Felson, R. B. (1993). *Aggression and coercive actions: A social interactionist view.* Manuscript in preparation.

Tedeschi, J. T., Schlenker, B. R., & Lindskold, S. (1972). The exercise of power and influence. In J. T. Tedeschi (Ed.), *The social influence process.* Chicago: Aldine-Atherton.

Tedeschi, J. T., Smith, R. B., III, & Brown, R.C., Jr. (1974). A reinterpretation of research on aggression. *Psychological Bulletin, 81,* 540–563.

Toch, H. (1969). *Violent men.* Chicago: Aldine.

Wills, T. A., Weiss, R. L., & Patterson, G. R. (1974). A behavioral analysis of the determinants of mental satisfaction. *Journal of Consulting and Clinical Psychology, 42,* 802–811.

Zillman, D., Bryant, J., Cantor, J., & Day, K. (1975). Irrelevance of mitigating circumstances in retaliatory behavior at high levels of arousal. *Journal of Research in Personality, 9,* 282–293.

CHAPTER 6

Aggression: Interaction Between Individuals and Social Groups

Amelie Mummendey and Sabine Otten

A ggression and violence committed by and between social groups is a major problem within human societies. Social psychological approaches toward group aggression focus mainly on the individual level of analysis. Most of the research offers simple extrapolations from the individual level to the group level (one of the famous examples is the frustration–aggression hypothesis; Dollard, Doob, Miller, Mowrer, & Sears, 1939). However, those stressing the necessity of developing theories of intergroup behavior have become more vocal. For example, Tajfel (1978) emphasized the discontinuity between individuals acting as unaffiliated individuals and acting as members of a group. Like Sherif (1966), he stressed the importance of the structure of intergroup relations; beyond that, he postulated different psychological processes operating at the interpersonal and intergroup levels.

In social contexts, however, individuals think, feel, and act: "'Social' phenomena necessarily arise from and are maintained by human cognition and motivation" (Condor & Brown, 1988, p. 17).

In this chapter, we depart from separately analyzing aggression and violence as either interpersonal or intergroup. Rather, we systematically analyze the relation between the two contexts. We identify the variance of aggression as corresponding to the interpersonal–intergroup continuum. This conceptualization should allow identification of crucial variables that explain aggressive interactions either as interpersonal or intergroup behavior.

In the first part of this chapter, we outline our concept of aggression as a particular kind of social interaction; we also derive some thoughts about the relation of interpersonal to intergroup aggression and finally report some results of several preliminary studies.

Aggression as a Particular Kind of Social Interaction

After a longer discussion about the deficiency of former definitions, Baron (1977) proposed the following definition of aggressive behavior: "Aggression is any form of behavior directed toward the goal of harming or injuring another living being who is motivated to avoid such treatment" (p. 7). The problem with this definition is that it takes a third-party stance toward the behavior of the individual and ignores the perspectives of the two parties involved in the interaction. To identify a particular behavior as aggressive requires an examination of both the intentions of the perpetrator and the perceptions and evaluations of the victim. The identification of a behavior as aggressive involves a description of social interaction that takes into account both the perpetrator's and the victim's points of view.

There is little awareness among aggression theorists of the perspective that they use to identify the critical event. Usually, they use the perspective of the outside observer (e.g., the experimenter), who perceives that a perpetrator has performed an action that has negative consequences for a victim. However, the social consensus about the observer's perceptions and interpretations is taken for granted or is at least overestimated. It is not at all self-evident that different observers would agree on whether a particular event is aggressive. Even more crucial for aggression research, it is unlikely that the participants in an aggressive interaction would have interpretations of the situation similar to those of other participants, the experimenter, or other observers.[1] On the contrary, as we discuss later, it is the perspective-specific variability (i.e., the relativity of perception and

---

[1] Compare the discussion of the validity of aggression simulators such as the Buss-Berkowitz masculine type (Baron & Eggleston, 1972; Schuck & Pisor, 1974).

interpretation) that produces some of the typical features of aggression. For an adequate conceptualization of aggression and for a research orientation that is consistent with the definition of aggression just given, it is necessary to take into account not only the antecedent conditions that influence the perpetrator's behavior but also variables that influence his or her interpretation of the consequences for the victim. In addition, because the identification of an event as aggression necessarily presumes various inferences by the observer (e.g., about goals, intent, and consequences), antecedent conditions influencing these inferences should also be a focus of conceptual and empirical work. For an event to be identified as aggressive, someone—after interpreting selective information—must come to believe that the criteria specified in the definition are met. In Baron's (1977) definition, for example, there are two criteria: The perpetrator must have an intent to cause harm, and the victim must be motivated to avoid this harm. Several authors have pointed out a third criterion: There must be a violation of some norm (cf. DaGloria & DeRidder, 1977; Ferguson & Rule, 1983; Mummendey, Bornewasser, Loeschper, & Linneweber, 1982; Pepitone, 1981; Tedeschi, Smith, & Brown, 1974). The information necessary to decide whether the criteria of the definition are met are obtained from both the perpetrator and the victim.

We shall begin by describing the essential aspects of an aggressive interaction. An event identified as aggressive by an observer—whether that person is the victim or a third party—has the following characteristics (Mummendey, Linneweber, & Loeschper, 1984b):

1. A person [the recipient or victim] runs into conditions which [s]he wants to avoid. This means the recipient suffers harm or injury or would have suffered it if chance or luck wouldn't have prevented it.
2. Under ordinary circumstances, these conditions would have been avoidable. They wouldn't have occurred if another person or agent [the actor or aggressor] hadn't created them [cf. Arendt, 1970, and Bernstein, 1926/1980, for more details about the crucial role of avoidability of aversive events in violence and hostility]. The actor thus decided to perform an action causing these conditions, albeit having further alternatives of actions which might have produced less aversive conditions for the recipient. This means the actor caused the aversive consequences and is responsible for them.
3. To have created these aversive conditions for this recipient within that particular situation is evaluated as violating situationally relevant norms. A norm violation is

apparent, at least from the victim's perspective, and perhaps from the perspective of an outside observer as well. In the eye of the victim, her/his aversive state was caused by the aggressor, although [s]he could, and therefore should, have avoided it. (p.70)

The large variety of aggressive events have these characteristics in common. The pattern includes a particular relationship between the actor and recipient with respect to the critical action: The perpetrator's choice of the action is seen as the result of a more or less conscious or deliberate decision from among a variety of perceived alternatives. The choice of that particular action is—from the perpetrator's point of view—rational; that is, it is the most appropriate alternative among those that appeared to be available in a given situation.

The victim of the consequences created by the critical action, however, disagrees about the appropriateness of the perpetrator's choice. He or she imputes the availability of alternatives that may cause less aversive consequences in that particular situation. The thoughts of perpetrators and victims are similar to those that Ross (1977) identified in the "false consensus":

> Laymen tend to perceive a "false consensus," that is to see their own behavioral choices and judgments as relatively common and appropriate to existing circumstances while viewing alternative responses as uncommon, deviant and inappropriate. The intuitive psychologist's estimates of deviancy and normalcy and the host of social inferences and interpersonal responses that accompany such estimates are systematically and egocentrically biased in accord with [his or her] own behavioral choices. (p. 190)

Factors Influencing the Perspective-Specific Divergence

In an aggressive interaction, the interpretation and evaluation of the situational appropriateness of the critical action are a function of each participant's role in the specific interaction (i.e., whether they are the perpetrator or the victim). This divergence between perpetrator and victim has an impact on the further course of the interaction sequence. Retaliation for a provocation may be perceived as appropriate by the victim but not by the original perpetrator and so on. Whether the interaction continues, whether the conflict escalates, and whether the victim is compensated all depend on the degree of agreement between the perpetrator's and the victim's interpretations and evaluations.

If the participants have contradictory views about the aggressive interaction, then neither will be willing to consider or accept the arguments of the other. Each will claim that the other's behavior was inappropriate and will therefore—applying the norm of reciprocity (Gouldner, 1960)—feel entitled to retaliation.

Because divergent perspectives are important for the termination and resolution of aggressive conflicts, it is particularly important to identify conditions that have an impact on the extent of judgmental difference. On the one hand, what factors support the divergence and stabilize it over time, and, on the other, what conditions facilitate a convergence in the opponents' judgments?

Subjective Confidence: The Generation of Alternative Interpretations

In a previous experiment (Mummendey & Otten, 1989), we found no evidence that the perspective-specific divergence in the evaluation of inappropriateness was based on an perpetrator or victim-specific perception of the aggressive interaction and the embedding situation. Although the information available to participants was essentially the same, they selected and weighted differently aspects as relevant for the evaluation of the aggressive action. Therefore, the divergence in perspective should be primarily analyzed as a cognitive-motivational phenomenon rather than a perceptual one.

Kruglanski's theory of lay epistemology deals with the cognitive-motivational determination of judgments on a more general level (e.g., Kruglanski, 1980, 1988; Kruglanski & Ajzen, 1983). He claimed that the mechanisms postulated in his theory are applicable to describing all domains of human knowledge seeking (e.g., Kruglanski, Baldwin, & Towson, 1985). We use the theory of lay epistemology to systematize the search for determinants of the divergence in perspective. We consider factors that may affect the way individuals generate and validate hypotheses about given aggressive events.

A central factor in Kruglanski's theory of lay epistemology is subjective confidence. All knowledge consists of specific contents plus the confidence with which they are held. The generation and validation of hypotheses for a given event are terminated as soon as the layperson feels sufficiently confident in an explanation. The higher the confidence in a given judgment, the less willing is the layperson to take into account inconsistent information and alternative interpretations. High confidence is also accompanied by an increase in the polarization of judgments (see, e.g., Fraser, Gouge, & Billig, 1971; Myers & Lamm, 1976).

According to Kruglanski, the number and variety of hypotheses a person considers until he or she feels sufficiently confident and "freezes" a judgment depend on the individual's capacity to generate alternative hypotheses as well as on his or her lay epistemic motivation. The capacity is determined by the individual's prior experiences as well as by situational cues. Three types of motivations are proposed. Each individual is assumed to have a need for structure (i.e., an interest in quickly finding an explanation for the event in question). However, each person also has some fear that the explanation will be invalid. The fear of invalidity increases when the cost for false judgment is high. Finally, people have a preference for desirable conclusions. Their explanations are biased by their individual desires and by the beliefs they favored before the occurrence of the event in question (e.g., social stereotypes).

People with a high need for structure or a low fear of invalidity quickly feel confident with an explanation of a given event. They generate and validate only a few hypotheses and may overlook facts contradicting their own viewpoint. Finally, the preference for desirable conclusions predisposes a person either to continue or discontinue the generation of further alternative hypotheses depending on whether a given hypothesis corresponds to the person's desires.

According to this theory, a divergence in perspective is likely when the generation and validation of hypotheses are terminated quickly. This maintains the dissent between participants. If both parties rely on one of the first hypotheses generated, it is unlikely that they will take into account their counterpart's perspective. Arguments in favor of the opponent will probably be disregarded.

These points suggest a further step in the process of identifying factors that influence the degree of divergence in perspective. We next examine conditions that promote or inhibit generation of alternative interpretations about an aggressive interaction. In our preliminary model, we suggest a number of possible conditions that may affect the subjective confidence of each participant and therefore the level of dissent. We do not consider stable individual differences in the tendency to generate alternative explanations and evaluations, such as open versus closed mindedness, need for structure, and rigidity versus flexibility. Rather, we concentrate on more social psychological processes, including social consensus, empathy, reduction of consciousness, and changes in normative orientation.

Social Consensus

Readiness and willingness to generate alternative explanations and evaluations of a critical event and to admit doubts about one's own evaluation may decrease with an increase in perceived social consensus. Adherence to political and religious ideologies will also reduce tendencies to generate or accept alternative judgments when a hypothesis is consistent with the ideology.

Empathy

Empathy consists of viewing events from another's perspective. To look at the critical action from the perpetrator's perspective is to consider information leading to a judgment that the action was reasonable and relatively appropriate. An empathic victim might be willing to accept a perpetrator's account for his or her behavior, and—as a consequence—refrain from retaliation (Feshbach & Feshbach, 1969, 1982).

Characteristics of the relationship between the two participants may have an affect on their tendency to empathize with each other. The victim may be willing to accept justifications and apologies that are offered by the perpetrator or to generate alternative judgments and evaluations of the action. To do so, the victim must consider the situation, possible reasons for the action, constraints, and so on from the perpetrator's perspective. Alternatively, the perpetrator may consider the victim's situation and modify his or her judgment about the appropriateness of his or her action.

The willingness of the victim to consider the perpetrator's perspective may be negatively correlated with the amount of perceived harm, the perceived severity of the action, and the amount of anger he or she has experienced. The more the participants perceive themselves as similar to each other and the more they perceive themselves as dependent on each other, the more willing they will be to take the other's perspective (Hoffman, 1982; Miller & Eisenberg, 1988; Mummendey, 1987). Empirical evidence supports these relations (Brown & Tedeschi, 1976). There is a positive relation between the severity of consequences of an action and the amount of sanctions that are perceived as appropriate (Loeschper, Mummendey, Linneweber, & Bornwasser, 1984). At the same time, the degree of negative evaluation in terms of ascribed aggression and punishment decreases significantly if the perpetrator offers an apologizing explanation. In other words, the perpetrator influences the victim's interpretation by offering information that is typically neglected by the victim (Brown & Tedeschi, 1976).

Interpersonal and Intergroup Aggression

Some of these factors can be used to examine the different perspectives of participants in interpreting and evaluating aggressive interactions in interpersonal and intergroup situations. Before doing so, we give a survey of some theories and experiments concerned with the effect of social groups on behavior. The contending theories emphasize the effect of the group situation on either the individual's state of consciousness or adherence to emerging or salient norms.

States of Consciousness

Following the mass psychology tradition (LeBon, 1895; see Reicher, 1982), various social psychological approaches have suggested that individuals engage in more norm violations and irrational and impulsive behavior in groups than they do when alone. Some of the most influential theories of collective behavior attempt to explain this difference.

Early social psychological theories dealing with the social behavior of individuals acting as parts of larger groups take a very negative, pessimistic view of the influence of group membership (see Brown, 1988; Reicher, 1982). They postulate the so-called "group-mind thesis" that in a group, the individual becomes irrational, loses consciousness of the self as an individual, and is less concerned with morality. This change toward more primitive, deviant behavior is a result of anonymity, diffusion of responsibility, and feelings of increased power and invulnerability, as well as of unconscious, instinctive forces released by the group situation.

One of the best known theoretical approaches to the phenomenon of collective aggression is that of postulating deindividuating processes within social groups that lower consciousness about normative concerns and moral responsibility (Diener, 1980; Festinger, Pepitone, & Newcomb 1952; Zimbardo, 1969). Deindividuation is influenced by a number of input variables such as anonymity, diffusion of responsibility, changes in time perspective, and changes in states of consciousness. Deindividuation explains conditions that lead to seemingly meaningless and irrational kinds of violence and destruction. Individual control of motivational processes is efficient under normal conditions and guarantees orderly and rational behavior. Under conditions of deindividuation, however, that control is diminished. Crowds and other situations with large numbers of people provide favorable conditions for deindividuation. But, as Diener (1980) explained, deindividuation does not necessarily produce antisocial behavior:

> Deindividuation does not necessarily lead to destructive or antisocial behavior but does release the person from both societal norms and personal standards that normally influence behavior. However, what the person does when deindividuated will depend on his or her motivations and desires at the time and on situational influences such as the behavior of models . . . In other words, the person may perform behavior that he or she would usually inhibit but this behavior may be either prosocial, antisocial or morally neutral as judged by society's norms. (p. 231)

Changes in Normative Orientation

The behavior of models is one of the key factors in another theory of collective behavior. In their emergent norm theory, Turner and Kilian (1972) suggested that people in crowds behave in accordance with social norms that emerge in the collective situation. As soon as such a norm has emerged, there is a pressure against nonconformity. The individual's motive to conform to the "emergent norm" is a desire for social approval and fear of social disapproval.

Turner and Kilian (1972) stressed that the apparent uniformity in groups is an illusion experienced by outside observers as well as by individuals in the group. Within the group, there are typically only a few active individuals who behave distinctively, attract the attention of the majority of passive crowd members, and establish a new norm. Reicher (1982) summarized this process as follows:

> This norm itself is the product of the actions of a few active and conspicuous members, which, being perceived as the dominant mode of behavior, constrains the activity of the other members. Thus, a person behaves as he does in the crowd because that behavior is seen as appropriate or required. (p. 65)

The main distinction between emergent norm theory and the mass psychology/deindividuation approach is that in the former, collective behavior is treated as the product of normative orientation and adaptation. The crowd does not release the individual from conformity to norms but brings about new norms with which the individual feels obliged to conform.

The normative regulation of group behavior is also a central factor in Rabbie's (1982) theory of norm enhancement. In contrast to Turner and Kilian (1972), Rabbie did not stress the development of new norms in group situations but claimed that in intragroup interaction there is an increase in the salience and perceived legitimacy of already-existing norms. Group membership may support prosocial or antisocial behavior. Groups are more aggressive and more hostile than are unaffiliated individuals only if aggressive behavior is in accordance with the prevailing norm of the given situation. For example, radical neofascists may behave more violently in a group situation, whereas members of the peace movement may behave less violently. On the other hand, if perpetrators perceive their own aggressive behavior as legitimate punishment for a victim's norm-violating behavior, groups will give more intense punishment than will individuals.

Norm enhancement is caused by processes of social comparison as well as mutual support during intragroup interaction, both of which allow the generation of socially shared consensus concerning the prevailing norm. When norm enhancement takes place in groups, it may cause group members to react more aggressively to violations of relevant norms than would individuals acting alone.

Rabbie (1987) and Lodewijkx (1989) further developed their behavioral interaction models by proposing that *enhancement* refers not only to normative but also to emotional and motivational processes of individuals embedded in social groups:

> Intragroup interaction enhances the cognitive, emotional, motivational and normative orientations as [group members] try to cope with an uncertain environment . . . The level of emotional arousal in the group—e.g. how they feel about themselves and the other party— and the dominant normative orientations: how one ought to behave in intergroup conflict, will determine the nature of intergroup behavior. (Rabbie, Schot, & Visser 1989, p. 180)

As Rabbie (1982) pointed out, the empirical evidence that individuals behave more irrationally or immorally in groups than alone is rather weak. Only a few systematic comparisons have been made between individual and real group situations with respect to aggression.

Empirical Evidence

Mainly influenced by the concept of deindividuation, Jaffe and Yinon (1979, 1983) hypothesized a higher level of aggression for subjects acting in groups than for those acting individually. The authors used the Buss (1961) aggression machine and the teacher/learner paradigm for measuring aggression. Subjects were instructed that they could control the learning of a pupil (who actually was a confederate of the experimenter) by delivering electric shocks whenever the learner failed to answer a question correctly. Subjects were free to choose the intensities of the shocks. In the individual condition, each subject reacted to incorrect responses by the pupil. In the group condition, three subjects decided consensually on the intensity of the punishment. In the 1979 study, subjects first had to take the learner's role and were administered several punishments by the confederate. In this stage of the experiment, subjects should feel provoked and thus be provided with legitimation for retaliation. Roles were then changed, and subjects had the opportunity to deliver shocks to the confederate. In the 1983 study, subjects experienced no provocation at the beginning of the experiment; thus, aggressive behavior was not retaliatory but instrumental in the sense that its purpose was to improve learning.

Results of both studies showed that groups administered higher levels of electric shocks than did individual subjects. Jaffe and Yinon (1983) explained their results mainly in terms of the diffusion of responsibility among group members. They assumed that the subjects in groups delivered more extreme punishments because

> as compared with his isolated counterpart, our typical group member seemed also to feel less identifiable and detectable by outsiders . . . Feeling relatively anonymous and less liable for punishments and retaliation, he apparently experienced a lessened fear of punishment and sensed himself to be freer from this and other inhibitions which normally restrain antisocial behavior. (p. 274)

One criticism of these experiments challenges their relevance for the comparison of individuals' and group members' aggressive behavior. One may ask whether delivering electric shocks in the learning experiment paradigm constitutes aggressive behavior, given that subjects are told that they can use shock as a means for enhancing the learner's performance. Thus, two opposite motives are confounded: the intention to benefit and the intention to harm.

The experiments of Jaffe and Yinon (1979, 1983) were guided by the assumption that acting as a group member increases the aggressive behavior of individuals. In general, groups displayed a higher intensity of aggression than did individuals. Rabbie and his co-workers (e.g., Rabbie, 1982; Rabbie & Lodewijkx, 1987) took a less pessimistic view on group aggression. Their research question was, What are the relevant conditions that make group members behave either more or less aggressively than individuals? They hypothesized that normative orientations are especially relevant for differences between interpersonal and intergroup aggression: "Generally our position has been that groups are not inherently more aggressive than individuals but that it will depend on the dominant normative orientation in the group whether groups will be more or less aggressive than individuals" (Rabbie, 1982, p. 1).

These experiments by Rabbie and his co-workers, especially Lodewijkx (1989), provide support for the norm-enhancement hypothesis. In these experiments, a prisoner's dilemma game (PDG) or similar social dilemma game was used. Subjects played either alone or in groups of two or three against either a single person or another group. During the PDG, subjects could earn or lose monetary rewards. Each party could play either cooperatively or competitively. The game was constructed in such a way that, in the long run, cooperative strategies of both parties maximized their gains.

Subjects interacted with the fictitious other party by means of a computer screen on which the choices were indicated. In addition, there was an acoustic connection. Subjects could react to the decisions of the other party by delivering higher or lower levels of unpleasant noise (ranging from Level 1 "nearly imperceptible" to Level 6 "very pain-ful"). On the first trial, the fictitious other party chose first and behaved cooperatively. On the following trials, the choices were made simultaneously. Three conditions were estab-lished: (a) The other party promised beforehand to behave cooperatively but changed to a competitive strategy during the game, (b) the other party promised cooperative behavior and kept the promise, and (c) the other behaved competitively without having promised cooperation.

Results showed that there was no general tendency of groups to behave more ag-gressively than individuals. When the other party behaved cooperatively, subjects in the group condition were not less aggressive (as measured by the amount of noxious noise imposed on the other party), nor was there a difference in the aggressiveness of subjects in the individual or group context when confronted by a party that played competitively without breaking a promise. Only when the other party broke a promise to cooperate did group members react more aggressively than individuals. Rabbie explained these results as due to an increase in the salience of the dominant normative orientation of the group, in this case, the norm of negative reciprocity.

Looking critically at the two complementary approaches to the phenomenon of in-tergroup aggression (deindividuation, as represented by the research of Jaffe & Yinon [1979, 1983], and norm enhancement, as represented by the work of Rabbie and cowork-ers), the following becomes obvious: The concept of deindividuation seems to be based on a specific perspective; it is especially suitable to describe such collective acts that—from the perspective of an outside observer—appear to be irrational, harmful, norm de-viating, or even criminal. One would probably never refer to deindividuating states of mind to explain collective acts that, although inflicting harm on the victims, were legitim-ized as necessary and meaningful to protect or restore public interests, social order, com-mon welfare, or relevant social standards. One would, therefore, probably not argue that police officers using tear gas and hemming in and knocking down demonstrators are in a state of deindividuation. Yet, this is an example of collective behavior that involves violence.

The concept of deindividuation—like earlier theories about collective behavior—runs the risk of incorrectly generalizing from a value-laden, biased perspective (see Reicher, 1982). The norm-enhancement hypothesis, on the other hand, avoids value judg-ments. Within this framework, a wide variety of incidents of collective aggression can be understood without regard to whether observers view the group behavior as appropriate, brutal, violent, consistent with law and order, or contributing to the common good.

Subjective Confidence in Interpersonal Versus Intergroup Contexts

We now consider the implications of the lay epistemic process for differences between aggression performed by individuals and that performed by groups. What are the differences between interpersonal and intergroup interactions in the tendency of opponents to have subjective confidence and to entertain alternative interpretations and evaluations of behavior?

Interpersonal and intergroup behavior can be characterized as two poles of a continuum. In the interpersonal domain, the individual behavior and perception is determined by personal relationships and individual differences in attitudes and personality traits. In the intergroup situation, the social categories to which individuals belong affect their interactions. Homogeneity is overestimated, and variability of judgment and behavior toward the outgroup decreases. To differentiate interpersonal and intergroup interactions, one must start with a very broad conceptualization of social grouping as a self-categorization supported by social consensus (Tajfel, 1981; Turner, 1982; Turner, Hogg, Oakes, Reicher, & Wetherell, 1987). According to this approach, a group exits when "two or more individuals . . . perceive themselves to be members of the same social category" (Turner, 1982, p. 15) and when this categorization is shared by outsiders (Brown, 1988).

Research shows that several characteristics are typical of intergroup situations. Some of these characteristics are useful for explaining the proposed differences in aggressive interactions in interpersonal or intergroup contexts. As we outline, confidence in judgments and evaluations is expected to be relatively high in intergroup interaction.

Individuals are likely to perceive a consensus or homogeneity among ingroup members that supports their point of view. In other words, the amount of (false) consensus will be higher in the intergroup situation. The decrease of perceived variability in points of view, attitudes, and behaviors among ingroup members may promote a social consensus of interpretation and evaluation resulting in a solid confidence of having chosen the appropriate alternative (e.g., "Everybody would react like me in this situation").

Individuals are also likely to perceive a consensus or homogeneity among outgroup members. Homogenization of outgroup members means that each ingroup member is confronted with interchangeable opponents in an aggressive interaction. Reactions and evaluations can be generalized irrespective of individual differences.

The perceived similarity between opponents belonging to two different groups will be relatively low. The salience of the intergroup situation may enhance the perception of dissimilarity and decrease the tendency for each opponent to consider the perspective of the other.

For aggressive interactions, these characteristics of the intergroup context may support a decrease in the probability of either the perpetrator or the victim generating interpretations and evaluations of a critical event from the other's perspective. Therefore, it is expected that group members will be more divergent in their perspectives than will unaffiliated individuals when evaluating the appropriateness of the critical action.

In addition to cognitive aspects like accentuation of intragroup similarities and intergroup differences, other phenomenon become apparent during the process of group formation and the definition of social identity, including prototypical judgments and evaluation of outgroup behavior as inappropriate and offensive as compared with ingroup behavior as appropriate and defensive (cf. the concept of mirror image proposed by Bronfenbrenner, 1961). Such stereotypes influence not only the group but the individual members as well. The interpretation and explanation of events, including the justification of group behavior, are crucial elements of a group's ideology. These aspects of the group culture are available for individual members. In this respect, it is not necessary for participants in an intergroup incident involving aggression to generate individual explanations and justifications. Because of the support of group ideologies, individuals are likely to be confident about their interpretation and evaluation of the event. As a result, taking the perspective of outgroup opponents is extremely unlikely.

Empirical Evidence for the Perspective-Specific Divergence

We conducted several experiments to test different aspects of the more general assumption of a perspective-specific divergence between perpetrator and victim in evaluating the appropriateness of the critical action. First, we studied the relation between the judgments of the opponents of a single event. Second, we evaluated the influence of the sequential aspects of the interaction as the two parties shifted between roles as perpetrator and victim. In all these studies, subjects evaluated the critical action either after being asked to take an empathic perspective or another perspective they chose themselves. Judgments were given individually in one study and after a longer group discussion resulting in a social consensual evaluation in a second study.

The results appeared to be clear and unequivocal (for more details, see Mummendey, Linneweber, & Loeschper, 1984a, 1984b; Mummendey & Otten, 1989): Consistent disagreement was found between perpetrator and victim concerning the evaluation of the appropriateness of the action. The disagreement appeared in evaluating a single event, a sequence of two events, and longer sequences that involved one or more changes of the positions of perpetrator and victim. A general self–other divergence was therefore demonstrated, with the subject's own behavior being consistently judged as less inappropriate than the other's, irrespective of whether the event was an action or a reaction.

The Perspective-Specific Divergence in Interpersonal and Intergroup Contexts
Dupin and Schattenberg (1985) used a similar procedure to test the effects of different social contexts on the variability in the divergence of perspectives. Subjects viewed critical actions on a videotape that were either embedded in an interpersonal or an intergroup context. In one condition, the critical actions were performed by individuals. There were two intergroup contexts: one in which the participants were members of different groups (ingroup vs. outgroup) and one in which they were members of the same group (ingroup vs. ingroup). Because it was expected that individuals would have more empathy for members of their own group, the hypothesis was that the divergence of perspectives would be less in the ingroup–ingroup condition than in the ingroup–outgroup condition.

Results again indicated a clear divergence of perspectives: Perpetrators evaluated their behavior as less negative than did victims, irrespective of whether the behavior was an action or a reaction during the interaction sequence. Consistent with our expectations, the amount of divergence was significantly larger in the ingroup–outgroup context than in the ingroup–ingroup context. But unexpectedly, the divergence of evaluations in the ingroup–ingroup context was reversed. Perpetrators evaluated their own behavior more negatively than did their victims. These results are primarily attributable to the variation in judgments from the perpetrators' perspectives. Perpetrators evaluated their own behavior against a victim belonging to an outgroup as least negative but their own behavior against an ingroup member as most negative. This pattern of evaluations appeared irrespective of whether the critical behavior was an action or a reaction.

In a further study (Schruijer et al., 1989), written episodes of aggressive conflicts between natural groups were used. In a 2 × 2 factorial design, the group membership of perpetrators and victims was identified as either communist or fascist. All subjects were communists attending a party meeting in Bologna, Italy. Consistent with previous findings, a significant main effect of the perpetrator's group membership showed that a critical action by an ingroup perpetrator was evaluated as less negative than was the same action performed by an outgroup perpetrator.

The studies just described yielded consistent findings except for the reversal of perspectives in the Dupin and Schattenberg (1985) study. Concerning the results in the Schruijer et al. (1989) study, one can speculate on the basis of norm-enhancement theory that subjects perceived the ingroup perpetrator's behavior as normative or expected. If such were the case, then the perpetrator would not be evaluated very negatively; rather, the victim would be perceived as overreacting to the perpetrator.

Subjective Confidence and Perspective-Specific Divergence

To test whether and how the divergence in perspectives differs in interpersonal and intergroup contexts, Otten (1990) examined the effects of moderating variables derived from the theory of lay epistemology. The evidence presented earlier suggested that in intergroup contexts, opponents' evaluations would vary more than in interpersonal contexts. The application of the lay epistemic process to aggressive interactions suggested two hypotheses. First, a polarization of judgments would be positively related to increases in judgmental confidence. Second, the divergence in perspectives would vary according to subjects' lay epistemic motivations. The divergence should be especially pronounced for subjects with a strong need for structure given that this need leads to quick judgmental decisions. On the other hand, divergence should decrease when subjects have a strong fear of invalid judgments given that this fear leads to extensive hypothesis testing.

The different perspectives were established by an empathy instruction: Subjects—students between 13 and 16 years of age—were presented a videotape about an aggressive conflict in school involving two opponents. They were instructed to look at this videotape from the perspective not of an outside observer but of either the actor or the recipient. While watching the film three times, participants were to try to imagine the given episode as vividly as possible. Social context was manipulated by introducing the two protagonists in the film either by their first names (Thomas and Stefan) or avoiding individualized information (students from the same grade but from different school classes). In accordance with procedures used by Kruglanski and Freund (1983), the epistemic motivation was manipulated by adjusting either time pressure (need for structure condition) or evaluation apprehension (fear of invalidity condition).

In the first case, the necessity of quick judgments during aggressive conflicts was stressed combined with the information that subjects' reaction times would be measured. In the second case, the importance of reasoned judgments was stressed and participants expected that after completing the questionnaire they would have to discuss their evaluations with the experimenter. Subjects rated the inappropriateness of the aggressive interaction and how confident they felt about their judgments of appropriateness. To avoid a social desirability effect, reaction times were also recorded as an indirect measure of judgmental confidence. All questions were presented on a computer screen, and subjects indicated their answers on a keyboard.

Epistemic motivation had no effect on evaluations of the aggressive episode. Additionally, there was no systematic relation between subjective confidence (measured by either rating scale or reaction time) and polarization of judgments. On the other hand, there was the typical divergence in perspective in judgments on variables concerned with norm deviation. Perpetrators evaluated their behavior as significantly less negative than did their victims.

The divergence in perspective concerning evaluations of inappropriateness and intent completely vanished in the intergroup condition. This effect was due to the recipients' reactions towards the context manipulation: They evaluated aggressive actions embedded in an intergroup context as significantly less negative than they did those taking place in an interpersonal context. This difference was contrary to the expectations derived from theoretical as well as empirical work. How can the decrease of judgmental divergence concerning the intergroup aggression be interpreted?

One possibility is that there are context-specific normative expectancies concerning the opponent's behavior. There may be different normative thresholds for defining inappropriate behavior in either interpersonal or intergroup contexts. If expectations about the "normal" behavior of outgroup members are lower than are expectations about the behavior of unaffiliated individuals, then actions in the intergroup context will have to be more severe to be classified as norm deviating than will the same behavior embedded in an interpersonal context. In this study, critical actions were identical for both contexts, but it is reasonable to suppose that the same behavior may be perceived as inappropriate in one case and as normatively expected in another. The videotaped episodes showed behaviors like tripping another boy, throwing his bag on the ground, pushing him, and preventing him from entering the school building. These behaviors were apparently perceived as less serious when they were directed at people outside the group than when they were directed at people inside the group. If one accepts this explanation, the results of this study are consistent with the data obtained by Rabbie and co-workers (reviewed earlier). Group members were perceived more negatively than were unaffiliated individuals after a (perceived) provocation only if the initiating action violated group-relevant norms. Our argument is that in Otten's (1990) study, because the initiating action was not perceived as a serious violation of group norms in the intergroup context, the perpetrator was not perceived negatively.

The results were somewhat disappointing with respect to the theory of lay epistemology. Methodological problems may account for the negative findings. The measurement of a construct like subjective confidence is very difficult. What is interesting and probably decisive for the lay epistemic process is the experience of confidence in hypotheses during the process of knowledge seeking. Subjects in Otten's (1900) experiment rated their confidence after they gave a judgment. In this respect, the reaction times may be the more valid measures. However, questions have been raised about using reaction times as indicators of subjective confidence (see Wyer & Srull, 1988).

Normative Orientations in Interpersonal and Intergroup Contexts

To test the hypothesis of different normative thresholds for identifying inappropriate behavior in interpersonal and intergroup contexts, we conducted two further studies (Mummendey, Otten, & Wenzel, 1991). In these experiments, subjects once again evaluated aggressive interactions involving an initiating action and a reaction. These interactions were embedded in either an interpersonal or an intergroup context. Besides context, the severity of the aggressive interaction was varied (low, high). In the study by Otten (1990), the acts in question were of medium severity at most. Accordingly, on the basis of the normative threshold interpretation outlined above, it was expected that judgments regarding mildly aggressive behaviors would be more positive in intergroup contexts than in interpersonal ones. On the other hand, for severe norm deviations (i.e., challenging behavioral expectancies in both contexts), differences between intergroup and interpersonal contexts should vanish or even be reversed.

Because the main focus in this study was the effect of situational context, perspective was not varied. Schoolchildren experienced the aggressive episode from the position of an observer who was present during the interaction but was not directly involved in the conflict. In the intergroup condition, subjects evaluated an aggressive interaction between two schoolboys who were introduced as belonging to two different cliques. In the interpersonal condition, the two participants were introduced by their first names and it was added that "they know each other but are not close friends." Subjects judged the inappropriateness of both the initiating action and the reaction. The two studies were identical in design but used somewhat different samples (schoolchildren from either urban or rural areas). The results of these studies were quite consistent and are therefore discussed in common.

There was no evidence supporting the main hypothesis, which proposed a significant interaction between context and severity on the evaluation of either actions or reactions. Nevertheless, a more detailed examination of the results revealed that actions were evaluated negatively irrespective of social context. Reactions, on the other hand, were evaluated less negatively than were actions. In some cases, judgments of reactions tended toward the positive end of the ratings of appropriateness. However, when depicted as intergroup behavior, reactions were evaluated as more inappropriate than were the same behaviors embedded in an interpersonal context.

Because actions are always evaluated more negatively than reactions, it seems obvious that in both contexts the norm of reciprocity (Gouldner, 1960) must be relevant. But at the same time, the reciprocity norm seems to be interpreted in a different way for interpersonal as compared with intergroup behaviors. For at least the episodes described in our studies, in the intergroup context, it was probably less appropriate to answer a provocation with aggressive retaliation. This fits very well with DeRidder, Kumar, and Schruijer's (1991) studies concerning (intergroup) norms of redress including not only reciprocity but also much more positive forms of conflict resolution. They examined conflicts in an industrial context as well as between ethnic groups in India and found that in the majority of cases, subjects did not retaliate but preferred positive, constructive reactions or ignored the provocation.

Although at present our results are restricted to a specific social institution (i.e., school) and a specific sample (i.e., schoolchildren), it seems necessary as well as promising to conduct further research about normative orientations in interpersonal and intergroup aggressive interaction sequences.

Conclusion

Compared with an interpersonal context, the intensity and quality of aggressive interactions in intergroup contexts appear to be more violent, more intense, and more spectacular. Individuals acting in groups are believed to engage in more immoral, irrational, and impulsive behavior than are individuals acting independently. Anonymity, deindividuation, and diffusion of responsibility are considered to be important variables in the variation in the intensity of aggression in different social contexts. We prefer a complementary position. We have argued that aggressive interactions are regulated by the same general principles in interpersonal and intergroup situations. Perpetrators do not abandon rationality. Rather, they consider their own behavior as relatively appropriate and reasonable. But it is the social context that provides conditions that crucially affect the interpretation of what is rational. Identical actions are interpreted and evaluated very differently depending on the social context or, more precisely, depending on the social relationship between the participants. In our context, opponents' belonging to either identical or different groups seemed to be especially important.

We have discussed several studies conducted to explore the impact of social context on divergence in judgmental perspectives that clearly indicate that aggressive interactions are interpreted and evaluated differently when embedded in either interpersonal or intergroup situations. At the same time, however, these studies demonstrate that the direction of this effect may vary. More research is needed to develop clear-cut predictions about the influence of social contexts on the divergent perspectives of participants in aggressive conflicts.

References

Arendt, H. (1970). *On violence.* New York: Hartcourt, Brace & World.

Baron, R. A. (1977). *Human aggression.* New York: Plenum Press.

Baron, R. A., & Eggleston, R. J. (1972). Performance of the "aggression machine": Motivation to help or harm? *Psychonomic Science, 26,* 321–322.

Bernstein, F. (1980). *Der Antisemitismus als Gruppenerscheinung* [Antisemitism as a group phenomenon]. Koenigstein/Ts., Germany: Jüedischer Verlag im Athenaeum Verlag. (Original work published 1929)

Bronfenbrenner, U. (1961). The mirror-image in Soviet–American relations. *Journal of Social Issues, 17,* 45–56.

Brown, R. (1988). *Group processes: Dynamics within and between groups.* Oxford, England: Basil Blackwell.

Brown, R. C., Jr., & Tedeschi, J. T. (1976). Determinants of perceived aggression. *Journal of Social Psychology, 100,* 77–87.

Buss, A. H. (1961). *The psychology of aggression.* New York: Wiley.

Condor, S., & Brown, R. (1988). Psychological processes in intergroup conflict. In W. Stroebe, A. W. Kruglanski, D. Bar-Tal, & M. Hewstone (Eds.), *The social psychology of intergroup conflict* (pp. 3–26). Berlin: Springer.

DaGloria, J., & DeRidder, R. (1977). Aggression in dyadic interaction. *European Journal of Social Psychology, 7*, 189–219.

DeRidder, R., Kumar, R., & Schruijer, S. (1991). Norms of redress. In R. DeRidder & R. C. Tripathi (Eds.), *Norm violation and intergroup relations* (pp. 147–170). Oxford, England: Oxford University Press.

Diener, E. (1980). Deindividuation: The absence of self-awareness and self-regulation in group members. In P. Paulus (Ed.), *The psychology of group influence* (pp. 209–242). Hillsdale, NJ: Erlbaum.

Dollard, G., Doob, L. W., Miller, N. E., Mowrer, O. H., & Sears, R. T. (1939). *Frustration and aggression.* New Haven, CT: Yale University Press.

Dupin, G., & Schattenberg, S. (1985). *Zur perspektivenspezifischen Beurteilungsdivergenz in aggressiven Interaktionen: Der Einfluß von interpersonalen versus intergruppalen Kontextbedingungen* [The perspective-specific divergence in the evaluation of aggressive interactions: The impact of interpersonal versus intergroup context]. Unpublished master's thesis, Westfälische Wilhelms-Universität, Münster, Germany.

Ferguson, T. J., & Rule, B. G. (1983). An attributional perspective on anger and aggression. In R. Geen & E. Donnerstein (Eds.), *Aggression: Theoretical and empirical reviews* (pp. 41–74). San Diego, CA: Academic Press.

Feshbach, N. D., & Feshbach, S. (1969). The relationship between empathy and aggression in two age groups. *Developmental Psychology, 1,* 102–107.

Feshbach, N. D., & Feshbach, S. (1982). Empathy training and the regulation of aggression: Potentialities and limitations. *Academic Psychological Bulletin, 4,* 399–413.

Festinger, C., Pepitone, A., & Newcomb, T. (1952). Some consequences of deindividuation in a group. *Journal of Abnormal and Social Psychology, 47,* 382–289.

Fraser, C., Gouge, C., & Billig, M. (1971). Risky shift, cautious shift and group polarization. *European Journal of Social Psychology, 1,* 7–30.

Gouldner, A. W. (1960). The norm of reciprocity: A preliminary statement. *American Sociological Review, 25,* 161–178.

Hoffman, M. L. (1982). Development of prosocial motivation: Empathy and guilt. In N. Eisenberg (Ed.), *The development of prosocial behavior* (pp. 266–286). San Diego, CA: Academic Press.

Jaffe, Y., & Yinon, Y. (1979). Retaliatory aggression in individuals and groups. *European Journal of Social Psychology, 9,* 177–186.

Jaffe, Y., & Yinon, Y. (1983). Collective aggression: The group–individual paradigm in the study of collective antisocial behavior. In H. H. Blumberg, A. P. Jare, V. Kent, & M. Davies (Eds.), *Small groups and social interaction* (Vol. 1, pp. 267–275). New York: Wiley.

Kruglanski, A. W. (1980). Lay epistemologic process and contents. *Psychological Review, 87,* 70–87.

Kruglanski, A. W. (1988). Knowledge as a social psychological construct. In D. Bar-Tal & A. W. Kruglanski (Eds.), *The social psychology of knowledge* (pp. 109–141). Cambridge, England: Cambridge University Press.

Kruglanski, A. W., & Ajzen, I. (1983). Bias and error in human judgment. *European Journal of Social Psychology, 13,* 1–44.

Kruglanski, A. W., Baldwin, M. W., & Towson, S. M. J. (1985). Die Theorie der Laienepistemologie [The theory of lay epistemology]. In D. Frey & M. Irle (Eds.), *Theorien der Sozialpsychologie. Bd. 3: Motivations-und Informations-verarbeitungstheorien* [Theories of social psychology. Vol. 3: Theories on motivation and information processing] (pp. 293–314). Bern, Germany: Huber.

Kruglanski, A. W., & Freund, T. (1983). The freezing and unfreezing of lay-inferences: Effects on impressional primacy, ethnic stereotyping, and numerical anchoring. *Journal of Experimental and Social Psychology, 19,* 488–468.

LeBon, C. (1985). *Psychologie des foules.* Paris: Alcan.

Lodewijkx, H. (1989). *Conflict and aggression between individuals and groups.* Unpublished doctoral dissertation. University of Utrecht, The Netherlands.

Loeschper, G., Mummendey, A., Linneweber, V., & Bornewasser, M. (1984). The judgment of behavior as aggressive and sanctionable. *European Journal of Social Psychology, 14,* 391–404.

Miller, P. A., & Eisenberg, N. (1988). The relation of empathy to aggressive and externalizing/antisocial behavior. *Psychological Bulletin, 103,* 324–344.

Mummendey, A. (1987). Aggression: Interaktion zwischen Individuen und sozialen Gruppen [Aggression: Interaction between individuals and social groups]. In M. Amelang (Ed.), *Bericht über den 35. Kongreß der Deutschen Gesellschaft für Psychologie in Heidelberg 1986* (Vol. 2, pp. 489–499). Göttingen, Germany: Hogrefe.

Mummendey, A., Bornewasser, M., Loeschper, G., & Linneweber, V. (1982). Aggressiv sind immer die anderen. Plädoyer für eine sozialpsychologische Perspektive in der Aggressionsforschung [Aggressive is always somebody else: Plea for a social-psychological perspective in research on aggression]. *Zeitschrift für Sozialpsychologie, 13,* 177–193.

Mummendey, A., Linneweber, V., & Loeschper, G. (1984a). Actor or victim of aggression: Divergent perspectives—Divergent evaluations. *European Journal of Social Psychology, 14,* 297–311.

Mummendey, A., Linneweber, V., & Loeschper, G. (1984b). Aggression: From act to interaction. In A. Mummendey (Ed.), *Social psychology of aggression: From individual behavior to social interaction* (pp. 69–106). New York: Springer.

Mummendey, A., & Otten, S. (1989). Perspective-specific differences in the segmentation and evaluation of aggressive interaction sequences. *European Journal of Social Psychology, 19,* 23–40.

Mummendey, A., Otten, S., & Wenzel, M. (1991). *Kontextspezifische Unangemessenheitsvorstellungen bei der Beurteilung aggressiver Interaktionen* [Context-specific perceptions of inappropriateness in the evaluation of aggressive interactions]. Unpublished manuscript, University of Münster, Germany.

Myers, D. G., & Lamm, H. (1976). The group polarization phenomenon. *Psychological Bulletin, 83,* 602–627.

Otten, S. (1990). *Determinanten der Beurteilung aggressiver Interaktionen: Zum Einfluß von sozialem Kontext, Perspektive und Urleilssicherheit* [Determinants of the evaluation of aggressive interactions: The impact of social context, perspective and judgmental confidence]. Münster, Germany: LIT-Verlag.

Pepitone, A. (1981). The normative basis of aggression: Anger and punitiveness. *Recherches de Psychologie Sociale, 3,* 3–17.

Rabbie, J. M. (1982, September). *Are groups more aggressive than individuals?* Henri Tajfel Lecture presented at the Annual Conference of the Social Psychology Section of the British Psychological Society.

Rabbie, J. M. (1987, August). *Armed conflicts: Toward a behavioral interaction model.* Paper presented at the conference "European Psychologists for Peace," Helsinki, Finland.

Rabbie, J. M., & Lodewijkx, H. (1987). Individual and group aggression. *Current Research on Peace and Violence, 10,* 91–101.

Rabbie, J. M., Schot, J. C., & Visser, L. (1989). Social identity theory: A conceptual and empirical critique from the perspective of a behavioral interaction model. *European Journal of Social Psychology, 19,* 171–202.

Reicher, S. D. (1982). The determination of collective behavior. In H. Tajfel (Ed.), *Social identity and intergroup relations* (pp. 41–83). Cambridge, England: Cambridge University Press.

Ross, L. (1977). The intuitive psychologist and his shortcomings: Distortions in the attribution process: In L. Berkowitz (Ed.), *Advances in experimental social psychology* (Vol. 10, pp. 173–220). New York: Academic Press.

Schruijer, S. G. L., Blanz, M., Mummendey, A., Tedeschi, J. Banfai, B. Dittmar, H., Kleibaumüter, P. Mahjoub, A., Madrosz-Wroblewska, J., Molinari, L., & Pettilion, X. (1989). *The group-serving bias in the explanation and evaluation of harm-doing behaviour.* Unpublished manuscript, Tilburg University, The Netherlands.

Schuck, J., & Pisor, K. (1974). Evaluating an aggression experiment by use of stimulating subjects. *Journal of Personality and Social Psychology, 29,* 181–186.

Sherif, M. (1966). *Group conflict and cooperation: Their social psychology.* London: Routledge & Kegan Paul.

Tajfel, H. (1978). Interindividual behavior and intergroup behavior. In H. Tajfel (Ed.), *Differentiation between social groups* (pp. 27–60). London: Academic Press.

Tajfel, H. (1981). *Human groups and social categories.* Cambridge, England: Cambridge University Press.

Tedeschi, J. T., Smith, R. B., & Brown, R. C. (1974). A reinterpretation of research on aggression. *Psychological Bulletin, 81,* 540–562.

Turner, J. C. (1982). Towards a cognitive redefinition of the social group. In H. Tajfel (Ed.), *Social identity and intergroup relations* (pp. 15–40). Cambridge, England: Cambridge University Press.

Turner, J. C., Hogg, M. A., Oakes, P. J., Reicher, S. D., & Wetherell, M. S. (1987). *Rediscovering the social group: A self-categorization theory.* Oxford, England: Blackwell.

Turner, R. H., & Kilian, L. M. (1972). *Collective behavior.* Englewood Cliffs, NJ: Prentice-Hall.

Wyer, R. S., & Srull, T. K. (1988). Understanding social knowledge. In D. Bar-Tal, A. W. Kruglanski (Eds.), *The social psychology of knowledge* (pp. 142–192). Cambridge, England: Cambridge University Press.

Zimbardo, P. G. (1969). The human choice: Individuation, reason, and order versus deindividuation, impulse, and chaos. In D. Levine (Ed.), *Nebraska Symposium on Motivation* (pp. 237–307). Lincoln: University of Nebraska Press.

PART THREE

Legitimation of Aggression

CHAPTER 7

Illusions of Anger

James R. Averill

A ggression takes many forms—child abuse, spouse battering, mugging and robbery, manslaughter, gang violence, urban riots, warfare. Regardless of its form, aggression is often attributed to anger. To attribute a response to anger is not to provide just a description; it is also to provide an explanation ("I did it because I was angry"), a justification ("I couldn't help it; you made me angry"), and even an implied threat ("Do that again, and I will become angry").

To understand many episodes of aggression, therefore, one must understand what is meant by *anger*. Nothing would seem to be simpler. Anger is one of the most frequently experienced emotions; moreover, we seldom have difficulty deciding when we are angry or understanding when others are angry at us. Yet, when asked to state what we mean by anger, we are often at a loss for words. For purposes of theory and research, therefore, the temptation is great to stipulate a definition of anger, thereby eluding the ambiguities of ordinary language.

One cannot deny the potential benefits of increased precision that stipulative or operational definitions sometimes provide. But scientific progress is based more on knowing when—not whether—to redefine a concept. Premature redefinition is more likely to lead to confusion than to clarity. Concepts of ordinary language are, after all, the survivors of a long evolutionary process. Words that are of little use soon become extinct (meaningless). Those that remain contain the wisdom—and folly—of a society gained over many generations.

Going further, I maintain (only half facetiously) that ontogeny recapitulates philology. As a child learns language, he or she also learns to behave in accordance with the rules and standards (folk theory) that lend everyday concepts their meaning. It therefore behooves us to try to understand the concepts of ordinary language before attempting redefinition.

The primary goal of this chapter is to understand how we use—and sometimes misuse—the concept of anger in everyday affairs and to explore the implications of the concept of anger for both theory and practice. As a tool or didactic device to explore the meaning of anger, I focus on the difference between feeling angry and being angry. More specifically, I argue that feelings of anger can be, and often are, illusory. Illusions have proved valuable in the study of perceptual phenomena; they can be similarly valuable in the study of emotions.

The arguments that follow can be summarized in four propositions:

Proposition 1: *Anger helps legitimize aggression.* Sometimes people do things "for no reason at all." But those instances are rare and typically involve inconsequential actions. Aggression, however, is not rare, and it is far from inconsequential. It cries out for legitimation. Under ordinary conditions, anger seldom results in aggression, at least not physical aggression (Averill, 1982). Nevertheless, anger can serve to legitimize aggression in two ways. First, because anger is an emotion (passion), people presumably cannot control their anger and hence cannot be held fully responsible for the consequences of their behavior while angry. This is what Solomon (1976) has called the *myth of the passions.* Second, if anger is justified, the target is presumably responsible for initiating the incident. Anger involves an accusation of wrongdoing directed at the instigator.

Proposition 2: *Anger is often identified (incorrectly) with feelings.* When pressed, laypeople frequently define anger as a kind of feeling. Such a conception seems reasonable in view of the frequent interchangeability of such expressions as "I feel angry" and "I am angry." During the height of behaviorism, the conception of anger as a feeling was rejected—correctly, I believe, but for the wrong reasons. Behaviorists dismissed feelings as epiphenomena, of little interest in their own right. With the success of the "cognitive revolution" in psychology, feelings have once again become central to psychological discussions of emotion. Sociologists and anthropologists, too, commonly conceive of emotions in terms of feelings, as indicated by the sample of quotations presented in Table 1.

The return of feelings as a phenomenon of interest is important given that how people behave frequently depends on how they feel. There is, however, a difficulty with

TABLE 1

Selected Quotes on Feelings and Emotions

From psychology

Because emotions are subjective experiences, like the sensation of color or pain, people have direct access to them, so that if a person is experiencing fear, for example, that person cannot be mistaken about the fact that he or she is experiencing fear. (Ortony, Clore, & Collins, 1988, p. 9.)

Emotion is like other perceptual experiences, such as the experience of distance or of objects, and as such it is private and can only be studied through indicators. (Leventhal, 1984, p. 271)

From sociology

Emotion . . . is a biologically given sense, and our most important one. Like other senses— hearing, touch, and smell—it is a means by which we know about our relation to the world, and it is therefore crucial for the survival of human beings in group life. (Hochschild, 1983, p. 219)

Feelings are sensations of the lived body. (Denzin, 1990, p. 88)

From anthropology

"Emotion" can be thought of as a subset of "feeling." (Levy, 1984, p. 401)

To speak of the emotional life is to talk about *felt* experience. (Shweder, 1985, p. 183)

---

any formulation that identifies emotions with feelings or that postulates feelings as essential (i.e., necessary if not sufficient) conditions for emotion.

Proposition 3: *Angry feelings can be illusory.* We like to think of feelings as somehow incorrigible. A person whose feelings are called into question might well respond, "I know how I feel, and if I feel angry, who are you to say that I am not?" Yet, as I will argue later, angry feelings can be illusory. By this, I do not mean simply that a person's anger is sometimes unjustified. Illusory anger is unjustified, but the reverse is not necessarily true—unjustified anger might or might not be illusory. *Unjustified* refers to the grounds or reasons for thinking and acting as we do; *illusory* refers to a certain kind of conscious awareness. Unjustified anger can be corrected once the false premises are pointed out. Illusions are not so easily corrected.

Illusory anger can be contrasted with anger that is "real," "true," or "objectively verifiable." These latter concepts differ among themselves in important respects; such differences are not, however, crucial to the present analysis. Hence, I use the terms almost interchangeably, depending on the context. Very briefly, illusory anger can be defined as the conscious awareness of being angry even though the experience has no correspondence in objective reality.

Proposition 4. *Anger is not an event, either psychological or physiological, that occurs within the mind (or body) of the individual.* The conception of anger as a feeling is only one variant of a broader thesis, namely, that anger is an ongoing (occurrent) response that takes place within the individual. The exact nature of the presumed response varies from one theorist to another. In addition to feelings, anger has been conceived of as an intervening "drive" variable, as a pattern of physiological arousal, as a way of appraising a situation, or as some combination of these. In each case, for the presumed event to be judged a true or accurate representation of anger, there must be some external frame of reference against which it can be compared. That external frame of reference, I argue, is what is meant by *anger,* the putative object of angry experiences.

I Feel, Therefore I Am—But Not Necessarily

In this chapter, I touch on each of the four propositions just outlined. From a practical point of view, my main objective is to explore some of the ways that anger is used to legitimize and hence facilitate aggression, even under inappropriate circumstances (Proposition 1). Theoretically, I am most concerned with the conceptualization of anger as an interpersonal rather than an intrapsychic phenomenon (Proposition 4). I begin, however, with Propositions 2 and 3, namely, angry feelings and their sometimes illusory nature.

As the quotations in Table 1 illustrate, emotional feelings are often identified with sensations (particularly proprioception) or are conceived of as analogous to bodily sensations. Although I believe that the analogy is more misleading than informative, it is worth pursuing briefly. Can a person feel angry without being angry? Compare this question with the following: Can a person see an object that is not present? Can a person hear voices when there are no voices to be heard?

Terms such as *feeling, seeing,* and *hearing* are ambiguous in that they have a dual reference. On the one hand, they imply a conscious state of the individual; on the other hand, they imply an independently existing state of affairs, namely, that which is felt, seen, or heard. Usually, these two referents covary. When I hear voices, for example, there are voices to be heard. Under unusual circumstances, however, the covariance breaks down. Given normal hearing and acoustics, I sometimes hear voices when no one is speaking (a positive hallucination), and, conversely, I sometimes fail to hear voices when someone is speaking in a clearly audible fashion (a negative hallucination).

Positive and negative hallucinations are among the symptoms of severe psycho-pathology. However, under special conditions (e.g., hypnosis), they can be induced in nor-mal people. In mild or attenuated form, they are also a common part of everyday experience. Driving along the highway at night, I see shadows that the moon casts on the road. Suddenly, I see an animal looming in front of me. I slam on the breaks. The "animal" turns out to be just another shadow. My imagination has played a trick on me.

When, as in this last example, the experience has some partial basis in fact (shad-ows on the road), it is more common to speak of illusions rather than hallucinations. But the principle is the same. Under certain conditions, subjective experience has little or no correspondence to objective reality.

How does one determine "objective reality"? In the case of hearing voices, that is easy. Is anyone speaking? Can others hear the voice? Can the voice be recorded for later playback? If the answers to questions such as these are negative, then there are grounds for concluding that the experience is at best illusory. But there is a complication. Let us assume that the person who is hearing voices is a shaman and that the voice he hears is the voice of a god. No one else can hear the voice because the god speaks only to and through the shaman—on that, all true believers agree. In such a case, the voice might still be considered real, at least by believers, even though no physical stimuli can be identi-fied. This illustrates an important principle that I address later: It is community standards as much as the physical environment that determines whether an experience is consid-ered real or illusory.

If this principle is applicable to hearing voices, which is a relatively simple experi-ence, how much more applicable must it be to emotional feelings, which are highly com-plex. Are there illusions of anger, that is, partial or inappropriate responses to a situation that do not qualify as anger in an objective sense but that are nevertheless experienced as anger? Without doubt.

I draw on the legal treatment of crimes of passion—homicides committed out of anger—to illustrate in a concrete way the manner in which illusions of anger can and do occur. However, first, I make a brief aside on the use of legal conventions as a basis for argument.

The interface between psychology and the law is becoming an increasingly important subspeciality. Unfortunately, psychologists often view the relation in a rather one-sided fashion. For example, psychologists study (and often serve as expert witnesses regarding) the validity of eyewitness testimony, the influence of suggestion on recall, the assessment of competency, and the like. However, there also is much that psychology can learn from the law. Courtroom trials are natural experiments in decision making. But more important for the purposes of this discussion, the law—especially common law—is social custom writ large. Therefore, legal proceedings provide an excellent means by which to explore the social rules and standards that guide even everyday decisions. This is particularly true with respect to such issues as the attribution of emotion, for example, in cases wherein homicide has purportedly been committed out of anger—the typical crime of passion.

A Tale Thrice Told

How does a jury decide whether a defendant was really angry at the time of a killing? Is it on the basis of the defendant's feelings at the moment? Or are there more objective criteria by which to make a judgment? Consider the following hypothetical case.

A Tale of Aggression

> Mary has been preparing a special dinner for her husband, George. The normal dinner hour comes and goes with no sign of George. The dinner starts to spoil. Eventually, George arrives, half drunk, having stopped off for a drink "with the boys." Mary scolds; George calls her a bitch. Mary dramatically throws the dinner in the garbage. George slaps Mary. Mary picks up a knife and shoves it between George's ribs. George dies. Mary is brought to trial.

This tale recounts the basic facts of the case as it might be recorded by a disinterested observer. Needless to say, no description can be completely objective. Such terms as *special dinner, drunk, scold,* and *bitch* carry connotations that are bound to influence the interpretation of the events described (in this case, probably more in favor of Mary than George). Nevertheless, few people would disagree that this was an incident of aggression. But aggression of what sort? The prosecution says murder in the first degree; the defense says voluntary manslaughter (a crime of passion).

A Tale of Murder

At trial, the prosecutor agrees that Mary had prepared a special dinner. She knew that George often stopped off for drinks after work, a pattern established long before their marriage. Moreover, she knew how George hated to be scolded, and she was only too familiar with his hot temper. His reactions were highly predictable. Building his case, the prosecutor points out that George had a life-insurance policy worth half a million dollars, with Mary as the beneficiary. Divorce would leave her penniless; widowhood would leave her rich. But more was involved than just money, according to the prosecutor. Mary was having a torrid love affair with Wayne, a former college boyfriend, now unemployed. She herself had been a criminology major in college and hence was familiar with the law of homicide. Moreover, she was a avid reader of mystery novels and even belonged to a club that devised and solved make-believe murder cases. This time, the prosecutor claims, Mary devised a very clever scheme—but for real, not for play. She tricked George into provoking his own death.

A Tale of Anger

Not so, according to the defense. Mary really loved George; she wanted him, not his money. The affair with Wayne meant nothing; it was the result of George's own indifference and indiscretions. Moreover, this was not the first time that George had hit Mary. There was a history of abuse, and the attacks were becoming more frequent and more violent. Mary did not know what to do. She did not want a divorce but neither could she stay in the relationship as it was. The special dinner, George's favorite, was an attempt at reconciliation. When George did not come home, Mary was very disappointed, and when he slapped her, something "snapped." Without realizing what she was doing, Mary picked up the knife and slew George in a fit of anger. At most, hers was a crime of passion.

There are three things to note about this tale thrice told. First, there is no disagreement about the basic facts of the case. Following the sequence of events described in the original story, Mary killed George.

Second, both the prosecution and the defense account for the facts by placing them in the broader context of George and Mary's relationship, their past histories, and future goals. The prosecutor builds one story; the defense, another. Even at this level, there is little disagreement as to the facts, for example, that George had abused Mary in the past, that he had a large life-insurance policy, that Mary was having an affair with

Wayne, that she did not want a divorce, and that she was an avid mystery fan. The disagreements come at the level of emphasis and interpretation: Which facts are important, and which can be ignored?

Third, much depends on which account the jury accepts. If the jurors believe the story told by the prosecutor, Mary could be sentenced to life in prison (which usually means about 15 years actually served). On the other hand, if they believe the story told by the defense, Mary would probably spend no more than a year or two in prison, and immediate probation would be a good possibility. Obviously, the jury's decision is not a trivial matter.

How is the jury to decide whether Mary was really angry at the time of the killing? To answer this question, a distinction must be made among three kinds of variables: (a) emotional reactions, (b) emotional states, and (c) emotional syndromes. (See Averill, 1990, 1991, for further discussion of these three kinds of variables.)

An emotional *reaction* is the actual set of responses manifested by an individual when in an emotional state. Examples of emotional reactions are facial expressions, physiological changes, overt acts, and conscious experiences (feelings). Grimaces and cutting remarks are common angry reactions.

An emotional *state* is a temporary (episodic) disposition on the part of an individual to manifest one or another emotional reaction. It is important not to confuse a disposition with its manifestation. For example, an angry person may do a great variety of different things while angry, including things that have little or nothing to do with anger per se (such as reading a book or joking with a friend). Stated somewhat differently, no one type of reaction is, by itself, a necessary or sufficient condition for being in an angry state. While angry, one person might attack; another person, or the same person on another occasion, might withdraw in silence. Some reactions are, of course, more representative of an angry state than are others. The representativeness of a reaction is determined by the emotional syndrome.

An emotional *syndrome* is the most difficult kind of variable to illustrate in a short space. Unlike emotional reactions and states, emotional syndromes transcend the individual. They exist "out there," so to speak, in the form of a set of rules or representations. Put another way, emotional syndromes are theoretical entities, accounts that people give of behavior based on our folk theory of emotion. Like their counterparts in the natural sciences (e.g., atoms or quarks in physics), folk-theoretical constructs help make the world intelligible. But unlike scientific constructs, folk-theoretical constructs such as anger are part of the moral order, not just the "natural" order; they are valuative as well as descriptive. More important for the present discussion, folk-theoretical constructs, at least those that refer to human behavior, serve as vehicles by which behavior is generated; they are prescriptive as well as valuative. To draw an analogy, folk-theoretical constructs are to scientific constructs what social myths and ideologies are to scientific theories.

With these distinctions in mind, I now rephrase the question with respect to Mary: Were her reactions at the time of the killing sufficiently representative of the syndrome of anger such that the jurors might reasonably conclude that she was in an angry state? The jurors have a matching problem: Only if there is a match between Mary's behavior (including her appraisal of the situation) and the syndrome of anger can they conclude that Mary was really angry at the time of the killing.

Legal Criteria for Attributing Anger

The law stipulates four major criteria for deciding whether a person was truly angry at the time of a killing: adequacy of provocation, the heat of passion, insufficient cooling time, and a causal connection between the provocation and the crime. Together, these criteria help constitute anger as a syndrome within the legal system. Two of the criteria—adequacy of provocation and insufficient cooling time—are judged on the basis of the so-called "reasonable-man test." This test basically asks, Was the provocation sufficient to arouse an ordinary member of the community to anger so intense that it might lead to homicide? And, again, according to community standards, was there insufficient time for the anger to dissipate before the act was committed? In answering these questions, the actual state of mind of the defendant is irrelevant.

The reasonable-man test provides objective criteria (the norms and standards of the community) against which the feelings and reactions of the defendant can be compared. If there is a match, the defendant may be considered to have been in an angry state; if there is no match, the defendant is not judged to have been angry, regardless of his or her feelings at the time. (Compare this with the example of the shaman who hears voices. If his experience conforms to community expectations, the voices may be considered real; if the experience does not conform, the voices may be dismissed as illusory.)

Returning to the case of Mary, suppose that she did feel angry at the time of the killing. Would one then conclude that her's was a crime of passion? Not if one found the prosecuting attorney's account convincing. Mary might have been suffering from a positive illusion. The converse situation is also possible (and more likely). Suppose at the time of the killing, Mary felt nothing in particular—her mind literally "went blank." Would one therefore conclude that she was not angry at the moment? Not if one found the defense attorney's account convincing. Mary could easily have been suffering from a negative illusion; that is, she could have "blanked out" and been angry without feeling it.

We can now begin to see why crimes committed out of anger are treated so leniently in courts of law. If the anger is accepted as real—that is, if it passes the reasonable-man test—blame is shifted toward the target for provoking the episode. The angry person is, in a sense, doing his or her duty by correcting some perceived wrong. In traditional ethical teachings, anger was counted among the seven deadly sins because it often leads to excess; however, a failure to become angry in the face of wrongdoing also was considered sinful. In the words of the 17th century divine, Thomas Fuller, "Anger is one of the sinews of the soul: He that wants it hath a maimed mind, and, with Jacob sinew-shrunk in the hollow of his thigh, must needs halt." Of course, in the case of homicide, the angry person has gone too far. The crime of passion is still a crime ("sinful"); the reasonable man has proven himself to be not entirely reasonable.

Anger in Everyday Affairs

At this point, it might be useful to introduce some data on more commonplace incidents of anger. At whom do people typically become angry? For what reasons? And to what ends? With regard to the first question, anger is primarily an interpersonal affair. Based on surveys of everyday angry episodes, the target of anger is typically another person (most often, a friend or loved one), a human institution, or the self (Averill, 1982, 1983). On the occasional instance when the target is an inanimate object, the object is typically imbued with human characteristics ("The damn car had no right to break down in the middle of a rain storm!").

The interpersonal nature of anger might seem so trivially obvious as not to warrant mention. Yet, the obvious is often the easiest to ignore. For example, theories of anger that emphasize frustration (or pain) as an adequate stimulus ignore the fact that not any kind of frustration induces anger. Anger-inducing frustration is primarily that caused by another human being or a social institution, that is, by someone or something that can be held responsible. This point becomes even more evident when one considers the provocations to anger.

Table 2 presents data from two groups of subjects who completed detailed questionnaires describing the most intense episode of anger experienced during the previous week or, if none was experienced during the week, the most recent episode prior to that

TABLE 2

Perception of the Instigation by Angry People and by Targets

Perception to the investigation	Angry person[a]	Target[b]	Significance difference
A voluntary and unjustified act	59%	21%	<.01
A potentially avoidable accident or event	28%	28%	ns
A voluntary and justified act	12%	35%	<.01
An unavoidable accident or event	2%	15%	<.01

Note. From "Studies on Anger and Aggression: Implications for Theories of Emotion" by J. R. Averill, 1983, American Psychologist, 38, p. 1150. Copyright 1983 by the American Psychological Association.
[a] $n = 102$.
[b] $n = 80$.

(see Averill, 1982, 1983, for details). One group of subjects (a mixed sample of community residents and university students, $n = 102$) described an episode in which they became angry at another person; the other group (university students, $n = 80$) described an episode in which they were the target of another person's anger. Different episodes were involved (i.e., the angry people and the targets were not describing the same set of incidents).

Nearly 90% of the episodes described by angry people involved either an act that they considered voluntary and unjustified (59%) or else a potentially avoidable accident (e.g., due to negligence or lack of foresight, 28%). About 50% of the instigations reported by targets also fell into one or the other of these two categories. In other words, roughly half of the targets accepted blame for instigating the incident. (See Baumeister, Stillwell, and Wotman, 1990, for similar findings.)

The data presented in Table 2 actually underestimate the accusatory nature of anger, at least as far as the responses of the targets are concerned. In their open-ended comments, more than half of the targets who denied any wrongdoing (i.e., by claiming that the instigation was either justified or an unavoidable accident) also made reference to the imputation of blame inherent in the other person's anger. Two common explanations offered by these "innocent" targets could be paraphrased as follows: "I understand why this person became angry, but I still had a right to do what I did" and "It couldn't be helped."

Using hypothetical scenarios, Gergen and Gergen (1988) also found that the most frequent response to someone else's anger was an acceptance of blame, as indicated, for example, by an apology or expression of remorse by the target (instigator). This is the culturally expected response (assuming that the anger is justified), and it typically brings an episode to an end. The second most frequent response observed by Gergen and Gergen was for the target to reframe the incident, making it appear less blameworthy (e.g., "I only did it because I thought it would be helpful to you"). Unless the reframing is accepted by the angry person, this type of response typically leads to a continuation of the episode. The third and least frequent response was for the target to reject entirely the implication of the other person's anger and to become angry in return. This type of response can easily lead to an escalation of hostilities on both sides.

Turning now to the outcome of a typical angry episode, both the angry people and targets studied by Averill (1982, 1983) tended to rate the long-term consequences as more positive than negative. This is illustrated in Table 3, which presents the percentage of episodes in which targets ($n = 80$) experienced one kind of consequence or another. Seventy-six percent of the targets said that they came to realize their own faults because of the other person's anger. Furthermore, the target's relationship with the angry person was reportedly strengthened more often than it was weakened (in 48% vs. 35% of the episodes), and the targets more often gained rather than lost respect for the angry person (in 44% vs. 29% of the episodes).

When considering the data in Table 3, an important caveat must be noted. Positive consequences occurred primarily when the anger conformed to community standards, that is, to the rules that help constitute anger as a syndrome. The following is a list of some of the important rules of anger. (A more complete list can be found in Averill, 1982.)

1. A person has the right (duty) to become angry at intentional wrongdoing or at unintentional misdeeds if those misdeeds are correctable (e.g., due to negligence, carelessness, or oversight).
2. Anger should be directed only at persons and, by extension, other entities (one's self, human institutions) that can be held responsible for their actions.
3. Anger should not be displaced on an innocent third party, nor should it be directed at the target for reasons other than the instigation.

TABLE 3

Target's Perception of Longer-Term Changes or Consequences Brought About by the Angry Episode

Type of change	% episodes[a] in which change occurred "somewhat" or "very much"
You realized your own faults	76
You realized your own strengths	50
Your relationship with the angry person was strengthened	48
You gained respect for the angry person	44
You did something that was good for the angry person	39
You did something that was for your own good	38
Your relationship with the angry person became more distant	35
You lost respect for the angry person	29

Note. From "Studies on Anger and Aggression: Implications for Theories of Emotion" by J. R. Averill, 1983, *American Psychologist, 38*, p. 1151. Copyright 1983 by the American Psychological Association. The figures add to over 100% because the consequences are not mutually exclusive.
[a]$n = 80$.

4. The aim of anger should be to correct the situation, restore equity, and/or prevent recurrence, not to inflict injury or pain on the target or to achieve selfish ends through intimidation.

5. The angry response should be proportional to the instigation; that is, it should not exceed what is necessary to correct the situation, restore equity, or prevent the instigation from happening again.

6. Anger should follow closely the provocation and not endure longer than is needed to correct the situation (typically a few hours or days, at most).

7. Anger should involve commitment and resolve; that is, a person should not become angry unless appropriate follow-through is intended, circumstances permitting.

These rules provide a brief synopsis of some of the major features of anger as an emotional syndrome. Rules 1–3 specify the adequacy of provocation and the link between the provocation and the target; Rules 4 and 5 concern the nature and purpose of the response; Rule 6 relates to the time course of events and corresponds roughly to the "insufficient cooling time" and "heat of passion" criteria for crimes of passion. Rule 7 (commitment and resolve) is perhaps the only one that requires further elaboration. The person who says, "I am angry, but I don't intend to do anything about it" can rightfully be asked, "Why not?" And if a reasonable answer cannot be given, either in terms of situational constraints or personal inhibitions, then the veracity of his or her anger or the strength of his or her character may be questioned. This rule finds application in many "consciousness raising" techniques. Convince people that they are angry and you have gone a long way toward convincing them, rightfully or wrongfully, that action is appropriate and necessary.

These rules of anger probably seem self-evident. This is not because they are universally or necessarily true, as might be the case if anger were simply a legacy of our biological heritage. Rather, they are culturally based norms that, when internalized, become part of our "second nature."

This last point may best be illustrated by comparing anger with an aggressive emotional syndrome from another culture. Rosaldo (1980) described the emotion of *liget* among the Ilongot, a people of the Philippines. One manifestation of liget is the taking of heads. Rosaldo sometimes translated liget as "anger," at other times as "vital energy" or "passion." Like anger, liget can be occasioned by insults, slights, and other affronts to the self or by the violation of social norms. However, the most important occasion for liget is the taking of a head. Then intent on such occasions is not necessarily to harm or punish the victim. Rather, the taking of a head is a way for a young man to establish his place as an equal member of society; it is an occasion for celebration, not condemnation. The identity of the victim is largely irrelevant—a man, woman, child, anyone will do, preferably a stranger. Liget also finds expression in a variety of nonaggressive ways. For example, male liget is implicated in both courtship and childbirth; "concentrated" in the sperm, it makes babies. Liget also helps stimulate work and provides the strength and courage to overcome obstacles.

From this brief description, it is clear that liget is not the same emotion as anger; it is constituted by a different set of rules. Only a well-socialized Ilongot, one who has internalized the rules of liget, could know what it feels like to be liget. The same can be said of anger within our own culture. The rules of anger do not simply regulate how we feel and behave when angry; they help constitute anger as an emotional syndrome.

To summarize briefly, anger (qua emotional syndrome) is a folk-theoretical construct, an account given of behavior. As an account, anger comprises the rules that determine its own nature and applicability. If the rules are misapplied, one may say that the anger is unjustified, but if they are violated too egregiously, one may refuse even to recognize the response as real anger, regardless of how intense or sincere the feeling of anger might be.

The Subjective and the Real

At this point, several ambiguities need to be clarified. Anger is a subjective phenomenon. Subjectivity is part of the meaning of emotional constructs. Therefore, to imply that anger (or any other emotion) has an objective existence that transcends the individual would seem to imply a logical contradiction. How can anger be subjective and yet objectively real?

The contradiction is only apparent. For one thing, it capitalizes on an ambiguity in the term *emotion.* As discussed earlier, *emotion* can refer to emotional reactions, states, or syndromes. Usually, the context makes the intended meaning clear. However, it is easy to assume that what applies to one meaning of emotion also applies to the other meanings. That assumption is an example of what Ryle (1949) called a *category mistake.* Only emotional syndromes have existence that transcends the individual and hence can be objective in that sense.

For another thing, the notion of subjectivity (and, by implication, objectivity) is also ambiguous. Even when applied to emotional states and reactions, *subjectivity* can be interpreted in two different ways. The first way involves what Calhoun (1989) called *epistemological subjectivity.* It is illustrated by such statements as "You can't trust John's judgment; he is too subjective." The implication is that John is biased, irrational, or even deluded in his judgment. Emotions can be subjective in this sense, but so, too, can ostensibly rational arguments.

The second meaning of subjectivity involves what Calhoun (1989) called *biographical subjectivity*. It is illustrated by such statements as "I find that picture disgusting" or "Your attitude makes me angry." Statements like these do not necessarily imply a biased or irrational judgment. They do, however, imply that the instigating conditions are evaluated in relation to the subject's own interests and values.

Calhoun (1989) argued that biographical and not epistemological subjectivity distinguishes emotional from nonemotional states; that is, emotional accounts make events meaningful by placing them within the context of the individual's own history and goals. Her argument is persuasive, but an important qualification needs to be added. People are not simply free to choose their emotions on the basis of their personal history, interests, and values alone, as Calhoun seems to imply. What is most characteristic about emotions is not their biographical nature but their relational nature (cf. Frijda, 1986; Lazarus, 1991). And it is society, more than biography, that determines the kind of subject–object relations that constitute the various emotions.

Put somewhat differently, the personal-biographical subjectivity of emotions is a particularization of a social-historical subjectivity. What is important to the individual is, to a large extent, a product of socialization, the internalization of the norms and values of society. And, as already described, when a person's emotional state and reactions match community standards (as reflected in the rules of anger), then they may be considered objectively real, even if they are biographically subjective.

In speaking of emotions as relationally subjective but objectively real, I do not wish to reify anger as some kind of ghostly entity that haunts our interpersonal relationships. As indicated earlier, anger (as a syndrome) is a folk-theoretical construct, a kind of story we tell to account for certain kinds of behavior, including (but not limited to) aggression. I now expand on that point briefly, especially with regard to the issue of truth and verifiability.

Sarbin (1986) described how people, when asked to give an account of how they feel, typically tell a story, a self-narrative. He used the example of a (hypothetical but familiar) athletic champion. When asked how he or she feels after winning a contest, the champion will usually respond with a few uninformative exclamations such as "It's incredible" or "It's a wonderful feeling." He or she will then launch into a story about the rigors of training, the role of fellow athletes, family support, the meaning of the contest, future plans, and so forth. (See also Gergen and Gergen, 1988, for a discussion of emotions as self-narratives, with a special emphasis on anger and hostility.)

In the case of the anger story, the central theme is "Don't blame me; it's the instigator's fault. Besides, I couldn't help myself." To feel angry is to tell the story to oneself—and to become so engrossed that it is experienced as real or true, even if the experience is illusory.

What makes a story or account so engrossing? The primary factor is the motivation of the person. Conscious experience is not just something that happens; it is a complex process, something one does. In a sense, emotional feelings can be conceived of as a form of self-presentation, but to one's own self, not just to others (cf. Laux & Weber, 1991). Of course, if the presentation is to be convincing—to have what is sometimes called *narrative truth*—other factors besides motivation must be involved (Gergen & Gergen, 1988). Among the more important criteria for narrative truth are the following: (a) the story must be based on fact and not fiction; (b) the facts must be related to one another in a coherent manner, thus forming a plot; and (c) the plot must be intelligible within a broader social context or belief system. The relation among these three criteria is bidirectional, not one way. As in the case of George and Mary, the same facts can often be interpreted in different ways. The story as a whole specifies which facts are to be considered important and which are to be ignored as trivial, depending on how they contribute to the overall plot. In the final analysis, narratives depend for their verification, at least in part, on debate and dialogue, and not just on proof in the traditional sense.

As this brief description suggests, a narrative approach to truth does not differ greatly from the traditional scientific method (cf. Rorty, 1980; Shotter, 1984). But be that as it may, my main point concerns the potential conflict between the motives or goals that an individual might have for accepting a particular narrative account and the goals sanctioned by society. People who commit aggression often have good reasons to account for their behavior in terms of anger and to accept their own account as true. Whether others accept their anger as real or illusory depends not on how keenly it is felt but on how closely the behavior conforms to accepted standards of conduct, for example, as reflected in the rules of anger.

Implications for Aggression and Violence

At the outset of this chapter, I suggested that anger is often used to explain or legitimize a wide variety of aggressive acts, from child and spouse abuse to urban riots (cf. Proposition 1). I also suggested, on the basis of evidence presented elsewhere (Averill, 1982), that in the normal course of events, anger only rarely results in aggression, at least the kind of aggression that involves physical harm. These two assertions must now be reconciled.

Aggression is part of our prototype of anger, but prototypes can be misleading. They often represent idealized or exaggerated states of affairs that are seldom realized in practice. Prototypic parents, for example, love and protect their children. Real parents seldom live up to the prototype, and some actually neglect and abuse their children. Similarly, although the prototype of anger implies aggression, the implication is more one of potentiality than actuality. In fact, according to Rule 6 (listed earlier), anger should not result in aggression except under exceptional circumstances. The proper goal of anger is to correct a perceived wrong, not to hurt the target. Yet, the threat of aggression, should other means of redress fail, lends anger some of its potency and effectiveness, thus reducing the actual need for aggression.

The link between anger and aggression is, however, even more complex than these remarks suggest. Consider another metaphor. As a syndrome or folk-theoretical construct (narrative account), anger can be likened to an architect's blueprint. The availability of a blueprint does not cause a building to be constructed, but it does make construction easier. In fact, without a blueprint, there might not be any construction at all, or at least the form of the construction would be quite different. Emotions, I have argued elsewhere (e.g., Averill, 1980, 1984, 1990, 1991), are social constructions. They, too, need "blueprints." In the case of anger, the blueprint is the set of norms and standards embodied in the rules of anger, such as those listed earlier.

The availability of anger as an account facilitates the behavior of which it is an account. I have illustrated this phenomenon with respect to crimes of passion. Less dramatically, the same phenomenon can also be observed in laboratory studies of aggression. In a typical experiment, one group of subjects is angered (e.g., by unwarranted criticism, the arbitrary administration of punishment), and another group is treated in a neutral fashion. The influence of some extraneous variable on aggression is then assessed (e.g., unexplained physiological arousal, the presence of weapons, or an aversive stimulus). Typically, only subjects who have been angered, or who have been given some other legitimizing rationale, tend to respond with increased aggression in the presence of the extraneous variable. (For a review of relevant research, see Averill, 1982, chap. 6; Baron, 1977).

One common interpretation of findings such as these is that anger "causes" aggression. I will say more about the issue of causality later. For the moment, suffice it to note that anger no more causes aggression than a blueprint causes the construction of a building. (Or perhaps it would be more accurate to say that anger causes aggression in much the same way that a blueprint causes the construction of a building.)

Ideally, anger should facilitate aggression only under conditions of adequate provocation and then only to the extent needed to correct the wrong. Unfortunately, the ideal is not always matched in practice, in which case anger becomes an excuse rather than a justification for aggression. I emphasize this point because of the current trend to treat anger as a intrapsychic event that must be discharged or released. Locating anger within the person rather than as a part of the social order not only conflates emotional syndromes with emotional states and reactions but encourages a "let it all hang out" attitude. Pent-up, repressed, or suppressed anger has been postulated as a cause of diverse physical and psychological disorders, including depression, hypertension, and cancer, to mention only a few. The expression of anger, advocates of this perspective contend, has a curative (cathartic) effect. Unfortunately, a response cannot simply be labeled as anger without endorsing—no matter how unwittingly and unintentionally—its exculpatory implications.

Not surprisingly from the present perspective, empirical research has not been kind to the catharsis hypothesis (Tavris, 1984). More often than not, the uninhibited expression of aggression on one occasion simply facilitates subsequent aggression. The old adage that practice makes perfect is as true of aggression as it is of any other type of behavior. And if the aggression is given the appearance of legitimacy by calling it anger, subsequent aggression is made even more easy.

Implications for Research and Theory

The foregoing analysis has implications for research and theory as well as for practice. One of the first objectives of research should be the identification of the system of rules that helps constitute anger as an emotional syndrome. This has been one focus of my own research, not only with respect to anger (Averill, 1982, 1983) but with respect to other emotions as well, including love (Averill, 1985), grief (Averill & Nunley, 1988), hope (Averill, Catlin, & Chon, 1990), and generalized stress reactions (Averill, 1989). Once the rules of various emotions are identified, we are in a better position to explore how they get misapplied, as in emotional disorders (Averill, 1988), and how they can be altered creatively to produce more adaptive emotional syndromes (Averill & Nunley, 1992; Averill & Thomas-Knowles, 1991).

Social rules are not to be confused with simple regularities in behavior. Rules carry sanctions—they are the "shoulds" and "should nots" of behavior. Anger is basically a moral concept. Psychologists, in particular, are wont to divorce anger from its moral underpinnings. The consequence is not simply to strip the concept of much of its meaning but (as in the "let it all hang out" attitude discussed earlier) to promote an inadvertent legitimation of aggression.

On a more theoretical level, when anger is divorced from the social order, it loses its external moorings and becomes anchored within the individual as a strictly intrapsychic phenomenon—at least that is the way most psychologists have come to conceive of anger. A short conceptual step then leads to the assumption that anger is either an internal cause of aggression (in the traditional sense of efficient cause—one event producing another) or a process that occurs in parallel with aggression (like two trains running on adjoining tracks—one emotional and the other cognitive). If I understand him correctly, these are the positions adopted by Berkowitz in his early (1962) and later (1990) writings on anger and aggression. By contrast, the present argument assumes that a person who displays aggression while in an angry state is doing one thing (aggressing angrily), not two different things, either sequentially or simultaneously. To repeat, anger (as a syndrome) is a folk-theoretical construct—an account we give of behavior. Accounts are not efficient causes or parallel processes that run their course within the individual, although they can—like an architect's blueprint—influence the nature, form, and incidence of behavior.

Conclusion

In one fashion or another, I have now touched on each of the four propositions outlined at the outset of the chapter: (a) anger helps legitimize aggression; (b) anger is often identified (incorrectly) with feelings; (c) angry feelings can be illusory; and (d) anger is not an event, either psychological or physiological, that occurs within the mind (or body) of the individual. Other than to reiterate these propositions, I will not attempt to summarize an already condensed discussion. As indicated earlier, the first proposition is the most important from a practical standpoint, and the last is the most important from a theoretical perspective. However, practice and theory cannot be separated without loss to each. The second and third propositions (which have to do with angry feelings and their sometimes illusory nature), although of considerable interest in their own right, have served primarily a didactive purpose. In the final analysis, a proper understanding of anger must extend beyond the self. The origins and functions of anger are to be found in the realm of social interaction, not in the realm of intrapsychic events, whether those events are conceived of in terms of conscious feelings or bodily reactions.

References

Averill, J. R. (1980). A constructivist view of emotion. In R. Plutchik & H. Kellerman (Eds.), *Emotion: Theory, research and experience: Vol. 1. Theories of emotion* (pp. 305–339). San Diego, CA: Academic Press.

Averill, J. R. (1982). *Anger and aggression: An essay on emotion.* New York: Springer-Verlag.

Averill, J. R. (1983). Studies on anger and aggression: Implications for theories of emotion. *American Psychologist, 38,* 1145–1160.

Averill, J. R. (1984). The acquisition of emotions during adulthood. In C. Z. Malatesta & C. Izard (Eds.), *Affective processes in adult development.* Newbury Park, CA: Sage.

Averill, J. R. (1985). The social construction of emotion: With special reference to love. In K. Gergen & K. Davis (Eds.), *The social construction of the person* (pp. 89–109). New York: Springer-Verlag.

Averill, J. R. (1988). Disorders of emotion. *Journal of Social & Clinical Psychology, 8,* 247–268.

Averill, J. R. (1989). Stress as fact and artifact: An inquiry into the social origins and functions of some stress reactions. In C. D. Spielberger, I. G. Sarason, & J. Strelau (Eds.), *Stress and anxiety* (Vol. 12, pp. 15–38). Washington, DC: Hemisphere.

Averill, J. R. (1990). Emotions as related to systems of behavior. In N. L. Stein, B. Leventhal, & T. Trabasso (Eds.), *Psychological and biological approaches to emotion* (pp. 385–404). Hillsdale, NJ: LEA.

Averill, J. R. (1991). Emotions as episodic dispositions, cognitive schemas, and transitory social roles: Steps toward an integrated theory of emotion. In D. Ozer, J. M. Healy, Jr., & A. J. Stewart (Eds.), *Perspectives in personality* (Vol. 3a, pp. 139–167). London: Jessica Kingsley.

Averill, J. R., Catlin, G., & Chon, K. K. (1990). *Rules of hope.* New York: Springer-Verlag.

Averill, J. R., & Nunley, E. P. (1988). Grief as an emotion and as a disease. *Journal of Social Issues, 44,* 79–95.

Averill, J. R., & Nunley, E. P. (1992). *Voyages of the heart: Living an emotionally creative life.* New York: Free Press.

Averill, J. R., & Thomas-Knowles, C. (1991). Emotional creativity. In K. T. Strongman (Ed.), *International review of studies on emotion* (Vol. 1, pp. 269–299). London: Wiley.

Baron, R. A. (1977). *Human aggression.* New York: Plenum.

Baumeister, R. F., Stillwell, A., & Wotman, S. R. (1990). Victim and perpetrator accounts of interpersonal conflict: Autobiographical narratives about anger. *Journal of Personality and Social Psychology, 59,* 994–1005.

Berkowitz, L. (1962). *Aggression: A social psychological analysis.* New York: McGraw-Hill.

Berkowitz, L. (1990). On the formation and regulation of anger and aggression. *American Psychologist, 45,* 494–503.

Calhoun, C. (1989). Subjectivity & emotion. *Philosophical Forum, 20,* 195–210.

Denzin, N. K. (1990). On understanding emotion: The interpretive–cultural agenda. In T. D. Kemper (Ed.), *Research agendas in the sociology of emotions* (pp. 85–116). Albany: State University of New York Press.

Frijda, N. H. (1986). *The emotions.* Cambridge, England: Cambridge University Press.

Gergen, K. J., & Gergen, M. (1988). Narrative and the self as relationship. In L. Berkowitz (Ed.), *Advances in experimental social psychology* (Vol. 21, pp. 17–56). San Diego, CA: Academic Press.

Hochschild, A. R. (1983). *The managed heart.* Berkeley: University of California Press.

Laux, L., & Weber, H. (1991). Presentation of self in coping with anger and anxiety: An intentional approach. *Anxiety Research, 3,* 233–255.

Lazarus, R. S. (1991). *Emotion and adaptation.* New York: Oxford University Press.

Leventhal, H. (1984). A perceptual motor theory of emotion. In K. R. Scherer & P. Ekman (Eds.), *Approaches to emotion* (pp. 271–291). Hillsdale, NJ: Erlbaum.

Levy, R. I. (1984). The emotions in comparative perspective. In K. R. Scherer & P. Ekman (Eds.), *Approaches to emotion* (pp. 397–412). Hillsdale, NJ: Erlbaum.

Ortony, A., Clore, G. L., & Collins, A. (1988). *The cognitive structure of emotions.* Cambridge, England: Cambridge University Press.

Rorty, R. (1980). *Philosophy and the mirror of nature.* Oxford, England: Basil Blackwell.

Rosaldo, M. Z. (1980). *Knowledge and passion: Ilongot notions of self and social life.* Cambridge, England: Cambridge University Press.

Ryle, G. (1949). *The concept of mind.* London: Hutchinson.

Sarbin, T. R. (1986). Emotion and act: Roles and Rhetoric. In R. Harre (Ed.), *The social construction of emotions* (pp. 83–97). Oxford, England: Basil Blackwell.

Shotter, J. (1984). *Social accountability and selfhood.* Oxford, England: Basil Blackwell.

Shweder, R. A. (1985). Menstrual pollution, soul loss, and the comparative study of emotions. In A. Kleinman & B. Good (Eds.), *Culture and depression* (pp. 182–215). Berkeley: University of California Press.

Solomon, R. C. (1976). *The passions.* Garden City, NY: Doubleday Anchor.

Tavris, C. (1984). On the wisdom of counting to ten: Personal and social dangers of anger expression. In P. Shaver (Ed.), *Review of personality and social psychology: Vol. 5. Emotions, relationships, and health* (pp. 170–191). Newbury Park, CA: Sage.

CHAPTER 8

Good Violence and Bad Violence: Self-Presentations of Aggressors Through Accounts and War Stories

Hans Toch

A recent television interview featured an exoffender who had become an actor. The man charmed the interviewer and reminisced about his career as an unpromising delinquent. He had been imprisoned, he said, because he killed a fellow delinquent in a fight. The fellow delinquent had fought dirty, but he won.

"How did you feel after the fight?" asked the reporter. "I felt nothing," the actor snapped back. After an awkward pause, he corrected himself. "If I'd met the guy in hell," he said, "I'd have killed him again." These versions are somewhat discrepant, but both are revealing. The first says, "In my prime, I was an extratough S.O.B. who casually used violence and never gave it a thought." The revised version says, "I needed to redress acts of injustice."

Both portraits are designed to impress people, but in different ways. The first is meant to evoke a sense of titillation and awe. "You are in the presence," it announces, "of an unfeeling monster." The addendum invites empathy and understanding. "I was a monster," it says, "with a heart." The picture is one of disinhibition in a justifiable cause.

This chapter discusses self-presentations by violence-perpetrating men that are designed to garner approval of or to minimize disapproval by significant others. Violence self-portraits vary in emphasis over time and across audiences. Different reconstructions carry different connotations about the person's motives and personality makeup. These connotations are designed to impress different listeners and to affect their view of the aggressor. The self-portraits also aim at the aggressor's view of himself. This usually means that he must avoid noticing two related facts. One is the disproportionality of his own responses to instigating occasions, and the other is that of his loss of control. If a violent person is honest with himself, he has to say to his audience, "I have a propensity to make much of insignificant provocations" and "I keep losing my cool and exploding with rage." Both of these insights are needed if a personal violence problem is to be sensibly addressed, and most aggressors work hard at not coming up with them—at least, not with both insights simultaneously.

Official Accounts

If an aggressor admits his aggression to officials or other strangers, his accounts are often lopsided confessions. Some aggressors volubly highlight their own irrationality, whereas others play it down. Many offenders prize a reliable propensity to explode (Berkowitz, 1978; Peterson & Braiker, 1981). Rage reduces their culpability (see chap. 7) and makes violence something ego-alien and unintended, a product of states such as emotional lability or intoxication. One does not commit violence; one is driven to it. Overpowering anger becomes the equivalent of the time-honored claim that "the devil made me do it."

In institutional contexts like competitive sports, police work, and child rearing, more dispassionate violence is prized. Miscalculations by the aggressor ("I shot because I thought the suspect's comb was a knife") become more defensible than retaliatory loss of control ("The dirtbag asked for it when he gave me the finger"). When violence is presumed to be instrumental, anger denotes unacceptable overkill.

Public accounts are versions of incidents that are designed for system consumption, for the record, or for justificatory use. They reduce chances of disciplinary action or punishment. They also aim to sidetrack interventions, which rather than threatening to change the aggressor are invited to target disinhibiting conditions (e.g., alcohol abuse) or to limit themselves to education or training efforts. Training efforts are designed to make instrumental aggressors more discriminating about when and where they use aggression. This implies that violent acts have been largely mistakes that can be remedied with information.[1]

In referring to *public accounts*, I use the word *account* as it has been used in sociological writings. I do so because of the applicability of the concept to most self-descriptions of violence. The applicability results from the fact that the aggressors' self-descriptions must defuse condemnation of aggression, and "an account is a linguistic device employed whenever an action is subjected to valuative inquiry . . . a statement made by a social actor to explain unanticipated or untoward behavior" (Scott & Lyman, 1968, p. 46). Sociologists distinguish between two types of accounts, justifications and excuses. *Excuses* are defined as "accounts in which one admits that the act in question is bad, wrong or inappropriate, but denies full responsibility" (p. 47). The offender who describes himself as explosive, for example, claims that his feelings are irresistible constraints.

Justifications are "accounts in which one accepts responsibility for the act in question, but denies the pejorative quality associated with it" (Scott & Lyman, 1968, p. 46). The officer who asserts "I saw what looked like a shiny gun" implies that his perception should exonerate him from culpable homicide.

Private Accounts

Public accounts are not designed for audiences of intimates or peers, whose understanding and loyalty the aggressor expects. No self-respecting delinquent tells another delinquent, "I really can't imagine what came over me to make me violent. Everybody knows I wouldn't hurt a fly. I guess something must have snapped." No hockey player says to his team, "You can imagine my chagrin when I misjudged the distance between Big Pierre and myself and knocked his teeth out with my stick."

Scott and Lyman (1968) wrote that

One variable governing the honoring of an account is the social circle in which it is introduced . . . Vocabularies of accounts are likely to be routinized within cultures,

---

[1]*Such was the implication when Police Chief Gates reacted to the televised beating by Los Angeles police officers with the announcement "I've ordered up an examination of our training on the use of force, brick by brick." Training is designed to prevent errors of judgment. These are also implied by the chief's assertion that his department "may have encountered some problems because of the relative inexperience of many officers" (Stevenson, 1991).*

subcultures and groups, and some are likely to be exclusive to the circle in which they are employed. A drug addict may be able to justify his conduct to a bohemian world, but not to the courts. Similarly kin and friends may accept excuses in situations in which strangers refuse to do so. (p. 54)

Intimates are individuals who share one's values. They can be enlisted as allies against outsiders who may threaten the group when they threaten the aggressor. If it becomes an issue, intimates can back one's alibis, including denials of violence. To help them, one may avoid discussion of incidents. This enables the intimates to assert that they know of no violent behavior and cannot believe that it occurred.

Private accounts, however, often permit serious reviews of violence. They can be detailed narratives. But they cannot (by definition) be favorable reviews in which violence is savored. These latter narratives are war stories, and they are told when one expects that one's violence will be approved of by intimates, which is different from violence that risks disapproval. Violence in accounts is acknowledged to be "bad violence," whereas violence in war stories is "good violence." In reviews with intimates, bad violence is deescalated into not-so-bad violence and good violence is escalated to become better violence.

Discounting Violence

Violence is a (hopefully last) recourse in settling conflicts. This recourse, though, is different from other options that can be deployed. Sticks and stones break bones; peaceful resolutions do not. This difference can be a problem for violence users and their friends. The problem can be ameliorated, however: One can make violent options sound like nonviolent solutions. One way of doing so is by using euphemisms. Nowadays, wars are referred to with soothing phrases such as "the use of force" or "the exercise of military options." And people who are killed become "collateral damage" of the action.

Blurring occurs with all sorts of violence. In date rape (see chapter 10 in this volume), fraternity brothers can represent rapists as clumsy, ill-fated lotharios. Those who cry "rape," they can say, destroy reputations with scurrilous cheap shots. Confusions arise during the end game of dating. Fraternity members endorse the goal of "scoring" or "making out." To score is to persuade a date to become physically intimate. This is different from rape, the domain of criminal rapists. According to the brothers, the difficulty is that the line between rape and persuasion is overgenerously drawn by philistines who do not understand the intricacies of socializing.

The emphasis in such arguments is on commonalities that one sees between violence and purposive behavior with similar goals. There is a deemphasis of differences between violent and nonviolent means to the same ends. Its point is to gloss over the violence that violence does.

But this line of argument is not usable when violence is blatant and thus hard to ignore. How can one discount obvious brutality? A hoodlum's mother cannot dismiss a rape or a murder as boyish misconduct. However, one path she can take instead is to claim that the act is unrepresentative and therefore a fluke. "Tom is a good son," she may say. "He does good work in school and loves Buster, his baby brother. This stuff is not like him at all." She means by this that the behavior is discountable because it must have been imposed on her son by extrinsic and extraneous forces ("The kids he hangs out with get him into trouble").[2]

External pressures are seen to shape instrumental or expressive components of violence. They are blamed for confusion and lapses of judgment ("It was the end of my shift, and I was tired"). Anger thresholds are perceived to change because of stressful impingements ("You see dozens of your buddies killed, you shoot anything that moves"). There are also social pressures—such as from "the neighborhood gang"—that are assumed to exact compliant misbehavior as a price of membership.

Environmental determinism and ego dystonicity can be invoked in tandem or conjointly. In the case of the Los Angeles police sergeant involved in the Rodney King beating, interviews elicited the following ruminations:

> Mr. K's friends say the scars to his psyche and the habits he picked up while working the most crime-plagued section of Los Angeles, the 77th Street Division, where police work has been compared to a war, might have been transferred with him when he moved last year to the Foothill Division, a less-violent section of the city. (Egan, 1991)
>
> "He is a very gentle family man; in fact, I would describe him as the ideal Catholic family man," said Father Robert Rankin, a close friend of Mr. K and who is also the sergeant's

---

[2] Where relevant behavior patterns are difficult to ignore, the argument can rest on a reluctance to extrapolate from less serious to more serious explosiveness. "Jim blows up when other kids tease him," a mother might say, "but he wouldn't burn a building. Not with people in it" (Daniels, 1991).

parish priest. "As a policeman, he is under a lot of pressure, and he seeks relief in the activities of this church." (Egan, 1991)

All sorts of demands can be seen to have compelling effects, known to those who live with the same context. Strangers are not supposed to understand these effects, however, because "you had to have been there to know what it was like." Intimates know about violence causation because shared experience confers perspective. At extremes, this perspective endorses overkill.

Some intimates know, for example, that the aggressor's world is a dangerous one. They know that this world demands caution, vigilance, and readiness to act—that one has to carry weapons and be willing to use them. They know that one may have to strike first, before others have a chance. To the uninformed outsider, this looks like aggression, but intimates know that decisions have to be made fast. They know that an instant reaction can include killing a victim in a robbery if he or she makes a furtive move that looks threatening, and it can mean assaulting a person who stares belligerently at oneself or a friend.

Intimates can honor claims that sound implausible to nonintimates. Honoring such claims is partly a function of empathy that is based on commonality of experience. The experience has to do with constraints and opportunities of the environment and their power to preempt. The intimate buys the aggressor's story to the extent to which he buys the environmental determinism on which it is based. He may not like what the aggressor has done, but he can see how circumstances could have promoted or prompted his actions. Intimates can also allow for familiar psychological dispositions and weaknesses, which can be encompassed by self-effacing admissions and assertions such as "One gets excited in the heat of battle," "Everyone reacts when provoked," "There is a limit to how much stress one can take," and so forth. More often, the aggressor appeals to disinhibiting perspectives related to the experiences that he shares with intimates. Statements can be prefaced with "I know it was stupid but . . ." meaning "Under similar circumstances, you might have been similarly stupid."

Empathy claims are enhanced when someone highlights situations with which one is familiar and reactions that one has experienced (albeit to a lesser degree). Some scenarios—such as murders by battered wives or violence against unfaithful spouses caught in the act of being unfaithful—have widespread claims to empathy. Others—such as killing a police officer to avoid being arrested—have narrower appeal.

Empathy and Social Distance

Although aggressors invite empathy, they must discourage empathy with their victims. Victims can be discounted because of trends in their behavior ("You know what a loud mouth he was," "She was a terrible nagger," and so forth) or attributes that challenge temptation resistance, such as carrying large sums of money or dressing flirtatiously. Victims can also be devalued as part of a calculus that compares system reactions to different incidents. The extremes of such calculus are invidious hypotheticals such as "If you (or the victim) had been White (or non-White) or male (or female), the system would have reacted more harshly (or leniently)." More prevalently, the focus is on the relative social distance between the spectator, the aggressor, and the victim. Violence by a stranger against a loved one becomes more serious than that by a loved one against a stranger. The greater the relative distance one can achieve from the victim, the more one can discount his or her victimization.[3]

In a recent incident, sadistic youths attacked homeless men returning to their shelter. A week later, perpetrators of this incident were identified, and some of them were arrested. Reporters interviewed neighbors, who complained that the police had taken unseemly interest in a minor-league event. Some referred to past friction between residents and drifters and some to the roughness of the neighborhood. They implied that the police used the occasion as an excuse to roust people: "Not that maiming indigents can be justified, but why so much fuss?" By contrast, community members getting police attention received sympathy.

The neighbors did not dehumanize the victims (adjudge them as less than human) or engage in victim blaming (claim that they had "asked for it").[4] Such perspectives

---

[3]*Accounts contemporaneous with former President Bush's decision to attack Iraq noted that, according to White House aides, "Bush assumed that the American public's main concern would be the number of U.S. casualties, not the tens of thousands of Iraqis who stand to die or be maimed in a massive air assault, and that even the killing of thousands of civilians—including women and children—probably would not undermine American support for the war effort" (Aides say, 1990). The president's assumption was confirmed by subsequent developments. Despite a ratio of 1,000 to 1 of Iraqi to U.S. deaths, the former were greeted with a wave of national indifference.*

[4]*The term victim blaming has many connotations that are frequently confused with each other or somehow combined. One compound connotation, for example, is "If the victim had not done what he or she had done, there would have been no violence." In asking, "What business did she have walking through this neighborhood with a shopping bag?" the victim is accused of lack of sophistication. To say, "Her blouse was unbuttoned, and she drank like a fish" implies a burden on the aggressor's temptation resistance that is an incitement to violence. Other comments imply that the victim initiated the violent action by disregarding unambiguous warnings ("I says, 'face the wall and don't move,' but he moves") or not meeting the aggressor's needs ("She shoulda made that cheeseburger instead of giving me grief")—thus committing calculated suicide.*

When an incident is described so that the first move is assigned to the victim ("He started the war by disregarding our ultimatum"), the disproportionality of the aggressor's aggression is obfuscated. Any emphasis on nonviolent initiatives by the

delete the reprehensibility of violence or define violence as good violence. Rather, violence discounting distances us from the victim while it may simultaneously personalize the aggressor so that he can claim and mobilize empathy.

The Myth of Good Violence

Good violence is seen as good because it is instrumental in a good cause. Its archetype is dragon-slaying violence. Such violence has three attributes: (a) It counters bad violence (b) from nasty aggressors (c) who pick on helpless victims.

The requisites of good violence include measured deployments of dispassionate force. Indignation is permitted as a feeling, but rage is proscribed. A dragon slayer must be in control of his actions. He must also be a brave person who does not take foolish chances. He must dispense violence impersonally but effectively.

Dragon slaying is a popular scenario in fiction. In standard plots, it is the charge of the cavalry that prevents settlers from being scalped in midscalping. It is the police intercepting offenders in midrape or in the act of murdering. It includes the campaigns of freedom fighters or soldiers on the just side of just wars.

Such violence is a myth in that it occurs infrequently in life. Murderers do not murder in public, where police can see them. Soldiers do not meet dictators (or concentration camp guards) in trenches. And dragon slayers have even doubled as dragons (lynch mobs, pogromists), as did crusaders, vigilantes, and Indian fighters. Heroes have tackled easy marks. Others have lost their cool, lashed out in anger, or struck in fear.

Good violence is defined as such in the eyes of beholders. It earns medals, commendations, and accolades. It wins esteem from peers and admiration from intimates. It gains formal recognition, informal recognition, or both.

Violence becomes consensually good if there is concurrence about the worthiness of its goals and the appropriateness of its means (i.e., force) to achieving its goals. Consensus of this kind can be facilitated when one can write scenarios that depict targets who are unmitigated villains and aggressors who are public-spirited heroes. Partisan

---

victim constitutes victim blaming, even when the victim's actions are hostile ("He said my mother was a whore") or challenging ("You don't have the guts to shoot"). The concept does not apply to violent initiatives ("He upped and slapped me . . .") that boomerang (". . . so I flattened him") because these constitute victim precipitation, which makes the violence transactional.

On the other end of the spectrum, victim behavior may not be at issue. Victims can be blamed for being who they are, such as members of a group that has been classified as an outgroup, on the basis of vaguely specified past behavior.

interpretations evoke rival scenarios that exonerate villains, tarnish heroes, or reverse their roles. Both Iraqis and Americans in recent confrontations talked of "good against evil" and "deliberate brutal aggression," but each side was referring to the other. Each side adduced evidence for its dragon-slaying mission by pointing to a different phase of the developing conflict. This "Who is the dragon?" discrepancy arises in many escalating conflicts. In private disputes—such as with exspouses claiming martyrdom—intimates become carriers of divergent myths.

Some argue that history is the final arbiter of disputes, thus pinpointing heroes and villains. But victors write the history texts, unless revisionist versions supplant them. If force is used by authorities against citizens (including offenders), authorities are the historians through official accounts. Not surprisingly, authorities emerge as the shining knights. "Unsung heroes" infrequently arise because singing makes heroes of aggressors.

War Stories

Narratives relating to good violence (war stories) are reminiscences of incidents that actors define as commendable violence. Such reminiscences can be exchanged by participants in violent incidents or told by participants to nonparticipants. The exchange of war stories is an exercise in fraternal nostalgia. It evokes experiences of risks jointly faced and overcome. It resuscitates memories of adversaries who were gamely vanquished in battle and highlights danger, action, and heroic exploits. War stories describe experiential peaks, not the routines in which these peaks are embedded. Delinquents remember gang fights, not boredom on street corners. Veterans talk of battles, not of sloshing through mud or hacking through jungles. Police war stories highlight shooting and fighting, not nights spent on patrol.

The narratives deal with unrepresentative exceptions to eventless routines to mythologize violence-related vocations and avocations. They romanticize the actors' roles, downplaying emotions such as indecision and fear, that characterize states of mind at the time of the incidents. The goal is not to understand one's violence but to exploit it for secondary gains.

The shared experience is partly existential. We acted, therefore we were (and hopefully still are). To kill, shoot, crack skulls, or wield batons is to exhibit behavior that has impact. The impact is also consequential and can be advertised. The "those-were-the-days-my-boy" flavor that permeates reminiscing envisages no deception because the listeners are familiar with the contexts in which the actions took place. Nor are reminiscences designed to mislead or to stake fraudulent claims so as to garner admiration. The point of war stories is to accentuate memorable aspects of worthy violence. This requires placing the emphasis on the threat posed by opponents and on the appropriateness of actions that one took to neutralize these opponents. In the process, violent acts emerge as meritorious reactions to threats.

Morality Plays

War stories can function as morality plays. In these scenarios, violence has become an instrument of social control, a means for dispensing justice and redressing wrongs. The justice and wrongs are those of the group. The protagonists are our good guys and their bad guys, and the good guys make the world safer for us. The lessons of morality plays are fourfold: The first lesson is that offending the group does not pay; rival gang members who disrespect women, for instance, get their comeuppance. Second, justice cannot be indefinitely subverted; offenders who keep offending are bound to be challenged. Third, the group has champions; these champions can be depended on to exact righteous revenge. Fourth, when all else fails, violence is the tool for restoring order. Morality plays buttress the belief in a just world and make violence the means for achieving this world. The mythology is uniquely alive because it is personalized in the incidents.

In a balkanized world, war stories are also parochial and ethnocentric. The hero is "one of us," the target "one of them." "They" are nonintimates, but they have other attributes that make them alien. Aliens reject our norms. They invade our turfs, insult our women, defy our rules, and demonstrate that they are unregeneratedly undersocialized. The hero steps in where our socialization measures fail to demonstrate to deviants that our rules must be taken seriously.

Morality plays cement solidarity and promote ingroup socialization. The alien offender is full of runaway impulsivity. When he is violent, his violence is predatory and impulsive. The hero's violence is cool and calculated and designed to curb subversive aggressivity.

Selfless Aggrandizement

Heroes cannot advertise: The hero cannot seek admiration by using violence, because he is selfless. However, the hero does earn admiration, because he puts his life on the line on our behalf. In discussing their accomplishments, heroes face a dilemma. They must not appear to seek status through their war stories; this is unherolike. Their task is to self-effacingly shoulder the burden of acclaim.

The morality-play aspect of war stories solves the modesty problem. There is a point to the story, and the hero is not boasting when he tells it. The point pertains to the reprehensibility of the affront to the group and to the punishment deserved by the affront.

The hero describes the offender's behavior and recalls his own forbearance. The hero tells us that the offender's attention had been called to his transgression and that notice had been served ("The crud made loud remarks; I told him twice to cool it"; "This is the police, turkey—freeze, or you're dogmeat"; "This is our playground, you get your tails out of here"). Any action taken at this point becomes the fault of the transgressor for not taking the hint. The hero's hand has been forced by the offender, and he has license to act.

The hero disclaims credit for violence but takes credit for upholding the norms. He has taught a lesson to a recalcitrant offender and has deterred other offenders who might follow in his footsteps. The war story reinforces the lesson. It may also build the reputation of the hero, but this is a corollary of the ostensible goal.

Feeding Reputations

War stories aside, few heroes are oblivious to admiring glances in locker rooms, taverns, and other places where intimates congregate. Having acquired reputations, some heroes feel that they must live up to these reputations. They must feed them through new heroic acts, which they have to seek out. War stories take up the slack but tend to become stale over time. With time, it becomes harder to pretend that dated incidents retain their currency.

Reputation building is difficult because legitimate occasions for violence are statistically rare. The reputation builder must therefore become proactive to the point of generating incidents in which norms can be enforced and justice can be restored (Toch, 1969).

If the norm enforcer is lucky, his reputation may cause some of his intimates to enlist his enforcing services: "If there is trouble in the cell block," they say, "call Big John," or "I saw a Latin Killer cross Main Street—get Stiletto." Norm enforcers who are not in demand must invite themselves into situations in which they may not be wanted, defining transgressions that others do not see. The problem is that they can acquire a reputation for "stirring up trouble" and can discover that they are feared more than admired by peers.

A second problem that the proactive reputation builder faces is that there is a distinction between private conflicts and public conflicts that he can be tempted to ignore. This temptation exists because any affront to a role incumbent can be directed at him personally, at his role, or both. Norm enforcers are subject to challenge by other norm enforcers or norm-enforcing candidates. Shootouts result in defense of or in search of reputations. Thin-skinned egos react to slights. Intimates become familiar with such scenarios and become resistant to claims that the issue is one of honor and justice.

Aggressors discover that groups do not blindly endorse the violence of members. Groups do owe loyalty to dispensers of justice. They do not owe loyalty to members who seek credit for low-credibility accomplishments. Intimates strive for empathy with protagonists, but this does not mean that self-serving stories will be uncritically endorsed.

Implications for Research and Reform

This chapter has discussed accounts of violence by perpetrators of violence that are designed mainly for intimates or significant others. Intimates who listen to accounts of violence can be a resource for researchers and for agents of change. They can serve as mediators; they can correct for unempathetic perspectives; they can make us sensitive to contexts in which violent incidents occur.

Aggressors trust their intimates and expect fairness and understanding from them. Accounts of violent incidents meant for intimates are less likely to be blatantly exculpatory than are accounts designed for official consumption. Versions of violence causation in such accounts will be skewed, but the emphasis is predictable and accommodatable. We can predict that purposive aspects of action will be highlighted where possible. We know that common denominators between violent and nonviolent solutions will be stressed. We know that contextual pressures will be cited and that group norms will be invoked.

We can work with aggressors and intimates to round out these pictures. What did the aggressor expect when he entered the scene? What were his feelings at this initial time? Did he do or say anything that might have been misconstrued or resented? Could he have evolved hostile or angry feelings? How might the victim have felt, and how might he or she have construed the situation? How did the aggressor follow up on his approach, and how could this action be perceived or misperceived? Could he in turn have jumped to premature conclusions? Did he then have such feelings as anger or resentment? Was he still in control of the situation? Come to think of it, could he remember incidents in which similar scenarios unfolded with comparable results? Intimates identify not only with context-relevant facts but also with feelings and perceptions that contribute to escalating encounters—especially in settings familiar to them. Intimates know that the aggressor is human. They also sense that he has a disposition that contributes to confrontations, such as a thin skin, short fuse, or abrasive demeanor. Faced with a more complete account of an incident, intimates can fill in blanks and supplement details.[5]

Some believe that the value systems of intimates must be changed to enlist their cooperation. This is so if one proposes to turn the intimates into finks, judges, or prosecutors. It is not so if the task is to help them understand and prevent self-destructive acts of their peers.

The context of research and/or reform must be nonpunitive (information must have no adverse consequences); it must be educational (there must be learning and insight to be gained) and socially productive (participants must see themselves as contributing to human betterment.) These requisites are compatible with ethical endeavors at research and reform. Such endeavors must permit those who work with perpetrators of violence to tell them that, among other things, (a) they and their peers can learn something about themselves that they may find interesting, (b) their experience gives them expertise in the subject of inquiry, (c) products of their learning have application and (d) and can have impact that prevents people from getting hurt or getting into trouble, and (e) there is no possibility that what transpires in sessions can be used against members of the group.

Other incentives depend on the program and its resources. I once was involved in a program that offered police officers the opportunity to keep fellow officers from being fired. The program also helped the officers examine critical steps in their responses to dangerous calls, thereby reducing injuries to themselves and suspects, and assisted them in studying their own reactions to critical incidents. Most important, it afforded the officers the opportunity to enact violence prevention programs that they had designed and proposed (Toch & Grant, 1991). In another type of setting, we wanted to give violent offenders a chance to expand their repertoire of conflict-related behavior so as to avoid outcomes such as had resulted in their confinement (Toch & Adams, 1989). These are

---

[5]*Intimates often privately hold views that they do not advertise about an individual's violent propensities. A police officer, for example, may be quietly avoided as a partner by some of his or her colleagues. The officer may be viewed as abrasive, insensitive, explosive, and dangerous to society. No such hypothesis, however, will be communicated to superiors or outsiders.*

examples of interventions in which peers or intimates are enlisted to deal with problems of violence. Endeavors of this kind have also helped families with aggressive offspring (Patterson, 1974), saved marriages of batterers and their victims (Goffman, 1984), facilitated education in violence-infested schools (Goleman, 1987), and recaptured violence-ridden neighborhoods.

In each case, peers or family members have been mobilized to work with people who are responsible for violence. In each case, the intimates have studied the dynamics of violence as it unfolds in actual incidents. In each case, the goal has been to prevent violent behavior, thus helping the person and solving a problem. In other words, the loyalty, empathy, and experience of intimates has been deployed on behalf of salvageable aggressors but also on behalf of victims and of society at large.

References

Aides say Bush ready to attack. (1990, December 28). *Albany Times Union.*

Berkowitz, L. (1978). Is criminal violence normative behavior? Hostile and instrumental aggression in violent incidents. *Journal of Research in Crime and Delinquency, 15,* 148–161.

Daniels, L. A. (1991, March 21). Youth held in fatal Bronx fire had been at scene. *New York Times.*

Egan, T. (1991, March 19). Indicted sergeant was a hero in '89. *New York Times.*

Goffman, J. M. (1987). *Batterers Anonymous: Self-help counseling for men who batter women.* San Bernardino, CA: Batterers Anonymous.

Goleman, D. (1987, April 7). The bully: New research depicts a paranoid, lifelong loser. *New York Times.*

Patterson, G. R. (1974). Retraining of aggressive boys by their parents: Multiple settings, treatments and criteria. *Journal of Clinical and Consulting Psychology, 42,* 471– 481.

Peterson, M. A., & Braiker, E. (1981). *Who commits crime: A survey of prison inmates.* Cambridge, MA: Oelgeschlager, Gunn & Hain.

Scott, M. B., & Lyman, S. M. (1968). Accounts. *American Sociological Review, 33,* 46–62.

Stevenson, R. W. (1991, March 21). Los Angeles police chief orders training review. *New York Times.*

Toch, H. (1969). *Violent men.* Chicago: Aldine.

Toch, H., & Adams, K. (1989). *Coping: Maladaptation in prisons.* New Brunswick, NJ: Transaction.

Toch, H., & Grant, J. D. (1991). *Police as problem solvers.* New York: Plenum Press.

PART FOUR

Violence Against Women

CHAPTER 9

Violent Networks: The Origins and Management of Domestic Conflict

M. P. Baumgartner

A typical case of domestic violence appears at first glance to be a transaction between two individuals. One person annoys or offends another, who retaliates aggressively. The party who has been attacked may respond in kind or may rely exclusively
on nonviolent means to bring the confrontation to an end; in either case, it may seem to
onlookers that there is a principal aggressor and a principal victim. If third parties are
present or are invoked, they may intervene in reaction to the event that the two antagonists have brought about, but their involvement is incidental and remedial. When domestic violence is seen in this way, its occurrence may appear rooted solely in the
personalities or characteristics of the two parties most immediately involved or in the
nature of the relationship between them.

The principal argument of this chapter is that a better understanding of domestic
violence—and, by extension, of violence more generally—requires a recognition of the
crucial role played at every stage by people other than the immediate combatants. Human
beings in the real world are embedded in extensive social networks and are continually

For helpful comments on earlier drafts of this chapter, I thank Donald Black, Mark Cooney, Richard Felson, Allan Horwitz,
Steven Nock, Mark Stafford, James Tedeschi, and two anonymous reviewers.

adjusting their conduct in response to the dynamics of interaction within them. Unless the two individuals who exchange blows are living like Robinson Crusoe and his man Friday in utter isolation on a deserted island, their behavior cannot be fully explained without reference to the many other people with whom they regularly interact. Seen in this way, violence between two people appears to arise not only from features of their own relationship but also from the nature of the larger social environment in which they are contained. There are violent social arrangements and peaceful ones. In an important sense, domestic violence does not occur unless the social context in which family members find themselves encourages or allows it.

The evidence supporting this claim is drawn in the present case from an ongoing study of conflict and social control—both violent and otherwise—found in families located in a wide variety of past and present societies around the world. For these purposes, attention is paid primarily to violence between husbands and wives. Certainly other family members can and do engage in violence. Violence between spouses appears to be comparatively more frequent and severe, however, and has been relatively well described in the cross-cultural literature. It therefore constitutes an appropriate and useful focus, one that may reveal patterns common to every form of domestic aggression.

Origins of Domestic Conflict

In all societies, the great majority of violent acts arise in the course of ongoing conflicts or disputes. They may thus be understood as attempts at social control (see Black, 1983; see also Tedeschi & Felson, 1993). Although the sheer existence of a conflict does not guarantee that violence will occur—the parties may instead rely on such alternatives as avoidance, negotiation, mediation, adjudication, or even supernatural aggression through attempted sorcery or witchcraft—the absence of conflict largely ensures the absence of violence. One way that social networks can generate domestic violence, then, is by generating and exacerbating discord between family members.

It is abundantly clear in the cross-cultural literature that conflicts between husbands and wives frequently have their basis in the relationship of one or both parties to other people. Perhaps the most widely recognized circumstance of this type occurs when one spouse replaces the other with a new partner, thereby initiating major adjustments in the social networks of all three people involved. Adultery and desertion appear to be among the most common causes of intense conflict between spouses all over the world. Even before the betrayed spouse is aware of what is happening, the new relationship may be responsible for a dramatic increase in conflict within the marriage. So, for example, among the Azande of the Sudan, women sulk and pick quarrels with their husbands when they are having affairs with other men (Evans-Pritchard, 1974, p. 114), and among the Zinacanteco Indians of Mexico, men who wish to marry other women sometimes beat their wives to drive them away (Collier, 1973, p. 191).

Another way in which third parties may promote marital discord is when individuals outside the marriage actively encourage one spouse to punish another for some perceived offense. This is most likely to occur when the outside agitators are more closely tied to one spouse than the other and when they are already embroiled in conflicts of their own with the more distant partner. What happens in these cases, then, is that a person outside the marriage seeks to use one of its partners to further his or her own conflict with the other. If the attempt is successful, a new conflict is generated. This behavior is often seen in polygynous societies, where one wife may try to enlist the support of her husband in the course of her own dispute with a co-wife. A study of conflict among the Jalé of New Guinea, for example, suggested that over a fourth of all marital disputes there have their origin in quarrels between co-wives (Koch, 1974, p. 99). Examples of violent confrontations between spouses arising from trouble between co-wives abound in the ethnographic literature, and a statistical association between spousal violence and polygyny has previously been noted (Levinson, 1989, pp. 49, 89).

In-law relationships provide another source of friction that can result in conflict between spouses. A wife may quarrel with her mother-in-law, for example, and each woman may solicit support from the husband. If a man feels that his wife has mistreated his mother, he may seek to punish her. Even if he does not feel this way, the strength of his tie to his mother and community expectations of filial respect may discourage him from siding openly with his wife, thereby angering her and setting in motion a process in which her attempts to sanction him for failing to help her elicit countermeasures on his part. In-laws may use one spouse as a weapon against the other in additional ways as well. In Jalé society, for example, fathers and brothers may urge a woman to avoid sexual intercourse with her husband until he has given them a sufficient number of "marriage pigs" (i.e., has paid an adequate brideprice). Her refusal to sleep with her husband, however, may in turn cause him to beat her (Koch, 1974, pp. 99, 100). If, on the other hand, it is the husband who feels that his wife's family owes him a debt, he may beat his wife as a means of communicating his displeasure—not with her, but with her stingy relatives (Koch, 1974, p. 104).

The occasions on which third parties may act to provoke marital discord are superficially varied—a sister may inform her brother of his wife's infidelity and urge him to take action against her (e.g., Rosaldo, 1980, p. 170), two brothers may stand together in anger and physically chastise their wives for quarreling with each other (e.g., J. K. Campbell, 1964, p. 78), a man may beat his wife because she has neglected or mistreated his children (e.g., Warner, 1958, p. 71), or a woman may attack and drive away a husband who has attempted to rape her daughter from an earlier marriage (e.g., Landes, 1971, pp. 31–32). What these and many related incidents have in common is that in all of them, strong ties of intimacy and loyalty between one spouse and a person outside the marriage conflict with the intimacy and loyalty that bind that spouse to his or her partner. The discord that then breaks out in the marriage can be fully understood only in light of the discord that prevails in the larger social network in which the married couple is embedded.

If strained and hostile relations within a married couple's network can promote conflict in the marriage itself, it follows that warmth and friendliness in the network can discourage it. Societies in which people are closely linked in friendship and mutual support to their spouse's families, or in which the kin of husband and wife are linked in such a way to one another, appear to generate less domestic conflict than do those in which in-laws are separated by social distance and ongoing hostility. Thus, for example, among the Yanomamö Indians of South America, there is less hostility and violence in marriages between cousins than between two less closely related individuals. In the former case, in-laws are also blood relatives, and the greater degree of harmony and solidarity they enjoy is reflected in the greater warmth of the marriage itself (Chagnon, 1983, p. 113). It is reported that in some societies, families of married women make a deliberate effort to cultivate cordial relations with the women's husbands, in the hope that the good will they create will secure better treatment for the wives. Among the Sarakatsani shepherds of Greece, for example,

> A brother tries hard to win the good will of his sister's husband. He is anxious that she should receive good treatment among the strangers to whom he and his family have given her. And it is noticeable that in the early years of marriage while the bride is still unsure

of her position in the new family, her brothers often do more favours and good turns for the husband and his family than they receive in return. (J. K. Campbell, 1964, p. 139, see also p. 103)

Note that in this case, a brother of the wife may perform a service for a parent or sibling of the husband in an effort to affect the nature of the interaction between the spouses themselves. The Sarakatsani thus exhibit a practical knowledge of the significance of larger social networks in promoting marital harmony.

Management of Domestic Conflict

However friendly and peaceful the social networks in which couples are embedded, some marital conflict is bound to arise. The techniques of conflict management available to partners when this happens are many and varied. Among them are insults and criticisms, voiced either privately or publicly; expressions of distress such as sulking or moping; acts of avoidance, either temporary or permanent; efforts to inflict deprivation, such as when wives refuse to cook for their husbands or to sleep with them; the invocation of third parties, whether to mediate or adjudicate; and violent self-help, or the handling of a grievance by unilateral aggression (Black, 1983, p. 34, note 2).

In previous research, the decision to resort to violence in disputes with spouses has been found to be associated with such features of marital relationships as the economic subordination of wives and their difficulty in obtaining a divorce (Lester, 1980; Levinson, 1989). One study also noted a negative correlation between spousal violence and "wife-beating interventions" in which third parties act to stop aggression against women but suggested that this is incidental to other aspects of the husband–wife relationship (Levinson, 1989, pp. 98–102). By contrast, the present study suggests that the role of third parties is critical in determining the likelihood that spouses will use violence during conflicts with each other. Because the available literature is much more eloquent on the subject of violence committed by husbands against wives than vice versa, the evidence is especially clear concerning the former. In general, it indicates that the likelihood that a man will resort to violent self-help varies systematically with the amount of support that he and his wife are able to generate within their larger social networks. In particular, as the degree of support available to the wife increases, the likelihood of violence against her decreases. This is a function both of the absolute numbers of allies that she is able to attract and of the nature of the support that these people are willing to give her—ranging from mild censure of her husband at one extreme to the use of vigorous retaliatory violence against him at the other. The most vulnerable wife is one who stands alone against a husband who has recruited extensive support from other people. The next most vulnerable wife is one who stands alone against an equally isolated husband. In this sense, it is not just the marital relationship that generates violent self-help but the entire social network within which it is contained. Violence is most likely to occur against an individual who is isolated and has been abandoned by other people. It occurs where these others allow it to occur.

The most important predictor of support in any conflict situation—marital or otherwise—is the degree of intimacy and interdependence that exists between third parties and the principals in dispute (Black, 1993). When third parties are intimate with both disputants, they are likely to experience divided loyalties and to attempt to help both parties by bringing about an end to their disagreement. Partisan support, by contrast, "is a joint function of social closeness to one side and social remoteness from the other" (Black, 1993, p. 126). In cases of domestic conflict, this means that a wife, for example, who has her own set of close contacts separate from those of her husband is likely to enjoy their undivided support. The closer these people are to her and the more remote they are from her husband, the more immediate and extensive their partisan assistance is likely to be. In most societies around the world, this kind of support, if it is found at all, is provided by blood relatives of the wife who have maintained strong ties to her after her marriage but have remained more or less distant from her spouse. It is not the mere fact of a recognized kin connection that determines their involvement, however, but the actual nature of their links to both spouses. Thus, should members of a woman's family be tied to her husband by strong bonds of economic interest or male solidarity or should norms of avoidance introduce an element of distance into their relationship with the woman herself, the partisan support they are willing to give her will be attenuated as a result. Under some circumstances, friends or neighbors may assume the role of a woman's most active supporters. This happens when they are the ones closest to her and most distant from her husband.

Mutual Support

One scenario for marital conflict, then, occurs when a woman is surrounded by people who are relationally close to both her and her husband. In this case, third parties are likely to be reluctant to favor one spouse over the other; rather, they are likely to divide their loyalties and feel that each person is partly right and partly wrong. They are likely to intervene to prevent violence and to defuse hostilities, working all the while to facilitate a reconciliation between the parties. If they are slightly closer to one spouse than the other, they may tilt somewhat in that individual's direction, but as long as their ties to both sides are strong, they will tend to adopt a peacemaking role.

Such a pattern has been described, for example, among the !Kung Bushmen of Africa. There, small bands of closely related people travel and forage together in each other's close company. Should conflict break out between a married couple, other people rush to separate them and to restore peace. Domestic violence among the !Kung occasionally occurs, but it is neither frequent nor likely to be severe (see Marshall, 1965; Shostak, 1983).

Another example can be found among the Tikopia, inhabitants of a small Polynesian island. In Tikopian society, a woman's brothers maintain an active interest in her throughout her life and typically develop very close and supportive relationships with her children. Partly on the basis of their mutual interest in the latter, men and their sisters' husbands also tend to be on very good terms; conflict between brothers-in-law is said to be rare (Firth, 1957, p. 204), and men generally cooperate with their wives' families all of their lives (Firth, 1957, pp. 257–258, 468). Should conflict between spouses erupt, women are likely to go to their brothers' homes and stay there until they decide to return home on their own initiative or until their husbands ask them to come back. It is said that even the threat of this "may be sufficient to make a querulous or unjust husband see reason" (Firth, 1957, p. 122). The brothers whom they visit, however, appear to remain on good terms with the husbands and are unlikely to take any hostile action against them; evidently, they take for granted that the women will return to their marriages, although they do not force them to do so. In fact, divorce on Tikopia is rare, relationships between spouses are typically amiable, and mutual deference to the complaints of disgruntled spouses is held out as an ideal (Firth, 1957, pp. 119, 121, 122).

Although most situations in which mutual intimates come between disputing couples and act to promote harmony between them arise spontaneously from the patterns of interaction and interdependence found naturally in their larger network, at least sometimes systematic efforts are made to ensure that peacemakers are available. One interesting attempt of this kind is found among the Amhara of Ethiopia. There, at every marriage, two men are appointed to protect the bride from anyone who might attempt to harm her in the future—including most notably her husband—and to advance her interests in the new community she is about to enter:

> During the wedding ceremony, the *mize* or protectors are sworn in. The formula is for the bride's father to say to the bridegroom: "Call for us two guarantors for her eyes, head, and teeth," whereupon the *mize* step forward and take the oath to protect the bride from bodily harm. (Messing, 1959, p. 327; see also Messing, 1957, pp. 420, 465–466)

The protectors are usually chosen from the ranks of the husband's family, in large part so that they can be relied on not to undermine the marriage. They retain their loyalty to their own kinsman, the husband, but they are also linked to his wife by a special bond. In practice, the most that *mize* generally deliver to the women they are bound to protect is a kind of mediation or arbitration, rather than aggressive one-sided support. This is understandable in light of their close connection to the husband, but it does provide the wife with at least some assistance in marital disputes.

Partisan Support

An altogether different pattern of third-party intervention is seen when people offer disputing wives their partisan support. Generally, this arises from close bonds to the women that the husbands do not share. A woman's immediate kin—parents, siblings, aunts, uncles, and cousins—are most likely to champion her cause in this way, although under some circumstances they may not do so, although others may do so as well. The willingness of people to involve themselves on a woman's behalf reduces the likelihood that her husband will resort to violent self-help against her and reduces its likely severity should it occur.

Accordingly, women in societies around the world commonly prefer to live near their own families after marriage, although only some are able to do so. This is not simply a matter of matrilocality, strictly speaking, in which husbands move in with their wives' families at the time they are married. Rather, it is a matter of the women's ability to maintain close spatial and social bonds to their kin, something possible if the latter live nearby and remain involved with their female relatives under a variety of residential arrangements. Furthermore, it is something of ongoing significance to women, still relevant years after a marriage takes place, and it is something that can change over time. Finally, it is something that can be affected by the nature of the bonds that link a husband to his in-laws and to his own family. The fact that it is the accessibility and commitment of a woman's family to her over the course of time—rather than the nature of her immediate postmarital residence—that shapes the course of domestic violence can explain why earlier studies have disagreed about the extent to which matrilocality in and of itself predicts a lowered risk of physical aggression against wives (see J. C. Campbell, 1985; Levinson, 1989; Masumura, 1979; Schlegel, 1972).

In any event, the desire of women to be close to their families, and the protection such closeness can afford them, is evident in a diversity of societies. To note one example, Amhara women, despite the two guardians they are accorded from the ranks of their husbands' kin, would much rather be near their own relatives, knowing that these individuals will protect them in quarrels with their husbands even if they are in the wrong (Messing, 1957, p. 404). Similarly, Yanomamö women dread being married into distant villages where their brothers cannot protect them and where they are in fact more likely to be severely beaten (Chagnon, 1983, p. 113). Although women prefer the advantages that proximity to their kin provides, men often prefer to keep their wives isolated from such strong support. Many men would agree with the sentiment attributed to people in Korean villages that "the toilet and in-laws should be far from the house" (Brandt, 1971, p. 122; see also Abu-Zahra, 1976, pp. 165–166; J. K. Campbell, 1964, p. 147; Spencer, 1965, p. 36).

An example of a society in which women typically enjoy strong partisan support when they quarrel with their husbands can be found among the Lugbara of Uganda. In this setting, women usually move to their husbands' neighborhoods when they marry, but this is generally close enough to their own natal villages to allow regular visiting (Middleton, 1965, p. 44). They remain members of the lineage into which they are born all of their lives. Men feel a keen sense of responsibility for their sisters and daughters married elsewhere, and they visit them often to make sure they are well. Ties between in-laws, however, are typically distant and not infrequently strained (Middleton, 1965, pp. 58–59). When women dispute with their husbands under these circumstances, they can rely on assistance from their families, who will take them in and arrange their divorces if they desire it. Furthermore, their brothers may go immediately to assault their husbands (Middleton, 1965, p. 57). The net result is a striking degree of freedom for Lugbara wives.

Another setting in which women regularly received partisan support against their husbands existed in the traditional society of the Cheyenne Indians of the North American Plains. There, married couples generally resided in tipis pitched in the immediate vicinity of the wife's mother. Should conflict develop, the wife could anticipate support from her mother, father, brothers, and other relatives. They would take her into their homes and would allow her to move in with them permanently if they felt that her complaints against her husband were valid. (In the latter regard, the opinions of her brothers were crucial.) They might also use violence on her behalf. Thus, in one case, a disgruntled wife left her husband's lodge while he was away and moved in with her mother. When the husband returned, he came after her, confronted her, and struck her in the face. The woman's mother then turned on him in fury, saying that he had gone too far in coming to beat her daughter. She concluded, "The world won't come to an end if I beat my son-in-law." She thereupon stabbed him in the back with a knife and ultimately chased him to his own lodge with a hot branding iron, where she tore everything down and scattered his belongings outside (Llewellyn & Hoebel, 1941, pp. 182–183). In large part because of the support on which women could rely, "the position of the Cheyenne woman in the marriage bond had considerable strength," and Cheyenne women had "unusual power over their warrior husbands" (Llewellyn & Hoebel, 1941, pp. 181, 182).

Women in Burma also enjoy considerable autonomy and a comparative freedom from domestic violence that is rooted in large part in the support that they receive from their own families. Most live near their kin after marriage, and many actually live with them in the same dwelling, given that some newly married couples move in to the household of the wife's parents and old people commonly come to stay with their daughters. In any case, the tie between a woman and her family—especially her mother and sisters—is exceptionally strong and enduring. A woman's relatives can be relied on to assist her in any crisis, whether or not it arises from conflict. Men, on the other hand, have less to do with their natal families and do not equal their wives in the intensity of the support they can generate. Under these conditions, it is reported that the wife tends to be the dominant partner in a marriage. Not only does violence against women occur in only a minority of marriages and infrequently even there, but husband beating, although uncommon, is recorded in the ethnographic record. An anthropologist who lived in rural Burma linked the favorable treatment of Burmese women to the tendency of joint families to consist of parents and married daughters, contrasting the situation with that in India and China, where households of parents and married sons are the norm (Spiro, 1977, p. 283). Significantly, the one case of wife beating he has described in some detail involved a woman who had moved into her husband's village and was thus relatively isolated from her own family. She resolved the situation by returning to her mother's home and dissolving her marriage (Spiro, 1977, pp. 291–293).

The presence of large numbers of potential supporters available to women has also been used to account for the extremely low incidence of violence in the families of the

Mundurucu, a South American Indian group. There, women stay with their mothers and sisters all of their lives, and their husbands come to join them at marriage. Women spend their time surrounded by other women, working alongside them cooperatively in the daytime and sleeping in homes headed by senior female family members at night. Women are rarely completely alone with their husbands, and their strongest bonds and deepest loyalties are those shared with their own kin, especially their female kin. Under these circumstances, spousal violence is essentially nonexistent. A man who attempts to chastise his wife for any reason, even for adultery, is in a difficult position: "He, after all, may well be from another village and without close support, but his wife is surrounded by a whole group of kin" (Murphy & Murphy, 1985, p. 184). A similar situation prevails among the Shavante Indians of Brazil, where men also typically move in with their wives' families at marriage, living there for some time as outsiders. In this situation, violence against women by their husbands is very infrequent (Maybury-Lewis, 1967). In describing an exceptional case of violence inflicted by a man on his wife, an ethnographer who lived among the Shavante remarked that the victim "was obviously not living in the house of her kin or her husband would not have been foolhardy enough to adopt this tactic" (Maybury-Lewis, 1967, p. 94).

The frequency and severity of violent self-help against wives is sensitive to shifts in a woman's ability to attract support. If a previously well-supported woman finds herself isolated, an increase in violence is likely, whereas if a woman who was once alone finds herself among family and friends, violence is likely to decrease. This pattern can be seen in a case history reported from the Ojibwa Indians of North America, in which a newly married woman went with her husband to his community and lived there for some years. The woman's mother-in-law did not like her, and she had little support in her new home. During this period, her husband beat her on many occasions, pulling out chunks of her hair. Some time later, the husband accompanied his wife on a visit to her parents. While they were on the woman's home territory, the husband never fought violently with his wife, although he was often sullen and mean. When the husband decided to return to his own community, the woman refused to go and divorced him instead (Landes, 1971, pp. 100–101). Similarly, among the Samburu of Kenya, women typically live in their husbands' villages and are considerably cut off from their own families. Should a man live for a while near his wife's relatives, however, for this period of time "he is constrained to treat her with moderation" (Spencer, 1965, p. 36). When the couple moves away, the special constraint ends. The same pattern can be seen among the Kgatla of Botswana, where some couples live with a new wife's parents for the first few months of their marriage.

When they do so, this domestic arrangement affords women a degree of protection lost to them thereafter. A wife's family is reported to resist immediately any attempt on a husband's part to bully their daughter, and "they are actually entitled to claim an ox or goat from him as damages if he thrashes her while she is still under their roof" (Schapera, 1940, p. 103). A husband has more latitude in his behavior toward his wife once the couple establishes an independent homestead.

The appearance and growth of children can also provide a woman with support she was previously lacking. Although in some societies, young children may isolate their mothers and thus be linked to higher rates of spousal aggression against them (see, e.g., Straus, Gelles, & Steinmetz, 1980, pp. 179–181), older children are likely to be a benefit to their mothers when conflict arises. If the children are equally close to both parents, their intervention is likely to take the form of mediation (Straus et al., pp. 14–18). If, on the other hand, they are more strongly attached to their mothers, they may offer them partisan assistance instead. In either case, a woman often finds that her position in domestic conflict improves after she has grown children to watch out for her interests. Thus, in one reported case from the contemporary United States, a woman who had been beaten by her husband for years was ultimately defended by a son who had become old enough to protect her physically:

> After one particularly ugly incident [the son, then 14] took his mother and younger half brother by the hand and issued a warning to his stepfather: "You will never hit either of them again. If you want them, you'll have to go through me." It was the stepfather who blinked, and though his drinking continued, the violence at home ended. (Applebome, 1992, p. 60)

Awareness of the potential role of children may actually become a motive in childbearing; in contemporary Rwanda, for example, many women resist exhortations to practice family planning because, as a founder of a women's group there observed, "the more children you have, the more stable the marriage. The children become your strength against your husband—they will fight for you if he tries to hurt you" (Perlez, 1992, pp. 1, 12). One consequence of the protection afforded by children is that in many societies, violence against older women is less likely than that against younger ones.

Although the most vigorous partisan support a woman receives tends to come from her own close relatives, other people may assist her as well. Of special note in this context is the role played in some settings by "public opinion." If neighbors and others are sympathetic to a woman's position in a domestic conflict, they may attempt to help her by gossiping about her husband, ridiculing him, ostracizing him, or depriving him of a variety of favors and kindnesses. Behavior of this kind is said to discourage the use of violence against women in such diverse societies as those of the Koreans (Brandt, 1971), the Sarakatsanis (J. K. Campbell, 1964), the Cheyennes (Llewellyn & Hoebel, 1941), and the Tikopians (Firth, 1957). Sometimes, the support offered by friends and neighbors is quite vigorous. Among the Pokot of Kenya, women may assemble in an ad hoc group known as a "shaming party" to punish a man they believe has mistreated his wife; ganging up on him, they tie him up, remove his clothing, smear him with dirt, urinate on him, and leave him for other men to find (Edgerton & Conant, 1964). In parts of 18th- and 19th-century America, vigilante groups such as the Regulators and the Ku Klux Klan undertook to punish men who were known for cruelty to their wives. In some cases, these groups "delivered notes to the doorsteps of offenders: stop the mistreatment, these warned, or receive a whipping." In others, they actually flogged the husbands (Pleck, 1979, pp. 69–70).

The partisan support offered by family, friends, and neighbors can take a variety of forms. The greatest degree of help is embodied in two responses: either assuming the woman's economic support, at least temporarily, so that she can leave a husband with whom she is unhappy, or exercising violence against the husband on her behalf. In regard to the first of these, it has been established in earlier cross-cultural research that the availability of divorce reduces the use of violence against wives (Levinson, 1989, p. 88). The availability of divorce, however, is highly dependent in most societies on the willingness of a woman's kin to take her back from her husband and provide her with a home. If they will not do this, in most cases the woman has no alternative but to remain in her marriage, however unhappy she may be. Whether on a temporary or permanent basis, sheltering a woman and separating her from her husband provide her with opportunities avoidance that would otherwise be lacking, and, because a great deal of evidence from the study of conflict establishes that the possibility of avoidance lessens the likelihood of violence (see Baumgartner, 1988, pp. 60–66), this can be very significant help indeed.

The use of violence against offending husbands by a woman's supporters appears to be less frequent than assistance in arranging a separation, but there is suggestive evidence that it too may profoundly alter the nature of conflict between married couples. In one case recorded among the Cheyenne Indians, a husband was beaten by members of his wife's family for his previous violence against the woman. The family then kept the woman with them for some time until her brother finally decided that the husband should be given another chance. He warned the man, however, that he himself would fight alongside his sister should there be further trouble in the marriage; the woman's mother also threatened the man. In fact, the couple lived thereafter in peace (Llewellyn & Hoebel, 1941, pp. 182–183). Similarly, a case is recounted from Idaho in the 1920s in which a group of neighbors confronted a farmer they felt was mistreating his wife. At first the husband was defiant, sneering at the others and asking if any among them was "man enough" to make him stop beating his wife. After being attacked by the group, however, and threatened with future harm if he did not alter his behavior, the shaken man solemnly promised to forego violence in his home. The neighbors then shook his hand and congratulated him; one invited him to dinner (Pleck, 1979, pp. 70–71). Further evidence comes from the Samburu of Kenya. Among them, a married woman does not typically live near her relatives; when they are close enough to intervene in her marital conflicts, however, they often do so, physically punishing whichever spouse they judge to be in the wrong. The Samburu claim that the public beatings they administer to offending parties, including men who are brutal to their wives, have "a very high degree of success" in preventing future misbehavior (Spencer, 1965, p. 37).

The use of violence by a woman's champions represents strong support for her cause. Its occurrence raises interesting questions about the position that violence occupies in the conflict management strategies of women, suggesting that to consider only acts of violence actually committed by disputing wives themselves may miss something of importance in the conduct of many domestic disputes. Women may be responsible for inflicting significant violence on husbands in many cases in which they themselves do not raise a hand against them; they may inflict violence indirectly, through the agency of supporters—most often male—who do the actual aggressing for them. Women may solicit such support, urge their supporters on, and thank them warmly afterward. From the husband's point of view, the end result may be the same as if the woman had attacked him herself. The presence of supporters willing and able to use violence on behalf of a wife may more than compensate her for any disadvantage in size, strength, or fighting ability. In choosing whether or not to resort to violent self-help in disputes with wives, husbands must consider the possibility of such vengeance by proxy, as well as that of other sanctions imposed by people in the couple's wider social network.

It remains to consider the situation of women who receive little or no support from third parties when they are involved in conflicts with their husbands. These are the women who are most likely to be attacked and to experience repeated and severe violence. Some of them are simply left to fend for themselves against equally isolated husbands. Others—the most vulnerable—find themselves pitted against men who manage to attract considerable support for themselves.

No Support

A good example of a society in which high rates of domestic violence arise in a context of general social isolation is that of the Ojibwa Indians of North America. The Ojibwa live in "small, autonomous, and often hostile households" that scatter over great distances for up to nine months of the year to exploit scarce and widely dispersed natural resources (Landes, 1971, p. v). These small households typically consist of only parents and children, and sometimes grandparents as well, who for many months of the year are constrained to associate with each other alone. Even when larger numbers of people gather during the summer, "the individualistic economic and household structure of the winter prevails." Both men and women tend to be highly competitive and mistrustful of other people, even close relatives. In this social environment, "no one has the right to interfere seriously with the affairs of another couple, or of another domicile" (Landes, 1971, p. 85). And few people seem inclined to do so anyway, except perhaps a few close relatives who may occasionally be near at hand when trouble breaks out between a husband and wife. Even concern on their part is likely to be limited, given that parents, for example, are said to dread being asked for help by their married children. Among the Ojibwa, there is a "preponderance of stormy marriages, frequent divorces, and violent interludes" (Landes, 1971, p. 119).

In cross-cultural perspective, the degree of isolation experienced by Ojibwa couples is not common; in most societies, married individuals tend to live near and regularly interact with at least some other related adults. One context in which comparable isolation does occur, however, is in certain contemporary American settings. In a society as large and diverse as the United States, it is difficult to identify "typical" features of marital and network relationships that transcend lines of class, income, age, ethnicity, education, and region. Some couples are embedded in networks as supportive and protective as those found virtually anywhere else in the world. That said, it is clear that in many American communities, people lead very isolated lives, separated from family, without many friends, and thrown very much on their own resources. Under some conditions, these features of social organization may be perfectly compatible with domestic tranquility; when family members are separated from each other much of the time by the nature of their independent everyday routines, when they have the material resources to secure ample personal space and desired goods for themselves within the household setting, and when they can easily move away from a relative with whom they cannot get along—when, in short, family life is characterized by extensive individuation, autonomy, and privacy—many opportunities for avoidance are available, and much conflict is prevented and defused as a result. These dynamics appear to operate in contemporary affluent suburbs, among other places, and are associated with comparatively low rates of domestic violence (Baumgartner, 1988, chap. 3). On the other hand, when these conditions are absent and family discord cannot be controlled by avoidance, then isolation from the larger community becomes significant because it means that one important constraint against the use of violence—the presence of third parties motivated enough to intervene—is absent. Family, friends, neighbors, co-workers, and others may be unavailable, unaware, uninterested, or unsure of how to proceed. Lacking strong ties of intimacy and connectedness to the married couple, they are likely to take little action to prevent violence between them. Official third parties—such as police, prosecutors, and judges—are theoretically available to assume the role of intermediary or champion, and it is significant that appeals to these legal actors seem to arise most often from individuals who have no one else to whom to turn (see, e.g., Black, 1980). Much research shows, however, that agents of the state tend to be very reluctant to become actively involved in domestic conflicts (see, e.g., Black, 1980; Smith & Klein, 1984; Vera Institute of Justice, 1981). Lack of support and social isolation may thus go far toward explaining the apparently high rates of domestic violence that prevail in some American settings.

Opposition

If a socially isolated woman is more likely to be the target of violent self-help, this is especially so when her husband is well supported and she thus faces large-scale opposition. This is likely to occur when the man is surrounded by family and friends and the woman is unable to mobilize her own relatives for one reason or another. This is the situation, for example, of the Yanomamö women mentioned earlier who are unfortunate enough to be married into villages far from their original homes (Chagnon, 1983, p. 113). It also characterizes women among the Gurage of Ethiopia, who move to their husbands' place of residence after marriage and whose ties to their own families become greatly attenuated thereafter. The relationship between a married woman and her brother is said to be one of respect rather than affection, closely resembling that of in-laws (Shack, 1966, p. 119). The relationship of a woman to her kin is undermined by the fact that she is not allowed to visit them, even for short periods, without her husband's permission (Shack,

1966, p. 124). In her new home, she is subject to the close surveillance of her husband's family. In this society, a man "may strike his wife at the least provocation," and he may do so in large part because the woman's family will take no action against him (Shack, 1966, p. 125).

When a woman finds herself extremely isolated from sources of support while her husband is surrounded by numerous allies, she may come to suffer violence at many hands. Not only her husband himself but also members of his family or friendship network may use force against her. Thus, among the Gheg of Albania, where women enter tightly knit households of their husbands' kin when they marry and have comparatively little further contact with their own families, wives are apt to be beaten not just by their husbands but also by their husbands' senior male relatives (Whitaker, 1976). In India, too, violence against wives often has a collective character. Indian women traditionally leave their homes at marriage and move as daughters-in-law into the households of their husbands' parents. Their own families take very limited responsibility for their welfare thereafter; as a result, the women are in effect thrown on the mercy of their husbands' kin. When they leave their homes on their wedding day, they are told, "Now only your dead body can leave your husband's house" (Crossette, 1991). In neighboring Nepal, the related formula is for the bride's mother to tell the groom, "If you kill her [the bride] the sin is yours, if you keep her the merit is yours" (Bennett, 1983, p. 88). In India, if marriages do not turn out well, the entire family of the husband may inflict violence on the wife, even in some cases carrying out her premeditated murder. "Bride burnings," as incidents of the latter type are known in India, allow husbands to remarry without having to undergo the difficult process of divorce. In one such case reported recently, the victim was apparently poisoned by her mother-in-law and then set on fire (Crossette, 1991).

Violence appears to be especially likely in cases in which a woman's nearest relatives actually become part of the opposition and support her husband. To some extent, this can vary within the experience of a single family depending on the exact nature of the husband's grievance. Brothers who often support their sisters may turn against them if they are caught in adultery, for example. Among the Jalé, it is said that women in this predicament prefer to suffer a beating at the hands of their husbands rather than return to face their wrathful families (Koch, 1974, p. 108). In societies in which a woman's kin group receives regular gifts and payments from the husband, their tie to him may actually become more important to them than their tie to the woman. If this is the case, they may routinely take the husband's side in marital quarrels, perhaps forcing a woman who has come to them for protection to go back to her husband's home or even beating her themselves for her offense against him. Among the Azande of the Sudan, where women often seek assistance from their families, wise men attempt to develop close bonds with their in-laws, visiting them often and helping them out. Then, if their wives run away, the women's fathers will chase them back (Evans-Pritchard, 1974, p. 187).

One society in which a woman's relatives provide her with strikingly little support and not infrequently take her husband's side against her is that of the Australian Aborigines. In Aboriginal society, men regularly act collectively in ritual affairs and exhibit a strong and exclusive solidarity with each other, even killing women who intrude on their ceremonial activities. This provides a strong bond linking a woman's husband to her male relatives. The ability of the woman to attract support is further weakened by the extreme age differences common in Aboriginal marriages. Husbands are generally many years older than their wives, and in a society in which age confers significant status, this can discourage a younger man from intervening on behalf of his sister (see Hamilton, 1970; White, 1970). In any event, women can rely on little support from their male relatives. Among the Murngin, an Aboriginal group,

> No brother or father would interfere with a husband chastising his wife; indeed they would help him. . . . It is only under the most extreme provocation that a woman's clan would act; no instance was recorded by the author. (Warner, 1958, p. 110)

Similarly, among the Gidgingali, a closely related Aboriginal group, men traditionally intervened often in the quarrels of other men but were much less likely to play any role in disputes involving women. Men "felt some responsibility for their daughters, sisters' daughters, and wives' mothers, but were reluctant to intervene in quarrels between such women and their husbands" (Hiatt, 1965, p. 74). To the contrary, brothers were actually obligated to attack sisters who were insulted in their presence, whether by their husbands or anyone else. To avoid having to do this, men often left the scene when they realized that a dispute involving their sister was brewing (Hiatt, 1965, p. 117). The vulnerability of women in Gidgingali society to violence within marriage was paralleled by a distinctive vulnerability outside it as well: If two men quarreled over a woman, another man might attack the woman to bring the conflict to an end:

> The inference is that male opinion regarded it as better to attack a woman, and perhaps cause her death, than allow men to fight over her. In general, men were reluctant to support female interests against male interests. (Hiatt, 1965, pp. 139–140)

In cases in which women attempted violence against men, the men's relatives were quick to intervene against the women (Hiatt, 1865, pp. 107–108, 111–112). In traditional Aboriginal society, then, wives have tended to find themselves isolated in marital disputes and are left to deal with well-supported husbands. Under these circumstances, they have been unable to prevent considerable violence against themselves.

Conclusion

Evidence from a wide variety of societies suggests the crucial importance of a couple's network in determining the likelihood that one spouse will use violence against the other. When a husband and wife are surrounded by dissension among relatives and friends, their own rates of conflict escalate and there is a greater chance that one of them will have occasion to resort to violent self-help. Given that a conflict has emerged, the decision to use violence in prosecuting it is sensitive to the degree of social support that each party can generate. Violence is comparatively unlikely against a well-supported individual. Social support can provide an embattled spouse with economic leverage in a marital relationship, with an opportunity to escape an unhappy marriage, with a champion who will counter violence with violence, or with a mediator who will seek to secure peace on his or her behalf.

Some kinds of social arrangements naturally breed support for marriage partners; others do not. Intimacy seems to be a key factor in this regard. Mutual intimacy with both husband and wife is associated with peacemaking efforts; unilateral intimacy is associated with partisan support. To the degree that a woman has strong and close bonds with other people, she is likely to receive their help; to the degree that she receives their help, she is likely to be protected against violence in her home. Social networks in which women are isolated and cut off from others will typically generate little support for wives, and their susceptibility to violence will increase with the degree of integration and connectedness enjoyed by their husbands.

The evidence bearing on these patterns presented in this chapter comes for the most part from ethnographic descriptions of prevailing or typical domestic arrangements in entire societies. It is important to emphasize, however, that the relative support available to marriage partners in conflict varies in all societies from family to family, depending on a number of particular circumstances, and can furthermore vary from case to case and over time. Differences in support can therefore account not only for differences in the amount of domestic violence found across societies but also for differences between groups within a single society, between individual families within these groups, and between a single family at different points in time. The more precisely the support available to parties in conflict can be specified, the more precisely predictions about violence can be made.

Each social network is to some degree unique, and each is reponsible for the amount and severity of domestic violence occurring between its members. Support and opposition flow along channels defined by daily patterns of sociability, economic exchange, and collective action. To understand fully what happens in a given relationship, one must know how the people involved are connected to these channels. One analyst has observed that it is impossible

> to separate completely the discussion of one set of kinship ties from that of others in the same system; they are like a set of forces in delicately poised equilibrium; if one is disturbed, others must respond in adjustment also. (Firth, 1957, p. 205)

One might add that ties to friends, neighbors, and colleagues are all part of this larger equilibrium too.

Domestic violence, then, is bred of many interactions, not just the one that transpires between the person who inflicts injury and the one who sustains it. What is true of domestic violence must be true of other kinds of violence as well, wherever it occurs in human groups. Across contexts—including warfare in the international arena, confrontations between rival gangs, hostilities between labor and management in the workplace, struggles between racial and ethnic groups, and many others—the existence and relative strength of supportive networks appear to play a crucial role. An isolated and friendless nation is more vulnerable to attack than one with many allies and trading partners; organized and mutually supportive groups of workers are more likely to use aggressive tactics in labor disputes than are individual workers alone; members of numerically dominant ethnic groups typically inflict more violence on members of minority groups than the latter inflict on them, except when the latter have superior access to the support of the police and the military, and so on. In every individual case of conflict, the relative weight of support and opposition shapes the interaction between the parties and determines the likelihood of violence. In fact, there is reason to believe that social support and coalition formation—grounded to an important degree in relations of intimacy—critically fashion the nature of conflict and violence in nonhuman societies as well as in human ones (see, e.g., Allman, 1992; de Waal, 1989). In the former, as in the latter, individuals able to recruit extensive support appear more likely to initiate aggression against others and to deter aggression against themselves. The close link between alliance and aggression has suggested to some that the use of force may be "an ancient evolutionary strategy more closely tied to coalition building and harmony than to murderousness and wanton violence" (Allman, 1992, p. 59); ironically, from this perspective, aggression may be seen as a product of advanced sociality. It is thus important to focus attention on the many third parties and the many social transactions that define the contexts within which aggression occurs. A better ability to predict and explain violence will result.

References

Abu-Zahra, N. (1976). Family and kinship in a Tunisian peasant community. In J. G. Peristiany (Ed.), *Mediterranean family structures* (pp. 157–171). Cambridge, England: Cambridge University Press.

Allman, W. F. (1992, May). The evolution of aggression. *U.S. News and World Report, 112,* 58–60.

Applebome, P. (1992, March). Bill Clinton's uncertain journey. *New York Times Magazine, 141,* 26–29, 36, 60, 63.

Baumgartner, M. P. (1988). *The moral order of a suburb.* New York: Oxford University Press.

Bennett, L. (1983). *Dangerous wives and sacred sisters: Social and symbolic roles of high-caste women in Nepal.* New York: Columbia University Press.

Black, D. (1980). Dispute settlement by the police. In D. Black (Ed.), *The manners and customs of the police* (pp. 109–192). New York: Academic Press.

Black, D. (1983). Crime as social control. *American Sociological Review, 48,* 34–45.

Black, D. (1993). Taking sides. In D. Black (Ed.), *The social structure of right and wrong* (pp. 125–143). San Diego, CA: Academic Press

Brandt, V. S. R. (1971). *A Korean village: Between farm and sea.* Cambridge, MA: Harvard University Press.

Campbell, J. C. (1985). Beating of wives: A cross-cultural perspective. *Victimology, 10,* 174–185.

Campbell, J. K. (1964). *Honour, family and patronage: A study of institutions and morals in a Greek mountain community.* London: Oxford University Press.

Chagnon, N. (1983). *Yanomamö: The fierce people* (3d ed.). New York: Holt, Rinehart & Winston.

Collier, J. F. (1973). *Law and social change in Zinacantan.* Stanford, CA: Stanford University Press.

Crossette, B. (1991, May 3). Indian women's group takes on abuse cases that government neglects. *New York Times,* p. A8.

de Waal, F. (1989). *Peacemaking among primates.* Cambridge, MA: Harvard University Press.

Edgerton, R. B., & Conant, F. P. K. (1964). *Kilipat:* The "shaming party" among the Pokot of East Africa. *Southwestern Journal of Anthropology, 20,* 404–418.

Evans-Pritchard, E. E. (Ed.). (1974). *Man and woman among the Azande.* New York: Free Press.

Firth, R. (1957). *We, the Tikopia: Kinship in primitive Polynesia* (2nd ed.). Boston: Beacon Press.

Hamilton, A. (1970). The role of women in Aboriginal marriage arrangements. In F. Gale (Ed.), *Woman's role in Aboriginal society* (pp. 17–20). Canberra: Australian Institute of Aboriginal Studies.

Hiatt, L. R. (1965). *Kinship and conflict: A study of an Aboriginal community in Northern Arnhem Land.* Canberra: Australian National University Press.

Koch, K.-F. (1974). *War and peace in Jalémó: The management of conflict in highland New Guinea.* Cambridge, MA: Harvard University Press.

Landes, R. (1971). *The Ojibwa woman.* New York: Norton.

Lester, D. (1980). A cross-culture study of wife abuse. *Aggressive Behavior, 6,* 361–364.

Levinson, D. (1989). *Family violence in cross-cultural perspective.* Newbury Park, CA: Sage.

Llewellyn, K., & Hoebel, E. A. (1941). *The Cheyenne way: Conflict and case law in primitive jurisprudence.* Norman: University of Oklahoma Press.

Marshall, L. (1965). The !Kung Bushmen of the Kalahari desert. In J. L. Gibbs, Jr. (Ed.), *Peoples of Africa* (pp. 241–278). New York: Holt, Rinehart & Winston.

Masumura, W. (1979). Wife abuse and other forms of aggression. *Victimology, 4,* 46–59.

Maybury-Lewis, D. (1967). *Akwe-Shavante society.* Oxford, England: Clarendon Press.

Messing, S. D. (1957). *The highland plateau Amhara of Ethiopia.* Unpublished doctoral dissertation, Department of Anthropology, University of Pennsylvania.

Messing, S. D. (1959). Group therapy and social status in the zar cult of Ethiopia. In M. K. Opler (Ed.), *Culture and mental health: Cross-cultural studies* (pp. 319–332). New York: Macmillan.

Middleton, J. (1965). *The Lugbara of Uganda.* New York: Holt, Rinehart & Winston.

Murphy, Y., & Murphy, R. F. (1985). *Women of the forest* (2nd ed.). New York: Columbia University Press.

Perlez, J. (1992, May 31). In Rwanda, births increase and the problems do, too. *New York Times,* pp. 1, 12.

Pleck, E. (1979). Wife beating in nineteenth-century America. *Victimology, 4,* 60–74.

Rosaldo, R. (1980). *Ilongot headhunting, 1883–1974: A study in society and history.* Stanford, CA: Stanford University Press.

Schapera, I. (1940). *Married life in an African tribe.* Evanston, IL: Northwestern University Press, 1966.

Schlegel, A. (1972). *Male dominance and female autonomy.* New Haven, CT: HRAF.

Shack, W. A. (1966). *The Gurage: A people of the ensete culture.* London: Oxford University Press.

Shostak, M. (1983). *Nisa: The life and words of a !Kung woman.* New York: Vintage Books.

Smith, D., & Klein, J. (1984). Police control of interpersonal disputes. *Social Problems, 31,* 468–481.

Spencer, P. (1965). *The Samburu: A study of gerontocracy in a nomadic tribe.* Berkeley: University of California Press.

Spiro, M. E. (1977). *Kinship and marriage in Burma: A cultural and psychodynamic analysis.* Berkeley: University of California Press.

Straus, M. A., Gelles, R. J., & Steinmetz, S. K. (1980). *Behind closed doors: Violence in the American family.* Garden City, NY: Anchor Books.

Tedeschi, J., & Felson, R. (1993). *Aggression and coercive actions: A social interactionist view.* Manuscript in preparation.

Vera Institute of Justice. (1981). *Felony arrests: Their prosecution and disposition in New York City courts* (2nd ed.). New York: Longman Press.

Warner, W. L. (1958). *A Black civilization: A social study of an Australian tribe.* New York: Harper.

Whitaker, I. (1976). Familial roles in the extended patrilineal kin-group in northern Albania. In J. G. Peristiany (Ed.), *Mediterranean family structures* (pp. 195–203). Cambridge, England: Cambridge University Press.

White, I. M. (1970). Aboriginal women's status: A paradox resolved. In F. Gale (Ed.), *Woman's role in Aboriginal society* (pp. 21–29). Canberra: Australian Institute of Aboriginal Studies.

CHAPTER 10

Motives for Sexual Coercion

Richard B. Felson

T he study of rape tends to be segregated from the study of other forms of harmdoing. Although rape is a violent crime, general theories of aggression, violence, and crime are rarely applied to rape. In this chapter, I use a social interactionist approach to aggression to examine the possible motives for rape and other forms of sexual coercion. That theory interprets coercive behavior as instrumental behavior designed to compel and deter others, to punish people for perceived misdeeds, and to obtain desired identities. Following social learning theory (from social psychology) and control theory (from criminology), I also discuss the role of inhibitions (see Malamuth, 1986). For a man to engage in sexual coercion, he must not only have a goal that would be satisfied by such behavior but must lack the inhibitions that would prevent the behavior.

Sexual coercion involves the use of contingent threats or bodily force to compel a person to engage in sexual activity. The offender, or "source," in the language of social influence theory, is almost always a male, whereas the victim or "target" is usually a female.[1] When the offender uses contingent threats, he threatens to harm the target unless she engages in sexual relations. For example, a man may threaten a woman with a weapon, an employer may threaten to fire an employee, or a spouse may threaten to seek

---

[1] *According to the National Crime Survey, 7.3% rapes of people living in the community involved men raping other men.*

outside companionship or leave the marriage.[2] In the case of bodily force, a man may use his superior strength to force sexual activity on a woman, or he may impose sexual relations when she is unconscious or in a condition in which consent is impossible.

It is important (although sometimes difficult) to distinguish sexual coercion from the noncoercive means that a source may use to influence a target who is unwilling or hesitant to engage in sexual relations (e.g., persuasion, deception, self-presentation, reward, sexual stimulation, arranging conducive circumstances, or encouraging the target to become intoxicated). This distinction is sometimes blurred by researchers in their attempts to demonstrate high frequencies of sexual coercion (see Gilbert, 1991).

The three major outcomes of sexual coercion are sexual behavior, harm to the target, and domination of the target. It is unclear which one of these outcomes is the goal of the action and which outcomes are incidental. Although an incident can have multiple goals, in this chapter I assume for simplicity that for a given incident of sexual coercion, one goal (and one motive) predominates. I consider these outcomes in discussing the role of social influence, retributive justice, and social identity—three social processes involved in coercive acts generally—in sexual coercion.

The model depicted in Figure 1 attempts to clarify the argument regarding social motives. It suggests that contingent threats and bodily force, if successful, produce three proximate outcomes in an incident of sexual coercion. Any of these outcomes could be the actor's proximate goal. Each proximate goal is associated with a distal goal, and each can also be considered a means to that distal goal. In other words, attainment of the proximate goal satisfies some motive. I shall refer to the diagram as I discuss each of the motives.

Sexual Compliance

Females tend to be more selective than males in their sexual behavior, restricting their sexual activity to partners with whom they have positive feelings (Ellis, 1989; Shields & Shields, 1983; Thornhill & Thornhill, 1983). They are more likely than males to interpret sex in terms of romance rather than recreation (Gagnon, 1977). The fact that people with

---

[2]Note that some acts of coercion are legal and may be viewed as morally appropriate (e.g., when someone threatens to leave their spouse because of the lack of a sexual relationship).

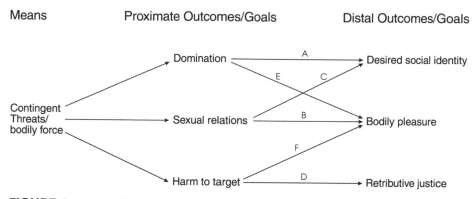

FIGURE 1 Alternative goals and motives for sexual coercion. Path A: Power motive. Path B: Sexual motive. Path C: Socio-sexual motive. Path D: Grievance motive. Paths E and F: Coercive-sexual motive.

sexual fetishes are almost exclusively male also indicates a strong sex difference in the ability to disassociate sexual response from interpersonal relationships (Gregor, 1990).[3]

As a result of sex differences in selectivity, it is not surprising that males are much more likely to attempt to influence females to have sex than the reverse, using a variety of techniques (Sorenson, Stein, Siegel, Golding, & Burnam, 1987). Furthermore, given that there can be conflict over sexual relations (e.g., a man may desire sex and a woman may be unwilling) and given that some people use force to get what they want, it would seem obvious that at least some sexual coercion is sexually motivated.

According to this point of view, the offender's immediate goal is to have sexual relations. He dominates the victim and accepts the victim's suffering as a consequence of his actions even though domination and punishment are not his goals. In other words, coercion is a means to an end, not an end in itself. He uses coercion for strategic reasons—to obtain compliance and to avoid apprehension.

Since the 1970s, most researchers have rejected sexual motivation as an explanation for rape and other forms of sexual coercion. This counterintuitive idea has been stated repeatedly and in the strongest possible terms without any reasonable evidence to support it (see Felson, 1991, for an explanation of the popularity of this idea).

---

[3]*These sex differences in sexuality may have a biological basis (e.g., Ellis, 1989; Thornhill & Thornhill, 1983). Because sex differences in sexual response have obvious reproductive consequences, one would expect them to have evolutionary significance.*

Palmer (1988) reviewed and criticized the arguments against the sexual motivation for rape (see also Hagen, 1979; Shields & Shields, 1983; Symons, 1979; Thornhill & Thornhill, 1983). In general, these arguments are based on spurious reasoning and the misreporting of evidence in those few instances in which evidence is reported. For example, the facts that force is used, that some rapes are premeditated, that some rapists experience sexual dysfunction, and that the victims are not always young have all been cited as evidence against sexual motivation. As Palmer pointed out, these facts say little or nothing about the motivation for sexual coercion. Furthermore, the age distribution of victims, as I discuss later, supports a sexual explanation.

Part of the confusion arises because of the failure to recognize that sexual motivation has social psychological as well as biological elements. It does not simply reflect the pursuit of physical pleasure nor is it the product of uncontrollable biological urges. Clearly, sexual behavior satisfies other goals as well. In other words, sexual behavior—whether coercive or consensual—is partly based on nonsexual motives (Gagnon, 1977). Both could ultimately reflect quests for power, status, or self-esteem. And sexual activity can bring these rewards for women as well as for men. These complexities led Felson and Krohn (1990) to describe the motivation for some rapes as "socio-sexual" rather than sexual. In Figure 1, Path B represents the relation between sexual relations and bodily pleasure, whereas Path C represents concerns for power. Note that this is different from the feminist approach, which suggests that domination is the immediate goal of the offender.

Sexual Aspirations

If sexual motivation involves social psychological processes, it should not be related in any simple way to sexual deprivation or satiation. Kanin (1965, 1967, 1985) argued that sexual aspirations or relative deprivation is a more important factor in sexual coercion. He found subjective sexual deprivation rather than actual sexual deprivation to be positively correlated with the use of sexual coercion by college men. College men who were dissatisfied with the frequency of their sexual activity, or who indicated that a higher frequency of orgasms was necessary for them to be sexually satisfied, were more likely to engage in coercive sexual behavior. In addition, college men who used sexual coercion were likely to have more sexual experience, presumably because they engaged in greater effort to obtain partners. Similarly, rapists who have been married reported a high frequency of marital intercourse and extramarital affairs (Gebhard, Gagnon, Pomeroy, & Christenson, 1965; Goldstein, 1973; Le Maire, 1956).

Access to willing, attractive females, even in a permissive sexual atmosphere, is restricted for most males. Kanin's research suggests that young men devote considerable effort to finding women who will engage in sexual relations. The fact that some men are willing to pay a high price to engage a prostitute also indicates that there are strong barriers to sexual access. Coercion gives males a very wide choice of sexual partners.

Situational Context

Another way to examine the motivation for sexual coercion is to examine the social interaction that immediately precedes coercive behavior. This is primarily relevant to coercion involving men and women who know each other. For example, it is important to determine whether coercion is used only with other techniques and whether it is used as a first or last resort. One would expect a male whose motive is to dominate or punish his victim to prefer coercive sex to consensual sex and to use coercive methods as a first resort. On the other hand, if sexual coercion is sexually motivated, then one would expect males to use coercion as a last resort with females they know, after other methods of influence have failed.

Evidence for sexual motivation is provided by Kanin's (1967, 1985) research on high school and college-aged men. He found that males who used sexual coercion were much more likely to use other methods to encourage sexual relations such as falsely professing love or attempting to get a female intoxicated. One assumes that these behaviors preceded coercive behavior. This evidence suggests that sexual coercion is used along with noncoercive techniques, that it is more likely to be used as a last resort, and that coercion itself has no special attraction for these men.

Sexual motivation is also apparent in incidents of rape among the Mehinaku Indians of Brazil (Gregor, 1990). There is a high level of promiscuity in the tribe. As in other societies, men show a much stronger proclivity to engage in sexual activity—they describe unwilling women as "stingy with their genitals"—and they initiate most sexual interactions. The men attempt to encourage women to engage in sexual relations frequently by offering fish in exchange. On occasion, when women refuse, the men use some level of coercion, described vaguely as "pulling," to force the women into the bush.

The nature of sexual scripts may also increase the use of coercion among sexually motivated males. The typical consensual encounter involves an implicit request by the male and compliance by the female. Rather than making an explicit verbal request, the male initiates intimate activity and proceeds to the next level of intimacy unless he meets resistance. Misunderstandings may result because males may misread ambiguous sexual signals (Goodchilds & Zellman, 1984; Muehlenhard, Friedman, & Thomas, 1985; Muehlenhard & Linton, 1987) or because of a general tendency for men to overestimate women's sexual interest (Abbey, 1982; Shotland & Craig, 1988). Females may also avoid expressing a firm refusal to avoid an embarrassing scene. When a female refuses a sexual overture, it implies rejection and violates rules of politeness (Goffman, 1955).

As a result of the sexual script, males may treat initial resistance as an opening bargaining position rather than as a final offer. This interpretation is not necessarily inaccurate as indicated by reports from college women that they sometimes engage in "token resistance" (i.e., they resist initially when they are actually interested in sexual activity; Muehlenhard & Hollabaugh, 1988). In these instances, females may believe that they decrease their power and status by giving in too easily.

There is also evidence that females are sometimes ambivalent about whether they want to engage in sexual activity or about the level of intimacy they desire (Muehlenhard & Hollabaugh, 1988). Knowing this, males may use persuasion or attempt to sexually stimulate females to influence them. Males may not view these tactics as aggressive or inappropriate and, as a result, their inhibitions may not be activated. Furthermore, during the "negotiation process," sexually aroused males may have lower inhibitions about using coercion and other techniques that violate their moral standards.

The role of sexual motivation was demonstrated in a study of 71 college students who had committed rape (Kanin, 1985). In every case, the rape occurred during a date after an intensive consensual sexual encounter, most commonly involving oral–genital sex. If date rapes occur when males are sexually aroused, it is likely that sexual motivation is involved.

Attractiveness

If sexual coercion is sexually motivated, then one would expect that those who are physically attractive would be more likely to be victimized. This issue has been examined indirectly in research on the age of rape victims. There is clearly a negative association between age and physical attractiveness if one excludes the very young for whom there are sexual taboos. The attraction of men for young women in consensual sex is apparently found in every culture (Thornhill & Thornhill, 1983). Homosexual men also show a preference for young men (Bell & Weinberg, 1978).

There is clear evidence of a very strong relation between age and rape victimization. According to the National Crime Survey, only 11% of the rape victims are 35 or older, and only 4% are 50 or older (Bureau of Justice Statistics, 1985). This same pattern is apparent in the rape of male victims. One could argue that this is related to the activity patterns of youth (Cohen & Felson, 1979). Young women are more likely to go out at night and to date, and their greater contact with a variety of men may put them at greater risk. In fact, they are more likely to be victims of crime generally (Bureau of Justice Statistics, 1985).

Although differential opportunity may be a factor, the evidence suggests that it is only a partial explanation of the age–victimization relation. Felson and Krohn (1990) attempted to control for differential opportunity by comparing crimes of robbery with crimes in which rape was committed in conjunction with robbery. During the robbery of a woman, the offender often has the opportunity to rape her as well. The evidence suggests that during a robbery involving a male offender and a female victim, a rape is more likely to occur if the victim is young. The average age of robbery victims is 35, whereas the average age of robbery–rape victims is less than 28. This suggests that rapists have a strong preference for youth, which suggests that they prefer physically attractive victims.

Interviews with rapists also suggest that attractiveness is an important factor in their selection of victims (Ageton, 1983; Queen's Bench Foundation, 1978). Additional evidence comes from a study of sexual violence in a prison for men (Lockwood, 1980). Lockwood found that most victims were young, slim White men. Interviews with inmates suggested that men who were young and slim were preferred because they were viewed as more attractive and as most highly resembling women. It is difficult to explain this pattern in terms of differential opportunity.

Sexual Coercion in Prison

Because heterosexual sexual access is either forbidden or severely restricted in prison and because many inmates are young and at the height of their sexual interest, it is not surprising that homosexual relations occur. The use of sexual coercion in part reflects the fact that prisons are filled with men who lack inhibitions about using violence. It may also reflect the reluctance of many heterosexual men to take the "passive role" in homosexual sex. In other words, there are many inmates willing to play the active role and relatively few willing to play the passive role. As a result, it is probably difficult to find partners to engage in consensual sexual activity. Powerful inmates who seek sexual satisfaction are likely to force weaker inmates to play the passive role. This is similar to the situation outside prison wherein there is a surplus of males and a scarcity of females interested in casual sex.

That a man's role in coercive encounters affects his power and status in prison does not necessarily imply that power and status are the goals of these actions. If power is the goal, then one would expect inmates to prefer unwilling over willing targets, and one would expect inmates to brag about incidents of sexual coercion to others. On the other hand, a sexually motivated offender is likely to prefer consensual to coercive sex and to use coercion as a last resort. Evidence that inmates use noncoercive as well as coercive techniques to influence other inmates to engage in sexual activity suggests a sexual motive (Lockwood, 1980).

Sexual Arousal and Violence

Some rape offenders may be sexually aroused by the use of coercion. This is represented in Figure 1 by Paths E and F, which suggest that harming the victim or dominating her may be associated with bodily pleasure. However, evidence from laboratory research on sexual arousal of rapists suggests that rapists are generally not more stimulated by violent sex than they are by nonviolent sex (e.g., Abel, Barlow, Blanchard, & Guild, 1977; Quinsey, Chaplin, & Varney, 1981). In these studies, films of violent and consensual sex were shown to rapists and to control groups, and penile tumescence was measured. The studies consistently showed that convicted rapists were no more likely to be sexually aroused by depictions of rape than they were by depictions of consensual sexual acts. Nonrapists, on the other hand, were less aroused by depictions of rape than by depictions of consensual sex. This pattern suggests that rapists differ from other men in terms of their inhibitions, not in terms of any preference for sexual violence. Unlike other men, the arousal of rapists is not inhibited by viewing sexual violence.[4]

In sum, there is some evidence to support the idea that many acts of sexual coercion are sexually motivated. Young men with high sexual aspirations are more likely to use sexual coercion as well as noncoercive techniques to obtain sexual compliance. In addition, sexual coercion tends to be used as a last resort in incidents involving people who know each other, after other techniques have failed. The ambiguity of consensual sexual scripts may also lead males to misread female resistance and to fail to realize that their behavior is offensive to females. Finally, the targets of sexual coercion tend to be

---

[4]*It is possible, however, that a small percentage of rapists are aroused by violence but that their preferences are not detectable in the relatively small samples that form the basis of this research.*

young, and youth is associated with attractiveness. Age differences in opportunity for victimization can only explain part of this pattern.

Sexual Coercion as an Expression of Grievances

Sexual coercion, like other forms of coercion, could reflect the expression of a grievance. Knowing the humiliation the victim will experience, some men may use sexual coercion as a form of punishment. The offender may be angry at the victim for some perceived misdeed, and he may believe that she deserves to be punished. In this case, the punishment is an act of retributive justice, and the harm to the victim is "just dessert" (see Path D in Figure 1).

This explanation suggests that males who engage in sexual coercion have been involved in a conflict with the victim beforehand and that they feel aggrieved. The social interaction is likely to be similar to homicides and assaults in which verbal conflict escalates, culminating in physical and sexual attacks. Another possibility is that males feel aggrieved when females resist their noncoercive attempts to encourage sexual activity and use sexual coercion as punishment. If men expect sexual relations for whatever reason and women refuse, the former may feel aggrieved.

One would expect that grievances are much more likely to be involved in incidents involving people who know each other (Black, 1983).[5] In particular, one might expect sexual coercion to be associated with conflicts between couples who are married, estranged, or involved in some other romantic or sexual relationship. Sexual coercion may be particularly common among estranged couples when the woman is no longer receptive to a sexual relationship. Men may use sexual coercion to punish women for insults, rejection, refusing to engage in consensual sex, infidelity, or some petty grievance. If homicides and assaults can involve petty grievances, so can rapes.

Nonstrategic Punishment

The strategic use of coercion is oriented toward compliance.[6] If men punish victims during incidents of sexual coercion for nonstrategic reasons (e.g., if they use gratuitous violence), it suggests that their immediate goal is to harm. An offender who values harm is

---

[5] *Grievances are possible between strangers, however (Wolfgang, 1958).*

[6] *The offender may also use coercion to discourage the victim from going to the police. Also, some rape victims report that the offender used violence to force them to take a more active role during the sex act (MacDonald, 1971).*

likely to harm the victim in a variety of ways: He may insult or humiliate the victim, and he may physically attack the victim even when she complies.[7] On the other hand, one would expect sexually motivated offenders to use enough threatening language to obtain compliance but otherwise treat their victims relatively well. They might even engage in acts of tenderness normally associated with consensual sex. Although such behaviors have been reported by rape victims, the frequency is unclear (MacDonald, 1971). No one has ever studied in a systematic way how men who engage in sexual coercion otherwise treat their victims.

There is evidence that physical violence tends to be used sparingly in incidents of sexual coercion (Amir, 1971). For example, Ageton (1983) found that only a small proportion of young men use much physical force during incidents of sexual coercion. Results from the National Crime Survey also indicate that there are relatively few injuries not related to the rape itself (Bureau of Justice Statistics, 1985). Finally, sexual coercion among college students rarely involves a physical attack (Koss, Gidycz, & Wisniewski, 1987).

Gratuitous violence sometimes does occur, however. If nonstrategic coercion reflects an expression of grievances, one would expect it to be more frequent in acts of coercion involving estranged couples and others who know each other. A number of studies suggest that this is the case (Amir, 1971; Koss, Dinero, & Seibel, 1988). For example, Felson and Krohn (1990) found that victims were more likely to be physically injured in instances in which the offender and victim were an estranged couple. This effect is observed even when offenders have a weapon (and thus a credible threat) and when victims do not resist. Presumably, in many of these instances, the offender rapes and beats up his exwife or exgirlfriend as an act of punishment.

Felson and Krohn (1990) provided evidence that rapes involving older offenders and victims are more likely to involve gratuitous violence and therefore a punishment motive and are less likely to involve sexual motivation. Using National Crime Survey data, they found that victims were more likely to be physically injured during a rape when offenders and victims were older. The positive association between age and violence was striking given that youths are much more violent during other crimes and in other contexts (Gottfredson & Hirschi, 1990). This pattern is consistent with evidence that sexual

---

[7]It is possible, however, that men who seek to punish the victim use sexual coercion but no other type of punishment. Still, one would predict that gratuitous violence is more likely when the offender values punishment rather than compliance.

motivation declines for men as they get older (Gagnon, 1977) and with the fact that youths are perceived as more sexually attractive. It suggests that incidents involving offenders with lower sexual interests and less sexually attractive victims tend to involve more gratuitous violence.

Grievances Against Groups

Another possibility is that some men are angry at women generally and that they express this anger through sexual coercion. In this case, the act of coercion involves a grievance against the general category of which the victim is a member. The evidence is mixed concerning the relation between sexual coercion and hostility toward women (Buss & Durkee, 1957; Koss & Dinero, 1987; Rada, Laws, & Kellner, 1976; Scully & Marolla, 1985). However, even if one were to find a relation between hostility toward women and rape, it would not necessarily imply that sexual coercion is an expression of this general hostility. It is also possible that negative attitudes toward women reduce men's inhibitions concerning the use of sexual coercion. For example, a sexually motivated man might use coercion if he lacks concern for women (Malamuth, 1986). This will be discussed further.

There are reasons to be skeptical of explanations of interpersonal violence that emphasize hatred for groups. Most incidents of homicide and assault are directed against individuals for whom the offender has a grievance. In spite of recent emphasis on "bias crimes" (i.e., crimes based on group prejudice), such incidents are quite rare. For example, in the United States, one might expect a high level of interracial crime based on group prejudices. Most crimes, however, including rape, are intraracial (e.g., Amir, 1971). In spite of the prejudice that some Whites feel toward Blacks, the incidence of Whites raping Blacks is extremely rare (South & Felson, 1990).

Interracial rapes committed by Blacks have sometimes been interpreted in terms of the perpetrator's hatred for Whites. It has been argued that some Blacks rape White women to obtain vengeance against White men (LaFree, 1982). The evidence does not support this point of view. First, South and Felson (1990) found that during robberies of female victims, Blacks were slightly less likely to rape the woman if she was White than if she was Black. If rapes by Blacks reflect their grievances against Whites, there should be a preference for White victims. Furthermore, they found no evidence that interracial rapes were more frequent in metropolitan areas in which there was greater interracial conflict or inequality (see also O'Brien, 1987). Although Lockwood (1980) found that

Blacks tended to rape White men in prison, he found no evidence that it reflected grievances against Whites.[8]

Deviant Targets

There is some evidence that men are more likely to use sexual coercion against women they consider deviant. For example, Amir (1971) found that about 20% of the rape victims he studied had "bad reputations," whereas another 20% had police records, many of them for sexual misconduct. Supporting evidence also comes from Kanin's (1985) study of the effect of date rape on the reputations of male college students. Relatively few of these young men (7–9%) believed that their best friends would respond favorably if they knew that the respondent attempted to coerce a "more or less regular date" to have sexual intercourse. On the other hand, the percentages were much higher for "bar pick-ups," "known teasers," "economic exploiters," and women with "loose reputations." For example, 81% of rapists and 40% of the control group indicated that they would get a positive response from their friends if the woman was a "known teaser." This suggests that some men believe that rape is justifiable against women who violate certain moral standards. Amir's evidence suggests that these women tend to be selected as targets.

There are at least two interpretations of these results. First, some men may feel personally aggrieved against these women and may attempt to punish them for their alleged wrongdoings. Second, it may be that men are sexually motivated but are disinhibited from using sexual coercion with women whom they perceive as deviant. In other words, they use the target's bad reputation as a justification for their behavior. This seems more likely given the evidence that men do not usually engage in nonstrategic violence and the evidence supporting sexual motivation. Furthermore, neither a "bar pick-up" nor a woman with a "loose reputation" is likely to cause the respondent or his friends to feel personally aggrieved.

In summary, there is indirect evidence that some acts of sexual coercion involve the expression of grievances. The use of gratuitous or nonstrategic violence during some of these incidents implies that men seek to punish the victim and not just gain compliance. That most incidents do not involve gratuitous violence suggests that punishment is not usually the motive for sexual coercion. However, some males may feel justified using coercion against females they perceive as not worthy of respect.

---

[8] White targets were preferred, in part, because they were viewed as vulnerable; they lacked support from third parties.

Power and Domination

By definition, power and domination are involved in all acts of coercion, sexual or otherwise. The issue is whether, as some feminists claim, power is the goal of sexual coercion, that is, whether men use sexual coercion *because* it allows them to feel dominant over female victims (Deming & Eppy, 1981).[9] Because there is no clear theoretical statement of this approach, it is difficult to imagine how it might be tested (e.g., Brownmiller, 1975).[10]

The aggression literature suggests a way that the power motive can be reconceptualized to make it testable and to connect it to a broader literature. That literature examines the role of social identities and impression management and suggests that those who engage in coercion are sometimes seeking to appear more powerful to themselves or others (Felson, 1978; Luckenbill, 1977; Toch, 1969). Some acts of sexual coercion could also reflect this motive. A man may seek to dominate a woman by compelling her to engage in sexual relations, thereby attaining a social identity as powerful (see Path C in Figure 1). He may demonstrate power to the woman he is bullying, to himself, or to some third party. He may also view his ability to control the target as an accomplishment.[11]

The emphasis of the literature on social identities and aggression, however, is on retaliation (Felson, 1978). It suggests that people retaliate when they perceive that they have been attacked to avoid appearing weak. Males may feel that they have been attacked when females reject their sexual requests. Because a female generally requires positive feelings before having sexual relations, her decision about whether to have sexual relations has identity implications for the male. By complying or turning him down, she communicates her evaluation of him. Her consent grants him special status, whereas her refusal denies him that status. (On the other hand, a male's decision to have sexual relations with a female does not necessarily imply anything about his feelings for her.)

---

[9]*Some feminists favor a more sociological version of the power thesis (e.g., Brownmiller, 1975). They argue that the function of sexual coercion is to control women and to keep them in traditional roles. Rape is attributed to a patriarchal social context that encourages coercive behavior against women. This approach does not focus on the goals of individuals but views offenders as acting unwittingly as agents of social control. Gregor (1990) described a form of group rape in a Brazilian Indian tribe that fits this description. The threat of rape is used to prevent women from observing certain male rituals. Because of their fear, the women complied with the rule, and a group rape had not occurred for 40 years. That such a pattern is rarely observed in other societies suggests that rape is generally not a social control mechanism developed by societies to control women.*

[10]*Groth, Nicholas, Burgess, and Holmstrom (1977) classified 65% of their sample of convicted rapists as motivated by power, but their classification scheme seems arbitrary. In particular, they give no evidence to distinguish power from sexual motivation. For a critique of their classification, see Palmer (1988).*

[11]*Some rapists report that they enjoy the power they exercise over their victims (Scully & Marolla, 1985).*

For this reason, males may view sexual noncompliance as an attack on their identity and may retaliate. They may also feel aggrieved and may punish females out of a sense of justice.

Some of the incidents involving estranged couples described previously may reflect this process. For example, a man whose wife has become involved with another man may feel that he has been made to appear weak and may attack his wife in retaliation. The "jilted lover" may use sexual coercion as well as other forms of coercion to save face. In general, sexual relations have profound status implications for men and women and are therefore a significant source of conflict.

If offenders are oriented toward power, then they should prefer coercive sex to consensual sex. To coerce the victim to do something he or she would not do otherwise demonstrates power. Thus, the power/identity explanation predicts that men who commit sexual coercion prefer resistance, whereas the socio-sexual explanation predicts that men who commit sexual coercion prefer compliance. For example, according to the power explanation, sexually coercive men prefer to date women who are uninterested in sexual relations. They do not attempt to influence women to have consensual sex using noncoercive techniques but use coercive techniques as a first resort. This profile is not consistent with Kanin's (1985) evidence, described earlier.

If some acts of sexual coercion involve impression management, then one would expect them to be affected by the perceived reaction of third parties, as are other forms of coercion (see Felson, 1978, for a review). For most audiences, however, men who use coercion against women are likely to be viewed negatively by an audience. Men who attack women are sometimes called cowardly, indicating that they are perceived as low in power.[12] Furthermore, evidence suggests that coercive incidents involving men and women (unlike intragender incidents) are less likely to escalate if there is an audience present (Felson, 1982).

The only direct evidence regarding the effect of third parties on sexual coercion comes from Kanin's (1985) study of the effect of date rape on the reputations of college students. Recall that relatively few rapists or nonrapists believed that they would enhance their reputation by using sexual coercion against a "more or less regular date." On the other hand, many rapists and, to a lesser extent, other men, indicated that they would get a positive response if the woman was some sort of deviant target. In general, it appears

---

[12] If retaliation reflects an attempt to recover self-esteem, it would not be affected by the presence of an audience.

that there are some audiences that respond favorably to the use of sexual coercion, at least against a deviant target.

Individual Differences

Most males have sexual interests, most have at least an occasional grievance with a female, and most would like to avoid appearing weak. However, most males do not use sexual coercion. Therefore, there must be some individual characteristics that distinguish males who use sexual coercion from those who do not. In part, males may vary in the strength of goals satisfied by this behavior. Thus, Kanin's (1985) work suggests that men who use sexual coercion tend to have high sexual aspirations. However, social learning theory and control theory suggest that learned inhibitions and disinhibitions are also important. Men who engage in sexual coercion are less likely to have certain inhibitions that would discourage this behavior.

One can conceive of two types of inhibitions (or disinhibitions): those related to women specifically (i.e., sexist attitudes) and those related to the use of coercion and exploitative behavior generally.

Sexist Attitudes

Considerable attention has been paid to the effect of sexist attitudes or "rape myths" on the use of sexual coercion. It has been argued that men who use sexual coercion tend to lack concern for women, view women as sex objects, believe that women want to be raped, or have some other attitude related to women. This reflects the feminist argument that sexual coercion is produced by sexism.

The evidence that sexist attitudes correlate with sexual coercion is mixed (Ageton, 1983; Howells & Wright, 1978; Rapaport & Burkhart, 1984; for reviews, see Koss & Leonard, 1984; Malamuth, 1981). However, even if cross-sectional correlations between certain attitudes and coercive sexual behavior could be demonstrated, their causal interpretations are unclear. It may be that men express these beliefs to justify their use of coercion (Koss, Leonard, Beezley, & Oros, 1985). For example, a rapist may report that the woman enjoyed the incident to justify his behavior. The issue is a general one in the attitude/behavior literature. The causal interpretation of correlations between attitudes and behaviors is unclear. Longitudinal research would be useful to examine whether such beliefs in fact have a causal impact on coercive sexual behavior.

If attitudes toward women do have causal effects on sexual coercion, it must still be determined whether attitudes toward women act as instigators or disinhibitors of sexual coercion. As indicated earlier, a man who is hostile toward a woman (or toward women generally) may use sexual coercion to punish her. In this case, his hostility instigates the attack, and his goal is to express his grievance. On the other hand, a man may have some other goal, but his hostility toward women may reduce his inhibitions about harming them.

There are at least two ways to determine whether hostility instigates or disinhibits sexual coercion. First, if a man engages in nonstrategic attacks against a woman, it would suggest that his goal is to punish her and that hostility is an instigator rather than a disinhibitor of his attack. Second, if attitudes are disinhibitors one would expect them to interact statistically with goals in their effect on behavior. For example, one might predict that the relation between sexual aspirations and sexual coercion to be stronger when men have negative attitudes toward women. A statistical interaction between hostility toward women and sexual aspirations would suggest that hostility removes inhibitions. On the other hand, if hostility toward women has only main effects on sexual coercion, it would suggest support for the punishment model. Supporting evidence for the inhibition argument comes from work by Malamuth (1986), who found interactions between sexual arousal to rape scenes and various attitudes in their effects on sexual coercion.

General Inhibitions

General inhibitions refer to inhibitions that are not specific to females; males who lack these inhibitions may not treat males any better than they treat females. According to this point of view, men who engage in sexual coercion are likely to be the same men who engage in other forms of coercion and in other exploitative behaviors. The argument is consistent with evidence that those who commit crime rarely specialize (Gottfredson & Hirschi, 1990).[13] The evidence regarding rape offenders reveals the same pattern: Few men specialize in rape. The criminal records of those who have been convicted of rape tend to be similar to the criminal records of those who have been convicted of other crimes (Alder, 1984; Wolfgang, Figlio, & Sellin, 1972).[14] Rapists are usually versatile

---

[13]Not only do they commit many different types of crimes, they also tend to drink and smoke heavily and be involved in traffic accidents. Gottfredson and Hirschi (1990) argued that low self-control is the common element is these behaviors.

[14]In addition, the social–demographic characteristics of rapists tend to be similar to those of other types of offenders (Alder, 1984).

offenders, committing property crimes as well as violent crimes. In addition, there is evidence that convicted rapists are similar to men convicted of other offenses in their attitudes toward women and toward women's rights (Howells & Wright, 1978).

If rapists are versatile offenders, then one would expect the characteristics of individuals that predict sexual coercion to be the same ones that predict involvement in crime and deviant behavior generally. Those who commit crime tend to have similar goals as the rest of us, but they lack certain internal and external controls (Gottfredson & Hirschi, 1990; Hirschi, 1969). Either they have failed to internalize certain moral inhibitions, or they lack self-control, or they do not have the social bonds to conventional society that increase the costs of engaging in criminal or deviant behavior. There is evidence that the same external controls that predict criminal behavior in general also predict sexual coercion (Ageton, 1983).

Conclusion

There is substantial evidence that many acts of sexual coercion are sexually motivated. For example, the evidence that offenders have high sexual aspirations, that they also use noncoercive methods to encourage sexual relations, and that they usually choose young women all point to a sexual motive. The use of coercive and noncoercive influence techniques may in part be based on sex differences in sexuality (whether learned or innate). That females are more selective than males creates conflict between the sexes and leads some males to use coercion to produce compliance. Similarly, strong sexual interests among prison inmates but a scarcity of inmates willing to play a passive role in homosexual encounters leads to the use of sexual coercion in prison.

Sexual coercion, like other forms of coercion, undoubtedly has a variety of motives, however. There is evidence that in some instances, the offender is motivated by a desire to punish the victim. This is suggested by findings that incidents of sexual coercion involving estranged couples or older offenders and victims are more likely to involve gratuitous violence. Although there is no convincing evidence that sexual coercion is motivated by power concerns, this seems a reasonable hypothesis given the importance of social identities in other forms of aggression.

The evidence is also clear that men who engage in sexual coercion engage in other forms of coercion, crime, and deviance. Explanations of sexual coercion must therefore incorporate insights from the general study of crime and deviance. If men who use sexual coercion are versatile offenders, we must examine those general factors that disinhibit their behavior.

There may also be situational factors that disinhibit the use of sexual coercion. In particular, it appears that some men justify sexual coercion against women whom they perceive as deviant. These women are viewed as "fair game." In addition, because of the nature of sexual scripts, men sometimes mistakenly believe that women are interested in sexual relations. They may treat initial resistance as an opening bargaining position rather than a final offer. They may pressure women if they sense any ambivalence. If men do not view their behavior as aggressive, then their inhibitions are not likely to be activated. In general, the negotiation process involved in consensual sexual relations is likely to result in at least some degree of coercive behavior.

In conclusion, a social interactionist theory provides a promising approach to the understanding of sexual coercion. Most important, it clarifies some theoretical arguments in the literature and suggests some testable hypotheses. Sexual coercion will be better understood when we apply general knowledge about coercion and crime to this behavior and avoid a narrow, ideological approach.

References

Abbey, A. (1982). Sex differences in attributions for friendly behavior: Do males misperceive females' friendliness? *Journal of Personality and Social Psychology, 42,* 830–838.

Abel, G. G., Barlow, D. H., Blanchard, E. B., & Guild, D. (1977). The components of rapists' sexual arousal. *Archives of General Psychiatry, 34,* 895–903.

Ageton, S. (1983). *Sexual assault among adolescents.* Lexington, MA: Lexington Books.

Alder, C. (1984). The convicted rapist. A sexual or a violent offender? *Criminal Justice and Behavior, 11,* 157–177.

Amir, M. (1971). *Patterns in forcible rape.* Chicago: University of Chicago Press.

Bell, A. P., & Weinberg, M. S. (1978). *Homosexualities: A study of diversity among men & women.* New York: Simon & Schuster.

Black, D. (1983). Crime as social control. *American Sociological Review, 48,* 34–45.

Brownmiller, S. (1975). *Against our will: Men, women and rape.* New York: Simon & Schuster.

Bureau of Justice Statistics. (1985). *The crime of rape.* Washington, DC: U.S. Department of Justice.

Buss, A. H., & Durkee, A. (1957). An inventory for assessing different kinds of hostility. *Journal of Consulting Psychology, 21,* 343–349.

Cohen, L. E., & Felson, M. (1979). Social change and crime rate trends: A routine activity approach. *American Sociological Review, 44,* 588–608.

Deming, M. B., & Eppy, A. (1981). The sociology of rape. *Sociology and Social Research, 64,* 357–380.

Ellis, L. (1989). *Theories of rape: Inquiries into the causes of sexual aggression.* New York: Hemisphere.

Felson, R. B. (1978). Aggression as impression management. *Social Psychology, 41,* 205–213.

Felson, R. B. (1982). Impression management and the escalation of aggression and violence. *Social Psychology Quarterly, 45,* 245–254.

Felson, R. B. (1991). Blame analysis: Accounting for the behavior of protected groups. *American Sociologist, 22,* 5–24.

Felson, R. B., & Krohn, M. (1990). Motives for rape. *Journal of Research in Crime and Delinquency, 27,* 222–242.

Gagnon, J. H. (1977). *Human sexualities.* Glenview, IL: Scott, Foresman.

Gebhard, P. H., Gagnon, J. H., Pomeroy, W. B., & Christenson, C. V. (1965). *Sex offenders: An analysis of types.* New York: Harper & Row.

Gilbert, N. (1991). The phantom epidemic of sexual assault. *Public Interest, Spring,* 54–65.

Goffman, E. (1955). On face-work: An analysis of ritual elements in social interaction. *Psychiatry, 18,* 213–231.

Goldstein, M. J. (1973). Exposure to erotic stimuli and sexual deviance. *Journal of Social Issues, 29,* 197–219.

Goodchilds, J. D., & Zellman, G. L. (1984). Sexual signaling and sexual aggression in adolescent relationships. In N. M. Malamuth & E. Donnerstein (Eds.), *Pornography and sexual aggression* (pp. 233–243). San Diego, CA: Academic Press.

Gottfredson, M., & Hirschi, T. (1990). *A general theory of crime.* Stanford, CA: Stanford University Press.

Gregor, T. (1990). Male dominance and sexual coercion. In J. W. Stigler, R. A. Shweder, & G. Herdt (Eds.), *Cultural psychology: Essays on comparative human development* (pp. 477–495). Cambridge, MA: Cambridge University Press.

Groth, A. N., Burgess, A. W., & Holmstrom, L. L. (1977). Rape: power, anger, and sexuality. *American Journal of Psychiatry, 134,* 1239–1243.

Hagen, R. (1979). *The biosexual factor.* New York: Doubleday.

Hirschi, T. (1969). *Causes of delinquency.* Berkeley: University of California Press.

Howells, K., & Wright, E. (1978). The sexual attitudes of aggressive sexual offenders. *British Journal of Criminology, 18,* 170–173.

Kanin, E. J. (1965). Male sex aggression and three psychiatric hypotheses. *Journal of Sex Research, 1,* 227–229.

Kanin, E. J. (1967). An examination of sexual aggression as a response to sexual frustration. *Journal of Marriage and the Family, 3,* 428–433.

Kanin, E. J. (1985). Date rapists: Differential sexual socialization and relative deprivation. *Archives of Sexual Behavior, 6,* 67–76.

Koss, M. P., & Dinero, T. E. (1987, January). *Predictors of sexual aggression among a national sample of male college students.* Paper presented at the New York Academy of Sciences Conference, Human Sexual Aggression: Current Perspectives, New York City.

Koss, M. P., Dinero, T. E., & Seibel, C. A. (1988). Stranger and acquaintance rape: Are there differences in the victim's experience? *Psychology of Women Quarterly, 12,* 1–24.

Koss, M. P., Gidycz, C. A., & Wisniewski, N. (1987). The scope of rape: Incidence and prevalence of sexual aggression and victimization in a national sample of students in higher education. *Journal of Consulting and Clinical Psychology, 55,* 162–170.

Koss, M. P., & Leonard, K. E. (1984). Sexually aggressive men: Empirical findings and theoretical implications. In N. M. Malamuth & E. I. Donnerstein (Eds.), *Pornography and sexual aggression* (pp. 213–232). San Diego, CA: Academic Press.

Koss, M. P., Leonard, K. E., Beezley, D. A., & Oros, C. J. (1985). Non-stranger sexual aggression: A discriminate analysis classification. *Sex Roles, 12,* 981–992.

LaFree, G. D. (1982). Male power and female victimization: Toward a theory of interracial rape. *American Journal of Sociology, 88,* 311–328.

Le Maire, L. (1956). Danish experiences regarding the castration of sexual offenders. *Journal of Criminal Law, Criminology, and Police Science, 47,* 294–310.

Lockwood, D. (1980). *Prison sexual violence.* New York: Elsevier.

Luckenbill, D. F. (1977). Criminal homicide as a situated transaction. *Social Problems, 25,* 176–186.

MacDonald, J. M. (1971). *Rape offenders and their victims.* Springfield, IL: Charles C Thomas.

Malamuth, N. M. (1981). Rape proclivity among males. *Journal of Social Issues, 37,* 138–157.

Malamuth, N. M. (1986). Predictors of naturalistic sexual aggression. *Journal of Personality and Social Psychology, 50,* 953–962.

Muehlenhard, C. L., & Hollabaugh, L. C. (1988). Do women sometimes say no when they mean yes? The prevalence and correlates of women's token resistance to sex. *Journal of Personality and Social Psychology, 54,* 872–889.

Muehlenhard, C. L., & Linton, M. A. (1987). Date rape and sexual aggression in dating situations: Incidence and risk factors. *Journal of Counseling Psychology, 34,* 186–196.

O'Brien, R. M. (1987). The interracial nature of violent crimes: A reexamination. *American Journal of Sociology, 92,* 817–835.

Palmer, C. T. (1988). Twelve reasons why rape is not sexually motivated: A skeptical examination. *Journal of Sex Research, 25,* 512–530.

Queen's Bench Foundation. (1978). *Rape prevention and resistance.* San Francisco: Queen's Bench Foundation.

Quinsey, V. L., Chaplin, T. C., & Varney, G. A. (1981). A comparison of rapists' and non-sex offender's sexual preferences for mutually consenting sex, rape, and physical abuse of women. *Behavioral Assessment, 3,* 127–135.

Rada, R. T., Laws, D. R., & Kellner, R. (1976). Plasma testosterone levels in the rapist. *Psychosomatic Medicine, 38,* 257–268.

Rapaport, K., & Burkhart, B. R. (1984). Personality and attitudinal characteristics of sexually coercive college males. *Journal of Abnormal Psychology, 93,* 216–221.

Scully, D., & Marolla, J. (1984). Convicted rapists' vocabulary of motive: Excuses and justifications. *Social Problems, 31,* 530–544.

Scully, D., & Marolla, J. (1985). Riding the bull at Gilley's: Convicted rapists describe the rewards of rape. *Social Problems, 32,* 251–263.

Shields, W. M., & Shields, L. M. (1983). Forcible rape: An evolutionary perspective. *Ethology and Sociobiology, 4,* 115–136.

Sorenson, S. B., Stein, J. A., Siegel, J. M., Golding, J. M., & Burnam, M. A. (1987). The prevalence of adult sexual assault: The Los Angeles Epidemiologic Catchment Area Project. *American Journal of Epidemiology, 126,* 1154–1164.

South, S. J., & Felson, R. B. (1990). The racial patterning of rape. *Social Forces, 69,* 71–93.

Symons, D. (1979). *The evolution of human sexuality.* New York: Oxford University Press.

Thornhill, R., & Thornhill, N. W. (1983). Human rape: An evolutionary analysis. *Ethology and Sociobiology, 4,* 137–173.

Toch, H. (1969). *Violent men: An inquiry into the psychology of violence.* Chicago: Aldine

Wolfgang, M. (1958). *Patterns in criminal homicide.* Philadelphia: University of Pennsylvania Press.

Wolfgang, M., Figlio, R. M., & Sellin, T. (1972). *Delinquency in a birth cohort.* Chicago: University of Chicago Press.

Index

About the Editors

R ichard B. Felson is a social psychologist with research interests in interpersonal violence and in the development of the self-concept. He is professor of sociology at the University at Albany, State University of New York.

James T. Tedeschi has been a professor of psychology at the University at Albany, State University of New York since 1970. His scholarly work has been devoted to the study of power and influence, self-presentation, and aggression.